After the Shooting Stopped:

the story of an UNRRA welfare worker in Germany 1945-1947

by

Susan T. Pettiss

and

Lynne Taylor

Note for Librarians: a cataloguing record for this book that includes Dewey Decimal Classification and US Library of Congress numbers is available from the Library and Archives of Canada. The complete cataloguing record can be obtained from their online database at:
www.collectionscanada.ca/amicus/index-e.html
ISBN 1-4120-3882-0
Printed in Victoria, BC, Canada

TRAFFORD

Offices in Canada, USA, Ireland, UK and Spain
This book was published on-demand in cooperation with Trafford Publishing. On-demand publishing is a unique process and service of making a book available for retail sale to the public taking advantage of on-demand manufacturing and Internet marketing. On-demand publishing includes promotions, retail sales, manufacturing, order fulfilment, accounting and collecting royalties on behalf of the author.
Book sales for North America and international:
Trafford Publishing, 6E–2333 Government St.,
Victoria, BC v8t 4p4 CANADA
phone 250 383 6864 (toll-free 1 888 232 4444)
fax 250 383 6804; email to orders@trafford.com
Book sales in Europe:
Trafford Publishing (uk) Ltd., Enterprise House, Wistaston Road Business Centre,
Wistaston Road, Crewe, Cheshire cw2 7rp UNITED KINGDOM
phone 01270 251 396 (local rate 0845 230 9601)
facsimile 01270 254 983; orders.uk@trafford.com
Order online at:
www.trafford.com/robots/04-1690.html

10 9 8 7 6 5 4 3 2 1

FOREWORD

The refugee crisis that plagued the European continent in the immediate aftermath of World War II was perhaps one of the most compelling parts of the story of Europe's postwar reconstruction. Literally, millions of people of all ages had been displaced from their homes, either by the Nazis or the war. There were six million displaced persons in the three western zones of Germany, most of them in the American occupation zone, and a further six or seven million in the Soviet occupation zone. And those figures did not include German refugees fleeing the advance of the Soviet forces in the east. This was just the number of non-German refugees or displaced persons (also known as DPs) in Germany. Most had arrived during the war, forcibly brought to Germany as prisoners of war, slave labour for German factories and farms, or as prisoners in the concentration camp system. Tens of thousands more had fled Eastern Europe as the Soviet army advanced inexorably westward, and they too had ended up in Germany. The DPs were of all nationalities, including Soviet, Polish, Lithuanian, Latvian, French, Dutch, Belgian, Estonian, Ukrainian, Jewish. It was a true United Nations. In fact they came to be referred to as UN nationals (as opposed to enemy nationals and ex-enemy nationals).

Confronted with millions of DPs, the Allies were faced with the task of caring for these people until they could be returned to their homes. The German government had collapsed in the face of military defeat and the Allies had temporarily divided Germany into four occupation zones (American, French, British and Soviet) until they could decide how best to reconstruct the country. The Allies were not completely unprepared and the flood of displaced persons came as no surprise. As early as 1943, the United Nations Relief and Rehabilitation Administration (UNRRA) had been established, with forty-four member states, expressly to provide care and maintenance for all United Nations displaced persons. While the task was monumental, if just because of the sheer numbers involved, the expectation was that repatriation would be straightforward and the period of interim care would be relatively short. The assumption was that all would return to where they had lived prior to the war. Thus, UNRRA was given a rather short life span, and it was originally to be disbanded at the end of 1946. Despite the best laid plans, UNRRA would continue operations until mid-1947, when it was replaced with another United Nations agency, the International Refugee Organisation or IRO, the immediate predecessor to UNHCR, the United Nations High Commission for Refugees, which deals with international refugee issues today. The last DP camp in Germany would not close until 1951.

What came as a surprise for the Allies and UNRRA were the difficulties that arose in trying to repatriate the DPs. Many willingly returned to their prewar residences, and there was a massive population transfer in 1945. However, after the dust settled, there were still some one million DPs left. For some, their place of residence in 1938 was now in a different country (as borders were shifted in the postwar territorial settlement) which may or may not have wanted their return, or where they themselves may or may not have wanted to return. In many cases, for the East Europeans, the changes had been fundamental. Their countries had fallen under the control of the Soviet Union. While many of these DPs wished to return to their homelands and did so, many others did not. Either they did not wish to live under a Communist regime and Soviet rule, or they saw better opportunities elsewhere. By January 1946, there were still some 700,000 such displaced persons in UNRRA camps in Germany and untold thousands more living outside of the camps. By far and away, the largest number were Polish (460,000), followed by Balts (140,000). "Balts" was the name given to those DPs from the Baltic republics of Latvia, Lithuania and Estonia. These people refused to return to their homelands because those had fallen under Soviet control, and they were vehemently anti-Communist.

The problem was soon compounded by what became known as the infiltrees. Jewish refugees from Eastern Europe began appearing in the western occupation zones of Germany in increasing numbers, and in increasingly well-organized movements. They were fleeing persecution in the east and sought to force Britain to open Palestine to them. Britain, at this point, had practically shut the door to Jewish immigration to Palestine, a British Mandate. Receiving a relatively hostile reception in the British Occupation Zone in Germany, they largely settled in the American Zone. In both zones, they became an additional responsibility for UNRRA.

These were the people UNRRA was directed to care for. UNRRA's position was a difficult one. While UNRRA was an organ of the United Nations, it found itself much beholden to the occupation forces governing the zones in which it was trying to work. This is because it operated in an occupation zone at the behest of the occupying forces. It was supplied by and supported by those forces. Thus, while UNRRA was not formally accountable to the occupation governments, in practice, it could not operate without the approval and consent of those governments. This put UNRRA in a awkward situation, occasionally, especially when UNRRA's policies ran counter to those of the occupying governments. They could face being shut down, or at least being threatened with it, through the withdrawl of support.

Their training was abysmal; as was their provisioning. They operated "on a wing and prayer", making it up as they went. For the initial months, because the upper echelons of the Administration provided no guidance, those in the field devised policy as circumstances demanded it. They begged, borrowed and confiscated what materials they needed in order to operate. They demanded, wheedled and parlayed to get what they needed from the occupying forces. Initially, there were no rules, no procedures, no directives--other than to bring succour to the DPs.

This was the situation facing Susan Pettiss, as she and Team 108 moved into Germany to bring order to chaos, and relief to the distressed. Her story provides us with a unique perspective on the DP problem in the American Zone in Germany and is testimony to the determination, ingenuity, exuberance and humanity of those hastily recruited international UNRRA staff who stepped in to deal with one of the largest refugee crises in modern times.

Lynne Taylor
University of Waterloo

The Occupation Zones
in Germany & Austria,
1946

FRIDAY, MARCH 17, 1945

It was St. Patrick's Day, 1945, when I wrote the following in my diary.

The voyage has begun! The good ship Kota Gede steamed out of Baltimore at nine o'clock this morning. The weather is perfect--beautifully clear and sunny, with enough snap in the air to make jackets comfortable. Everything seems to be propitious for a perfect trip.

To go back a little--to just a week ago--or even ten weeks ago. On January 2, 1945, training at UNRRA training center at the University of Maryland began. Ten weeks of classes in languages (German for me), lectures and lots of fun in everything, even the five mile hikes. Then after eight weeks, we were dramatically told to get ready for the trip. Mad dashing into Washington to Headquarters to sign all sorts of documents, check health examinations, shots, buy last minute purchases, etc. Governor Lehman, Director General of UNRRA and a former Governor of the State of New York, even bade us farewell impressively. We were all set for the final summons.

It came to me on Thursday night about nine p.m. when I was at Aunt Katie's apartment. There had been lots of rumors all day but nothing was confirmed until Miss Lindsey called to tell me that we were to report to Travel Section, trunks packed, and ready to leave the next day at four p.m. I dashed madly to the bus station, got back to College Park to find the dormitory in a turmoil. About five or six of us were in the group leaving. Everyone was in a hilarious humor, contributed to by our friends who were assisting us to pack. By one-thirty we were exhausted and gave up for the time being--so went to bed. The next morning was hectic. We were not supposed to have anyone know we were leaving but that was ridiculous. We heaved our trunks (foot lockers) in a truck, got a taxi and went into town about noon. Passports, tickets for New York, and final instructions were given to us. We dashed to the station to check our baggage about six p.m. since we were to leave on the eight o'clock train. While at the station a call came through telling us we would not be going that night--and probably not for several days. What a let down! I gathered my hand baggage and went to Aunt Katie's apartment.

Aunt Katie and her friend, Kathleen Small, were waiting expectantly, Kathleen with a lovely camellia for me. They howled when I told them the news. After a cocktail, Kathleen took us to a nearby restaurant for a marvelous dinner--the first of a long series of "last meals."

On Saturday I went to Headquarters, was told to "stand by," perhaps we were leaving. The rest of the girls had returned to College Park, had a marvelous party. After lunch word came that we were to leave Washington the following morning, on the seven o'clock train for Baltimore.

Sunday morning, after a frantic half hour worrying about who had my trunk check, we finally got off. We looked like refugees as there were no porters to carry our bags, so we each had hand luggage, musette bags, shoulder purses, and "Balkan Bunnies," those army issue khaki trench coats lined with faux fur.

In Baltimore we were given an address of the Holland-American Line office and told to report immediately. On arriving (nine in the morning) we were greeted by two officials and given details of our trip. We were to sail on a Dutch freighter and there were to be 23 women (the only passengers), 17 of us from UNRRA, 4 from the M.I.T. (Massachusetts Institute of Technology) Research Lab, one O.W.I. (Office of War Information) and one State Department girl. No male passengers. Accommodation would be good, meals regular and excellent. We would go in convoy, probably sail the next day. We were to be on board ship at two p.m.

Charity Grant, Polly Bakeman (my College Park roommate) and I had a room at the Belvedere Hotel where the gang stayed. That night Helen Zilka, Louise Guenther, Tally De Angeles and I had a "last dinner" with a huge steak and went to a movie. The next morning we gathered baggage and headed for the pier in a procession of taxis. There was the boat!!

We had prepared for a rugged trip, tough customs inspection, carrying our own baggage, etc. No one would allow us to touch our luggage. I was the first on--up the gang plank. At the top was standing a cute little Dutch officer, 3rd Mate, who introduced himself as Toni Wysmueller. Charity, Polly and I were assigned to Cabin 8. There were bunks for six, three stacked on each side, so by careful maneuvering we managed to arrange ourselves very nicely. All afternoon we explored the ship, met the officers, were checked in. Before supper the Chief Mate invited Tally and me to his cabin for drinks. Toni and Herman Auderbeck, the 2nd Mate, joined us. We also had drinks in the smoking room to celebrate our departure. This was Monday. We were then told that we would not leave that night, and probably not the next day. We could go into town if we wanted.

Tuesday, we dashed into town to make more last minute purchases. Since being on ship we had thought of lots of things. Had dinner at "Millers"--superb, and went to a movie, "A Tree Grows in Brooklyn." Arriving in time for supper, I was met at the gang plank by Toni--was told sailing was delayed and asked if I would go into town that night. Toni, Tally, the Chief Mate and I went to dinner, had a cocktail first at the Belvedere, then went to a night club, ended up by having coffee before returning to the ship.

Wednesday was more of the same. Went into town for lunch, did some shopping, went to a play, "Jacobowsky and the Colonel," got back to the ship for dinner.

Thursday
Were told we would probably sail that afternoon. Noon came. Night came, no signs of sailing. The customs officers didn't so much as peek at our luggage. The immigration officers checked us over. Rumor was we wouldn't sail until next day. Everyone had to stay aboard ship, though. Another farewell party in Toni's cabin. Had first boat drill.

And so on Friday we finally sailed. It was thrilling to pull away from the dock. All the crews on other ships yelled appropriate remarks to our crew about the cargo aboard (the women).

3

Chesapeake Bay was in its glory. Evidences of war were obvious as we cleared the harbor. And so we were all set!

UNRRA

When I read that diary entry, all the excitement of the time comes back in a flash. I was ready and eager to join the war effort, and to get as far away from Mobile as possible, and, most important, to start a new life. Though it is seldom mentioned nowadays, UNRRA had caused quite a stir when it was established. Well before World War II ended, wise individuals began planning for the repatriation and assistance of the millions of individuals in Germany and allied countries displaced from their homelands into prisons and concentration camps, and for use as slave labor. The chaos immediately following the end of World War I with clogged roads, epidemics, widespread hunger could not be repeated. We understood from listening to Hitler in the 1930s that World War II grew out of this hunger, disease, and displacement. It was to break this cycle of war that nations had come together before the shooting stopped to set in motion this organized international effort.

On November 9, 1943, representatives of forty-four countries gathered at the White House with President Roosevelt to sign a document establishing the first international relief agency in history. UNRRA was conceived while the United Nations itself was still in a gestative state. Former New York State Governor Herbert H. Lehman was selected as its first Director General and its Headquarters was established in Washington. The center for European recruitment and operations was set up in London.

UNRRA's mission was visionary and grand in scope. It was to provide for the immediate needs of the population from countries devastated by war including food, clothing, shelter, and medicine. Or, to quote from the official pamphlet distributed by the agency, the "sum total of UNRRA's objective" was the following:

> Get to the people the essentials to keep them alive and
> then give them some means to begin to pull themselves

up by other than their own bootstraps. And, finally, and
to as vast an extent possible, give them some boots....[1]

There was no background, tradition, system, common language or
currency for UNRRA. By the time we sailed for Europe, no
decision had even been made about a uniform. It was only when
we were in London that word came through that personnel would
wear the military uniform of their country, without insignias. A
patch on our shoulder and a little round patch on our caps with
UNRRA initials were our identification. This was because we had
not been recruited by our countries per se, nor were we official
representatives of them. Our loyalty, identification, and
accountability was to UNRRA. I, Susan Pettiss, became an
international servant.

In some respects, UNRRA was a magnificent unprecedented feat;
men and women of different nationalities, backgrounds and skills
coming together to meet impossible challenges. We often had
little beyond our own ingenuity to feed, cloth and shelter
thousands of refugees from every corner of Europe. At the outset,
no one knew what our mission would be. Not one of us truly had
the slightest idea how we would go about accomplishing it,
whatever it was.

However, I firmly believed, as did my colleagues, that peaceful
reconstruction of Europe must begin immediately. The mistakes
and perceived betrayals which followed World War I were not to
be repeated. We would, this time, achieve a permanent peace and
help to establish a unified world.

So the new year and my new life began on January 2, 1945. I
reported to the UNRRA Training Center at College Park,
Maryland, housed in a section of the University of Maryland,

---

[1] "The Story of UNRRA", issued by the Office of Public Information, United
Nations Relief and Rehabilitation Administration, 1344 Connecticut Ave. NW
Washington D.C., Feb. 15, 1948, pp.5-6.

relieved to be getting on with my life. I stayed in close touch with Aunt Katie, however, as College Park was, practically speaking, almost a suburb of Washington, only seven miles from the District of Columbia line. Public transportation on frequently scheduled buses took only about forty minutes from the University to the center of the city.

There were fifty of us Canadian and American recruits at any one time, with trainees departing to Europe as space on ships became available, but quickly replaced by new recruits. We were in our thirties or early forties, for the most part, and hailed from a variety of educational and occupational backgrounds. There were usually an equal number of men and women. None of us had accompanying attachments. We lived in a dormitory (women and men on separate floors), ate in a cafeteria, and spent the days in lectures and occasionally on hikes which usually ended in a local beer tavern.

A pervasive idealism infected both faculty and trainees. We all hoped to see established a true world community with new social systems and international relations. However, no one knew what to expect or how to prepare for the realities that would confront us. Thus, little practical training was offered. I guess the most useful information I picked up during those weeks was how to dispense meal or travel tickets to refugees loaded down with baggage in both arms. (You put the ticket in their mouths.) We did receive intensive language instruction, German for me, as I had already been assigned to Germany. I took a lot of kidding about my Alabama accent--as well as frequent advice that I get assigned to *southern* Germany.

This orientation period, however, served purposes other than training. It gave the faculty a chance to look us over and screen out misfits. It gave the State Department time to "clear" us, to prepare passports and other documents, to check health records, and to provide equipment. It also gave us, as individuals, time to adjust to our new lives.

For me, the idea of getting away from it all and into the arena of post-war Europe as a participant in efforts to pick up the pieces was intriguing--a great and socially acceptable escape.

However, I had not been prepared for the rapid swing in my personal life which began on that January 2nd. The dramatic events on a hot summer's night in Mobile made me realize that there was no safety or future in my marriage to an alcoholic, abusive husband. That night had precipitated my flight, ending at the home of my Aunt Katie in Washington D.C. After eight years as a married woman and a working woman in a traditional Southern setting, I suddenly found myself a part of a group of interesting, exciting companions who laughed a lot, had fun as well as serious "bull sessions" solving the problems of the world--all with a great sense of camaraderie. I realized at College Park that I had been bored most of my life.

I found, too, that I still had the capacity to attract men and to be rated as popular. For the first time in my life, I socialized with Afro-American men. As a white Southerner who had grown up in a racially segregated society, I was generally unaware of discord between black and white. That today seems inconceivable. As a social worker, I had associated as equals with black colleagues in an office setting. But at College Park, for the first time ever, I studied and socialized with people from other parts of the country, men and women from different backgrounds and different races. I remember standing in the cafeteria line with black men thinking, "Gee, I don't feel any different." And how surprised I was the first time I found myself dancing in the arms of a black man--surprised there was no difference, and no discomfort. Literally, color didn't matter. I was lucky, too. Those few Afro-American men (I don't recall any Afro-American women there at the time) were great guys. Ernest Griggs, for instance, later worked for the U.N. and I often saw him in New York. Herman Holiday was an ex-Olympic champion.[2]

---

[2] Our paths later crossed in Kenya. Sadly, my last contact was a visit with him in the New York Hospital where he died shortly afterwards from cancer.

I could sense a page turning in the book of my life at College Park. As the end of the six-week orientation approached, my sense of excitement and the desire to get on with this great new experience mounted. Recruits were being sent out with no more than a day's notice. Tight security was in effect to conceal shipping schedules from the enemy. Finally when word came that I was a part of a group that would be leaving the next day there was relief, a day of mad packing and an impromptu costume party on our dormitory hall that night, women only. I dressed in army issue khaki-colored long johns (only something a man would have designed), a huge red flower pinned on my shoulder and my gas mask. We had been briefed that passage to Europe could be tough, with few amenities aboard ship; that the food would be questionable both in quantity and taste; and that there would be always the lurking presence of enemy submarines, so we knew that things could be dangerous. But, if anything, that seemed to just heighten our excitement. There were fond farewells, although in a "I may never see you again" mood.

The saga of the long drawn-out departure was reminiscent of Sara Bernhardt's farewell to the theater. Finally when the day came and we did put out to sea, it was almost an anticlimax.

AT SEA

Saturday, March 18th
We had arrived amidst fog, in New York harbor on Friday night. We could see little but the lights of the city and feel the presence of gray hulks of other ships lying nearby.

On Saturday morning the sunrise in New York harbor was an unforgettable sight. As the mist lifted we found ourselves anchored just off the shore of Brooklyn with the Statue of Liberty in the distance. We were completely surrounded by gray ships, all loaded. The harbor was busy all day--ships coming and going--patrol boats roaming around, planes patrolling and tugs puffing in and out.

On Saturday night a Coast Guard boat brought word for the Captain, the Chief Engineer and Gunnery Officer. All Sunday there was an air of expectancy. We were told they were to attend a conference at one o'clock at which they would be given details of the convoy. No one knew when we would sail until they returned.

The day was a lazy, interesting one. The weather perfect. Slacks and a sweater were sufficient. So much was going on in the harbor that the morning was spent learning landmarks on the New York skyline, and how to identify the different types of ships.

The Captain returned on board just before supper. We were to sail that night.

The evening left an unforgettable impression as a farewell to our native land. Dusk in New York harbor with only a softening veil of mist. The lights blinked on, one at a time, like jewels. The other ships were busy with activity--they looked as if they might be going with us. If we could have ignored them it would have been very peaceful. After dark some of us stayed on deck and sang. It was a happy parting.

Monday, March 20th, At Sea
I got up in time to see the sunrise on the ocean. We had slipped out of the
harbor while we slept. The day was sparkling and clear. The sight of a
vast number of ships all around us was astounding. All morning, ships
maneuvered into position in the convoy. It gave a great sense of security
to be surrounded as far as one could see. Blimps were along, an aircraft
carrier on the horizon, planes circled. It did make us aware that this was
a serious thing.

For the next fourteen days, our convoy zigzagged across the
Atlantic, wary of an encounter with submarines--the dreaded
German U-boats. Convoys, a system of escorted formations of
large numbers of ships, had been developed in World War 1 to cut
risks and provide the greatest protection possible. They were
initiated again early in World War II, with the US providing some
escorts even before their entry into hostilities. Supply lanes from
America to Britain were lifelines to that country, which was
completely cut off from the continent. They were the only supply
channels for food, equipment, weapons, and personnel.

Our convoy was comprised of sixty ships, we were told, giving us
a sense of security. We and a ship loaded with flour were
positioned in the center as "precious cargo." The secrecy of the
route and timing was of greatest importance. No outside lights,
for instance, were permitted at night, thus all our evenings were
spent in the lounge where windows were blacked out.

The *Kota Gede* had been at sea when the Netherlands was invaded
by the Germans so it was turned over to the British and sailed
under the British flag, carrying two radio operators who were
members of the British Armed Forces. It was not exactly what you
would characterize as a luxury ship, just an ordinary freighter in
neat, but rather battered condition--no spit and polish.

I was very fortunate in the assignment of my "hut-mates." Charity
Grant, a Canadian about twenty-seven years of age, was from a
distinguished family in education circles in Toronto. Her brother-
in-law was the current Canadian Ambassador to England. There

was no sign of elitism about Charity, however. With typical Canadian openness and a delicious sense of humor, she was a delightful companion. Polly (Pauline) Bakeman was a psychiatric social worker from New England whose deadpan dissertations invariably sent Charity and me into gales of laughter. We immediately bonded and laughed our way across the Atlantic. I suppose our levity was a mild form of hysteria--a combination of excitement, tension and uncertainty. Everything seemed funny and fun.

The pattern of days aboard ship took shape. We had worked out a schedule for ourselves. At nine we broke up into little groups to study French on deck. With a break at 10:30 for chocolate, we kept it up until just before lunch. It was getting colder so a little exercise was necessary for warmth. After lunch, a nap--then a bath (the technique was an art, with a pail). Tea at four. Supper. At night, bridge or poker.

The monotony was broken by frequent invitations from some of the crew to join them in their cabins for drinks.

The Chief Mate usually asks three of us, Tally, Helen and me to his cabin for a drink before lunch. The past few days our summons have been most amusing. One of the Javanese boys comes on deck or in the salon and will point to one of us and say brokenly "you--whiskey--Chief." It is somewhat embarrassing.

Initially the crew kept its distance. They had just made a Pacific crossing with a boat loaded with returning nurses and one more boat loaded with women was more than they could bear. Gradually, however, they relaxed and began to enjoy our company. It was a Dutch crew with the exception of an American Gunnery Officer and the two British radio operators.

Toni and I became known as something of a couple, albeit a platonic one. I was often invited to his cabin for drinks before supper, alone or with others. He was rather small, very dark-haired and had a mustache. While not handsome, he had an infectious smile, mischievous brown eyes and a lusty Dutch sense

13

of humor. His English was excellent, he was interesting and fun to talk to. He was unmarried, but only thinking of war's end, and getting back to Holland and his family.

The Weismuller family was a well-known seafaring family with the tradition that each son, following their education, have time at sea before settling down as members of the business. Toni had attended the Dutch Naval Academy for two years before his turn and was caught in the war. Now, nine years later and once on a torpedoed ship when only a few were saved, he was ready for a life on land.[3]

The waning winter weather made it seem a gray world. Choppy, slate-colored water and gray sky enveloping motionless gray ships passing on the sea in all directions gave a dreary look to the voyage. It seemed peaceful enough. But once the alarm was sounded for real. Rumor fairly crackled, like static electricity. Depth charges had been dropped, it was said, and flares seen on one of the other ships in the convoy--we were in dangerous waters. We were instructed to keep our life preservers with us at all times.

It was a glorious night – the full moon made the sea look like molten lead. It was interesting to note the reactions among the passengers. On the surface there was not much difference. There was even joking about it. We learned that some of the crew members planned to sleep in their clothes (most had been torpedoed at least once). Some of the girls packed their musette bags and kept them handy. Some said they didn't sleep all night. I'm such a fatalist that I'm afraid I slept quite soundly.

We had the sense that we were nearing the end of our voyage. In the meantime, the steward was outdoing himself with the food. We had luscious pastries, steaks, cheese, and Dutch and Javanese dishes.

---

[3] Later, after leaving Germany, I visited Holland and got in touch with him. He took me and my traveling companion to Baarn to meet his family and for a sail on the Zeider Zee.

Tonight we had some wonderful Javanese rice with shrimp, eggs and meat all mixed up in it (nasi goreng, a traditional Indonesian specialty).

The kitchen crew was Indonesian, mostly from the island of Java. This was understandable, for at that time, Indonesia was a Dutch colony.[4]

While we were in this limbo at sea, news over the radio was building excitement every day, as reports of the German retreat was coming through. The decisive Battle of the Bulge had begun on December 16th, just before the end of 1944. Hitler had been defeated in the Ardennes Forest in Belgium and the German troops had retreated with the Allies in hot pursuit in a push to the Rhine. This was to be the Germans' "last stand." It was crossed by Allied forces on March 7th, just before we sailed. The spring offensive was under way. The daily news bulletins were giving such glowing accounts of the retreat that it gave us hope that it might not be so long before we could get to our job in Germany.

Easter Sunday, April 1st
A most unique Easter--certainly different from any I have ever experienced. We had begun to feel the first thrill of anticipation of landing. During the night the color of the water had changed from deep blue to a soft green. We knew we were out of dangerous waters as far as submarines were concerned.

Several of us got up and held a short service together on deck. The mist kept the sunrise from showing but it added to the peacefulness, appropriate for the occasion. The rest of the day was spent in joviality. It was grey outside but that didn't dampen our spirits.... We knew we would arrive in port the following day. We saw lighthouses that night--

---

4 Little did I know that the introduction to Indonesian food and the few Indonesian words I picked up would have a lot of meaning to me three decades later when my career took me frequently to that country. On one of those trips, when in Jogjakarta, I discovered there was a section of the city named Kota Gede. Of course I had to go!

the ships in the convoy had lights on for the first time.

Our emotions as to arriving are mixed. Our sojourn aboard the Kota Gede has been so very pleasant--the lack of responsibility, the lazy existence, and the congeniality of everyone. We have made close friends and now have a very warm feeling for each other. On the other hand--new experiences and adventures call. We are all very excited.

LONDON

Monday, April 2ⁿᵈ
Land! Before breakfast I went on deck and saw it--seagulls, too! It is like a holiday aboard. Everyone is dashing around--taking turns in the cabins packing (only large enough for one at a time). The crew is rather excited too. Even the Javanese boys were dropping dishes.

About noon we sighted the Isle of Wight--at first only a jagged rise on the horizon. As we drew closer we could see green--then cliffs and trees and lighthouses. Our escort vessel then led us away from the convoy which continued out to sea.

It was a beautiful day--clear, mild, and the sea was milky green. As we drew nearer the shore the fields stood out brilliant green with the trees almost black by comparison. We knew it was spring. I shall never forget my first impression of England. We passed very close to a lovely old castle--Norris Castle, whose green lawns sloped to the sea--then to the little village of Cowes with its red brick houses with the irregular roofs. It was neat and quaint. The church spire was the outstanding feature of the landscape. It made it all look like something out of a fairy story. We anchored off Cowes along with many other ships--some military and some freighters, all either gray or camouflaged. We had seen several buoys marked "wreck" and some ship hulks in the water, otherwise there was no war-like atmosphere.

On ship there was a combined atmosphere of sadness and festivity. We knew it was our last night aboard. The dinner was superb. The Captain joined us and was quite jovial. The Junior Officers brought a Victrola into the dining salon and there was dancing. Later, quite later, a few of us gathered into the cabin of one of the Junior Officers. The scene was a fitting finale to the trip. There were about six young Dutch officers, mostly blonde except Toni, the young Scottish boy, Scotty, and Dick Adair, the American Gunnery Officer. The Dutch boys sang Dutch songs, both rhythmic and sentimental. They were so young, so handsome, clean and wholesome-looking.

Whereas this was the end of a cruise-like voyage for us, for the crew it was the promise of a beginning--a beginning of a life where it left off five years ago. To be back "home" again. To see parents, wives, sweethearts, family, friends again. To forget the daily fear of the dangers of war. We Americans didn't know the travails of occupation by an enemy so it was hard to conceive the real meaning of "victory" to those in cities, towns and villages soon to be free. The crew didn't speak of it much, but you could feel the suppressed sense of anticipation.

Tuesday, April 3rd, England
England! Another beautiful day. Breakfast--packed. The tender came alongside about 10:00 in the morning--the immigration officers checked our papers. Then the real farewell. The boys all got a kiss. We stood on the deck of the tender as it pulled away from the Kota Gede. The Dutch crew broke out in a nice Dutch love song. Tears were in all our eyes. The boys ran to the front of the ship and waved until we were out of sight. I will always have a very warm feeling for the Dutch.

We were only about an hour coming into the Southampton harbor. We were the first passengers to be brought into the harbor for two and a half years. It was in the worst blitzed part of England. It was only because the coast of Holland had been liberated a few days before that we were allowed to come in.

The effect of war struck us with a bang. Destruction was evident everywhere. Fortunately for me, it was not quite so raw because the rains and weather had washed it and moss and flowers were trying to hide it. Churches were skeletons. Buildings were just walls, window panes were out everywhere.

Then the train ride to London--only two hours--through beautiful country. Every inch was cultivated. Small emerald green carpet-like fields cut by hedges and trees. The villages were neat, houses red brick, all neat and regular. Spring was at its height. Flowers, trees in bloom. People on the train were friendly, cheerful and fairly well dressed.

Waterloo Station was crowded with men in uniforms of all nations and services--people seemed serious and purposeful--little greetings and good-byes. After a tedious wait to contact our headquarters we came in a funny little taxi to the American Red Cross Hostel--the only available place in London as it was Easter weekend and so many service people had leave.

We ran into some of the UNRRA men and they gave us our first view of London. For an hour we rode the subways from Picadilly to Oxford Circus to Charing Cross, etc. We came out at Green Park and looked into the sky to see searchlights focusing on a plane. There was a big red fiery looking reflection in Green Park. The effect startled us at first, making us think that a bomb had been dropped. We soon learned it was just practice. But it did give us some idea of the real thing.

People in England are happy, happier than they have been for five years. They smile--they tell us there will be no more bombing although a V bomb hit in the center of London five days ago. The food situation is better--they even had ice cream for the last two months, a great treat. Their clothing seems drab and worn but adequate. There are flower venders on almost every corner selling violets, tulips, daffodils.

The next twenty days were spent in London. My shipmates and I were joined by many friends and colleagues from College Park who had come over on troop ships, 'liberty ships,"[5] freighters, et cetera. There were always pals with whom to go sightseeing, dine, dance, attend concerts. The excitement of the experience and times was contagious, and for a Southerner with no previous exposure to Europe and knowledge of London only through storybooks, pictures, and newspaper reports, I was enthralled.

Because of the scarcity of housing, several of us were billeted in a rooming house at 50 Cadogan Place, a house rented by a Polish woman doctor who had been in London for the past five years working in a Polish hospital. I shared a room with Helen Zilka

---

[5] "Liberty" ships were wartime purpose-built ships to carry equipment and supplies to support the war effort. They were cranked out in a hurry and in large numbers to meet the wartime demand.

who was fast becoming my best friend. Our backgrounds were certainly different. Helen was a first- generation American (her parents, Czech immigrants), living in Chicago. I was a fourth-generation Alabamian. Both of my grandfathers had fought in Confederate armies. Helen and I were both social workers, however, and soon found that we enjoyed the same things, the same people, and thrived on fun and laughter. Slightly taller and heavier than I, Helen was an attractive young woman with a shock of black hair curling softly around her face setting off her dusky skin and always smiling brown eyes. We had bonded almost immediately.

At night the city was in semi-darkness.

The dim-out is an amazing state of affairs. Of course it is nothing compared to what the black-out was, so they say. No lights show from houses or shops--only dim street lights are seen.

The bomb damage in London was extensive. Rubble was neatly stacked, the streets clean and clear and life seemingly ignoring the open sores of war. Some people were still sleeping in the Underground. On a visit to St. Paul's Cathedral we found that...

...the interior is beautiful, if a little cold looking. The gold-leaf and mosaic almost unbelievable. The stained glass windows are all out and one chapel damaged by bombs. We went up the winding stairs to the "whispering tower" and on to the roof of the dome. The view of London and the Thames river is awe-inspiring. It was the first time that I could get any idea of the extent of destruction caused by the blitz. It is a miracle that St. Paul's was not blasted. For blocks in every direction buildings are demolished.

We had checked in at the UNRRA office immediately after arrival in London.

We reported for work in small groups. The morning was spent in receiving instructions, registering with the police, obtaining ration points and books. That first day news had come to us about our jobs. It was very serious. The armies which are taking more of Germany every day, were screaming for UNRRA to handle the displaced persons. We would only be in London two weeks, then to Granville, France, for more training under SHAEF (Supreme Headquarters Expeditionary Force)-- then to Germany. The greatest blow--no civilian clothes. We American women would wear khaki W.A.C. (Womens Army Corps) officers' uniforms, we would also have helmets, gas masks, tents, bedrolls, etc. It looks serious.

We had gained the impression that the UNRRA office was not very well organized. The staff didn't know quite what to do with us so were glad to have us see the city, get out of their hair, and not bother them. Periodically we had to turn up for a lecture or two and get further instructions.

I will say that I'm a bit disappointed in the caliber of the recruited personnel in England--they are old, stodgy and hardly fitted for the job ahead. There seems to be a lot of vagueness, inefficiency in this E.R.O. (European Regional Office of UNRRA).[6]

I had to remind myself that the British had been on the battlefront for five years and most of the able personnel were deeply engaged in survival and war-related activities.

Unbeknownst to us in the field, there were also obstacles at higher levels. The US military was of two minds about whether it really wanted UNRRA in Germany or not. It had hesitated to call in UNRRA because it thought UNRRA would interfere with its own operations. However, when finally faced with the hordes of DPs (displaced persons), the military realized it couldn't and didn't want to be responsible for their organization and care. At that point, the military authorities began demanding that UNRRA send up teams immediately, if not yesterday. UNRRA, on the other hand, being badly under-funded and not wanting to over-commit itself when badly short of essential supplies and

---

[6]The E.R.O. managed UNRRA's operations on the European continent.

transport, had delayed recruiting and training teams until the military authorities had informed it of how many teams were needed, and where. And if it would be adequately supplied. The result, when the call came in finally, was panicked chaos.

I must say that any thoughts and actions about the job in Germany seemed suspended during this three-week immersion in the world of London. We made the most of it. Some of our comrades had been to London before and so could guide us. The usual attractions for tourists were now for us; adventures, exploration of sights and scenes of history and legend.

The impact of the contrast between the world of war and the sights and sounds of the fascinating city of London was dramatic. The juxtaposition of wartime and so-called normal life was a constant.

By night the bomb damage wasn't so ghastly and the silhouettes were magnificent. Attended service at Westminster Abbey. We got there about a half hour early. Many of the windows were gone--sandbags were evident everywhere--otherwise no bomb damage. The service was most impressive--the pageantry superb, the robes, the choirboys with their red and white costumes. I shall never forget the thrill that went through me when the organ first pealed forth and rang out among the rafters.

There were walks through Hyde Park, shopping on Regent Street, visits to the Tower of London.

London is full of American officers--all nice clean looking boys in well-fitting uniforms.

We went to concerts--The London Philharmonic at the Royal Albert Hall, the theater to see *While the Sun Shines*, Alfred Lunt and Lynn Fontaine in *Love and Idleness*, a noon-day concert at the National Art Gallery. We saw *Gay Rosalinda* (Johann Strauss' *Der Fledermaus*) and a movie *Henry V*, produced by and acted in by Laurence Olivier.

One of my most vivid memories was the day at Kew Gardens with Helen as my companion.

Kew is almost indescribable. I shall always remember this day when I see lilacs--"Down to Kew in lilac time!"--they were in full bloom, the flowering plums, apricots and cherries were at their height. The trees reminded me of Japanese prints. There were beds and beds of tulips in bloom, roses, pansies, rhododendrons, camellias, and hundreds of other flowers. Lovely walks wandered through the woods where bluebells were blooming. The gardens were filled with people lying on the grass, under the trees and sitting along the river. We walked for two hours and still didn't cover the garden. We had tea in the garden at the Pitt House under a flowering plum tree. After tea Helen and I took a trolley to Hampton Court and went to the castle. It is the first honest-to-goodness castle I have ever been in. It looks so perfect that I would have expected it could almost be a movie set. It was very interesting inside--that part through which we were allowed to go. Part is now given over to apartments for widows of indigent notables.

On the other hand there were constant reminders of the war. In addition to the gutted buildings, boarded-up windows, streets of row houses where some were gone, like missing teeth, there were ominous sounds.

On Saturday, April 14th I noted...
...for an hour bombers have flown over London on their way to Berlin (we presume). They had carried out a terrific raid the previous night. Again on April 15th, lots of planes had been going over all day--headed for Germany. Air resistance is reportedly nil and Berlin in shambles.

Again on April 15th...
...planes were overhead about midnight until the air fairly vibrated.

The reality of the war at the front was brought home most vividly by stories from friends. On arrival in London, I had looked up Demouy Spottswood of Mobile to give him news of his family whom I had seen just before leaving Washington. He was a Major in the Civil Affairs Division of the US Army. Over dinner one night he told me of his recent experience.

He had gone into France shortly after the Normandy Invasion to plan for the feeding of civilians. The Army didn't think it very important at first. When Patton's army went through Paris in such a hurry Demouy was given 36 hours to formulate a plan for feeding Paris. Fortunately the need at the time wasn't as great as anticipated. The people suffered greatly later on. And now Demouy was to leave on the 15th to go to Vienna. This was surprising to me (April 5th) because Vienna had not fallen (it was April 5th when we had this conversation). The Russians were within 30 miles of it.

On Saturday, April 14th, my diary read...
Vienna fell yesterday to the Russians. It is amazing how Demouy had been ordered weeks ago to proceed to Vienna on April 15th.

I was in touch with another Mobilian, Les Taylor, a cousin of my former husband.

Les (a physician) is now Lt. Colonel Taylor, Chief Surgeon of the 216th General Hospital in Warminster. He had wired that he would be in town that afternoon. Les had been in England a year--is quite anxious to get home again. His hospital is on property of the estates of Lord Bath, rented by the US. The capacity is 1500 and there is a complete turnover each month. In one month they handled 2700 casualties. In all this year they have only had six deaths. He described the way the wounded are treated--care on the field within a matter of minutes--then treatment at a base hospital. There the wounds are left open with penicillin on them. They are then flown back to the base hospitals in England for closing of the wounds, operations, etc. There is plenty of blood plasma, so that there is little suffering and quick recovery. It all sounds miraculous.

I had expected our soldiers to have the need to unburden their tales of battle. Quite the opposite. They wanted to talk about everything but the war. What kind of clothes were girls wearing at home? (Nylon stockings and hats, hats, hats!) What movies were playing? (*Meet Me in St. Louis* with Judy Garland starring.) They wanted to flirt with women, and dance, and drink wine, and laugh with them. We were happy to oblige. For instance, there was an evening with two American officers who were on seventy-two hours' leave from the front.

Went to the Quartermaster's Store for my uniforms. After trying on and assembling almost everything, I started out struggling with both mine and Helen's packages since she had a conference. A very nice officer helped me--got a cab and asked me to lunch. We first went to the Ritz Hotel but it was too crowded--went on to the Piccadilly Hotel.

He was from North Carolina, now in the 313th Regiment of the 79th Division of the 9th Army. He asked me to go out that night. I said " I have a friend (Helen)," and he replied, "I have a friend, too," so the four of us went out together. He was awfully nice--this was the last night of their 72-hour leave.

At eight o'clock he and his friend from Kansas arrived. He had made complete plans for the night. We had a drink. They hadn't tasted rye in years and practically fell on my neck when I produced some. We were taken by taxi to Lansdowne House--a lovely restaurant with music. Reservations had been made (in the name of General Twining, their commander). A marvelous dinner with champagne. After dinner we went to the Coconut Grove, a private club they had joined for the night (again, in the name of General Twining). They had bought three bottles of scotch, at $30 each (so we learned later). The night ended at 4:00 a.m. They were two nice American boys--had been in the army since 1940-- both married, both lonely for nice girls. They said it was the nicest evening they had had since leaving the States. They were both in the Normandy invasion, had gone across the Rhine and had been in the thick of fighting, although they didn't talk much about it. It was encouraging to see that they were still normal, natural American boys even after their experiences.

The whole London experience was like a dream, something which in my wildest imagination would never happen to me. Only those in the South wealthy enough to afford "The Grand Tour" could expect to go to Europe. My great grandfather, William Stewart, had taken his wife and three daughters to Europe, had been caught there by the Civil War, and lived in Paris until the war's end. When he returned to Mobile, he found his cotton brokerage business, home and everything gone. My father had died when I was ten, leaving my widowed mother to bring up the three children and educate us during the Depression, which wiped out any idea of travel or adventure. Given that my maiden name was "Thames," London had a special meaning to me. Still, seeing my name everywhere was startling.

And money in London had no significance. We never made decisions on what we did or where we went based on cost. First of all, because of the constraints of war economics, luxury activities were relatively cheap. In a letter to my mother I mentioned, ·

For once in my life I seem to have enough money. I had a $100 check waiting for me--got $200 for uniforms of which I only needed about $80. We can't take but $50 (in French currency) with us and having no place to deposit the balance I almost have to spend it. I can assure you that is not a burden.

In those days, too, it was still customary for men to pick up the check, and there were plenty of men around willing to do it.

It was as if I had to continuously pinch myself to believe that I was in the country of Dickens, the Magna Carta, Queen Elizabeth, Shakespeare, Piccadilly Circus, Sir Thomas Beecham, Westminster Abbey, and the Thames River, and in the midst of war so vividly portrayed in recent radio reports, newspaper pictures, posters and movies. The word "history" took on a more intimate meaning.

Friday, April 13th
Roosevelt is dead! One of the girls came running up to the room as I was dressing to tell me.

I still remember the moment vividly. Having been a Depression youth, and social worker during the Roosevelt social revolution, I was both shocked and stricken with grief.

All day in London, you could sense a feeling of grief throughout the city. I had no idea how beloved he was. I had learned on the boat coming over that people throughout the world probably thought more of him than did the American people. One of the English shop-girls was telling me today that the English loved him more than they did Churchill. Churchill was all right as far as winning the war was concerned, but they didn't have the confidence in his principles in respect to peace. A great pity. All eyes are now on Truman.

And on the next day, Saturday,
Talked with an English waiter. He was so disturbed over Roosevelt's death--all the English are. The tributes in the papers and on the radio are incredible. At 11:00 a.m. everything stopped for two minutes of silence. All day long, in all churches, memorial services are being held. On Tuesday, services will be held at St. Paul's Cathedral. The English did certainly love and respect him. As one paper said, they consider Churchill the "strength" and Roosevelt the "faith."

Sunday, April 23rd, was the last day in London,
...sad--a meeting in the morning to receive passports, tickets and the SHAEF identifications, etc. Took heavy baggage down before breakfast. I had on my uniform for the first time. Felt very self-conscious. Did errands, told people good-bye, last minute purchases. Then Antoine's for a last beauty touch.

We left about ten on a boat train--traveled an hour and a half to New Haven to embark. The train was full of boat passengers, soldiers of all nationalities, some French civilians, Red Cross workers. We went through customs, embarked about midnight. All the women, about thirty of us, slept in one big room--double-decker bunks. We had tea and coffee before going to bed, so it was rather late. We weren't to sail until the next morning.

FRANCE

Tuesday, April 24th
Our boat pulled out of New Haven about nine in the morning--another
beautiful day, blue sky, milky green water. The white cliffs stood out
until we were far at sea--as impressive a sight as our first glimpse had
been. I was a little sad to leave England. I had loved every minute of it.

The boat trip only lasted from nine to one. It was interesting to see the
other passengers. It was too cold to stay on deck and nothing to do in the
limited space. We were told to keep life preservers with us at all times.

We met American soldiers who were glad to see American girls. There
was also a group of French officers only liberated from a prison camp on
Sunday, flown to England, and now (the next day) returning to France.
They had been treated fairly well because the nephews of Churchill,
Montgomery and a Polish general were in the camp. They had been
interned for five years.

The first sight of France was almost as lovely as that of England. We
pulled into Dieppe about one. It was green and gently rolling to the sea.
The destruction there was simply astounding. Most of the docks were
blasted away. Rows of shells of housing were left, very little was
untouched. We boarded the boat train for Paris. The train was nicely
upholstered, in good condition. Our compartment was shared with an
English Lieutenant going to Paris on leave. We stood at the window in
the aisle most of the day, looking at the countryside. It was fascinating--
bomb craters frequent and every little stone house or barn had gun holes
cut in them. Many were destroyed.

We arrived in Paris about seven--were taken in a large bus to the "Circle
International Militaire"--an Officers' Mess, for supper. It was an
elegant place--filled with American officers--a wonderful meal. On the
way to our hotel (Little Palace Hotel on Sebastopol Street) our bus driver
kindly took us on a slight tour, down the Champs Elysée, by the Arc de
Triomphe, to the Place de la Concorde, to the Tuilleries; and the Louvre

and the Notre Dame Cathedral. It was almost dusk and a teasing view of the city. Later Helen and I had the nerve to go on the Metro to the Champs Elysée and walk down it for awhile. There was not a taxi in Paris. There were some horses and buggies.

The next day...
...up at five. Left in the bus at six for mess at the Officers' Club--arrived at the station to catch a train before nine. I shall never forget that half-mile walk down the station platform carrying luggage. It was tough.

We women had all agreed that we would not ask the men or expect them to help us then or later, declaring a sort of feminine independence. So we had helmets and gas masks on our backs, duffle bags, purses, musette bags and coats. To this day it is a heavy memory.

This train wasn't at all like the one we rode the previous day. There were eight of us in the compartment--no cushioned seats. The aisles were crowded with people and luggage the whole day. It was a trip I shall always remember.

The distance was no greater than that traveled the previous day but it took us from nine in the morning until six at night. The tracks had been bombed and all bridges destroyed--recent repairs made it possible to get over them, but slowly. The reason we had to go all the way to Paris was because there was no coastal transportation from Dieppe to Granville.

The scenery, especially Normandy, was incredibly beautiful. The rolling countryside was as if tended by a million gardeners. The hedges, the trees, the green fields were in perfect neatness. The lilacs, buttercups, daisies and some unfamiliar flowers were everywhere. Cows, sheep, and horses added to the landscape. The houses were either gray plaster or stone with softly irregular tile or thatch roofs. Young men were not to be seen. The fields were being worked by women and old men. During the whole day I saw only one automobile although we followed roads the whole way. This peaceful countryside was quite often marred by signs of war. It was always possible to know when we approached a bridge by the bomb craters in the fields beforehand. Lovely orchards were pockmarked.

Especially in Normandy, complete villages were destroyed. One such, Argentan, actually did not have two walls of a house standing. It was complete debris. It was shocking. Others were badly hit. I got the impression that all of Europe will have to be rebuilt.

Our train was carrying many French prisoners of war who had been released only several days ago. They had been in prison for five years. The men were old looking, but sunburned and fairly healthy in appearance. At every station, crowds of serious people, mostly women (and always a priest) lined the platforms, anxiously waiting. The French seemed well organized. Each station had a well-marked "Center for Deportees"--often decorated with flags and flowers. The men would be met by what appeared to be a committee. There did not seem to be much jubilation or excitement though, almost a stolidness.

In our compartment there were several UNRRA girls and an UNRRA Frenchman. Additionally there was a returning prisoner of war and a French soldier. French was spoken almost entirely. I was particularly interested in the prisoner of war who was returning home. He said things had been pretty bad--water and potatoes to eat mostly. The Red Cross packages came once a week and kept them alive. If they worked for the Germans they got more to eat. He hadn't been treated too badly. He lived in the Saar Valley.

Watching the reception of returning prisoners was interesting. In Paris the officers had created much excitement--other French officers had greeted them with much kissing on each cheek, hand shaking, slapping of backs. Movie pictures were taken. In contrast, in the little towns most of the people were quiet, motionless and sad looking. Many men were put in trucks to go on to their own villages. Those who were met by families seemed deeply moved, but calm. And there were always the crowds of solemn people, waiting and hoping, I suppose, that each day their man would come. We arrived in Granville about six in the afternoon, very weary. Several of the fellows we knew met us at the station. Our baggage was heaved into trucks, we got in also, to be transported to the Normandy Hotel, just in time for supper.

I might mention that this was my first introduction to travel in trucks although this was to be a way of life for months and years to come. By trucks, I'm referring to army trucks, the ubiquitous two-and-a-half-ton trucks. Sometimes, there were benches along the sides of the rear section for passengers, sometimes it was covered with a green canvas top, particularly in bad weather. Slacks were a must. A well-padded rear helped.

Granville is a little dot on the map of the Normandy coast, a small village on the west coast of the Cherbourg peninsula. It was just below the beach where the US troops landed in the Allied invasion on June 6th just nine months before. Even after the beachhead was established, heavy fighting continued with slow progress. The British and Canadian forces moved north towards Belgium and the Netherlands while the US forces swept south, town by town until the real breakthrough when St. Lo fell on July 18th. Granville is just a few miles from St. Lo, which was virtually destroyed.

Though it had never been as fashionable as the better-known Normandy resorts of Deauville and Trouville, the town was beautiful and quiet, a simple and harmonious collection of white plaster houses and small cafes threaded along cobblestone streets that followed the hilly contours of the land.

The Normandy Hotel evidently at one time was an elegant resort hotel, directly on the beach. It was now camouflaged with drab paint--was bare of furniture and most windows were out. Its most interesting feature were the murals on the wall in the dining room--very large-sized paintings of voluptuous women. We were told they were originally nude, painted there by the Germans when the hotel was used as an Officers' Club. When the Americans came along they painted some clothes on the women. They were fierce! After supper there was registration--more showing of papers. After registration I went walking along the beach with some of the men and then to bed--on a canvas cot. I mean the kind without any spring or mattress --just canvas--with a bedroll on top--no sheets, my jacket in a pillowcase for a pillow.

I slept in wool socks and a woolen undershirt under a flannel gown, snuggled under a few scratchy brown Army blankets. And I was still cold.

The UNRRA Mobilization Center had only been set up about a month before our arrival and during that time had trained, assembled and equipped one hundred teams of thirteen members each. New arrivals to the Center went first to the Normandy Hotel in Granville (there were eighty-seven in our group). Those needed first, and those with some previous training, were sent on to Joulouville, a smaller village four miles away, where they were billeted in a (former) Casino for about six days. A nearby building, a previous Children's T.B. Preventorium, was used partly for lectures and partly for those who had finished training and were assigned or about to be assigned to teams for departure. There was a tremendous movement of people at the Center--usually five hundred at Granville and five hundred at Joulouville at any one time, with an average turnover of three hundred every week. One of the perks was that we became eligible for P.X. issue, which then was a week's ration consisting of five candy bars, two packages of gum, five packages of cigarettes, and a bar of soap.

The conditions at all three residences were shocking.

The day after our arrival at the Normandy Hotel I found a notice just posted that a group of us were to be ready at three o'clock to transfer to Joulouville to begin training the following day. This time the accommodations were a little worse--three in a room, sleeping on canvas cots, window panes out, no furniture, no water most of the time. Rugged!

No water at all--no toilet facilities functioning--cold, no sheets, my jacket still serving as a pillow. My hands got so cold and blue I had to go walking to get warm.

It actually snowed one day.

The outlines of our job began to emerge. Lecturers brought word of field conditions and of responsibilities expected of us. On April 29th, we learned the Army was requesting twenty teams of four (Director, Administrative Officer, Welfare Officer and Driver) for the next week.

On May 2nd, we learned that two million DPs were already being cared for in Germany. Ninety UNRRA teams had arrived there and forty more to go out the next week, one of which I would be on. At a meeting of Welfare Officers I learned at that time there were thirty-two of us in all, with only two men. The nationality breakdown was interesting--twelve Americans, one Canadian, one Czech, four Belgian, nine English and eight French.

My first impression of UNRRA's personnel was somewhat of a shock--a lot of elderly British colonels, some still carrying their swagger sticks or tottering on canes. There were a few Belgian doctors and Dutchmen. Americans were in the minority. As time went on, however, the image changed.

Mostly men, mostly young (except the English), vital and energetic. Most of the Continentals have been in the armed services, in prison or concentration camps. Their true life stories beat all the fiction I have ever read.

And then there were the American soldiers, God bless them. A camp adjacent to the Casino was occupied by a company made up of G.I.s back from the front for R&R. On learning there were American girls among us, they sent an emissary to find out if a dance could be arranged.

And what a dance we had! Barrels of beer were produced and a French orchestra located. I jitterbugged for three hours without a break--no surprise, considering that the soldiers arrived in droves and there were only twenty of us American girls. It was a great success. Some officers came, but stood in the background. It was a "grunts" dance. Most of them had been overseas for three years and they had seen only WACs and nurses, with whom they couldn't mix socially because of rank.

The boys were hungry to just talk to the girls, to dance, flirt a little. One of the soldiers said he couldn't express how he felt about the Americans coming here--it is something like taking an old brass bucket and polishing a bright spot on it.

The unit next door literally saved our skins. We had no way to take baths, what with the water situation, so the G.I.s worked out an arrangement whereby they declared their showers off-limits for a couple of hours, set out guards and slipped American girls through the fence. Hot showers! We were in heaven! They had made a hole in the fence that divided the Casino from their camp, a hole that opened onto a walkway running the length of a shed which housed a row of showers. Mildewed curtains gave privacy, as did the high fence just on the other side of the walk. We felt badly about our non-American friends, but the opportunity was too great to miss. When we thanked one of the boys, he commented, "Since we are fighting for American girls, they sure can use our hot water."

Nearby was a French house which had been taken over and occupied by American officers, dubbed "the Villa." It was modern architecture, in good taste. It could have been a Palm Beach home. Having met some of the American UNRRA men and women at the dance, they were generous in sharing their open fire, steaks, peanuts, et cetera--all priceless amenities. They would send a jeep to pick us up on evenings. It was my first ride in a jeep.

Saturday, April 28th
Word had come over the radio that Himmler was asking for peace-- offering unconditional surrender to the United States and England--not Russia. And on Monday, April 30th. "News of importance--Mussolini shot and killed. Himmler made second offer of peace. Peace expected any moment." Up at the Villa that evening, just before we were ready to go home, a call came from the Colonel that an alert was on--there was a

possibility of an attack. We had to wait for quite some time. Nothing happened, however. There are still Germans on the Guernsey Island (one of the Channel Islands), just off our coast.

Often at night we would walk into the village of Joulouville, an old town with narrow, winding cobblestone streets overlooking a little harbor and bay. The clacking of the wooden-soled shoes (there had been no leather available since early in the war) of the villagers became a familiar sound. Since there was no electricity or heat in our buildings, we sought warmth and light, as well as congeniality, in the village cafes. It was my first real exposure to the international camaraderie which quickly developed over wine or Calvados, the local brandy distilled from apple cider. It tasted to me, at first, rather like gasoline. It was explained to us apologetically that we were getting the new, raw Calvados as the American army had exhausted the existing stock when it went through. Sharing jokes, singing French, Belgian, Canadian songs with my new companions, I could feel my world expanding.

Wednesday, May 2nd
News has come that Hitler is dead--that Germany is collapsing. Everyone is expecting peace at any time. Italian fighting has ceased.

May 3rd
The Germans in Denmark, Norway and Holland have surrendered--the only resistance left is in southern Germany.

Thursday, May 4th
Several of us walked to a cafe where everyone had an air of anticipation and were gathered around the radio every hour for news. At eight it was rumored that Churchill was to give big news over the radio, but no news.

The UNRRA teams were moving out every day--ten starting each morning, separating as they went across France. Trucks were always parked in front of the building, poised. The Army was finally asking for small "spear-head teams"--five members, a Director, Administrator, Welfare Officer, Doctor and Nurse--with two trucks, two drivers.

The whole process of creating and organizing the teams seemed very disorganized and unplanned, as did our training and preparation.

Thursday, May 3rd
Lectures by Col. Schottland who had flown in from SHAEF Headquarters (the Military Authorities) to talk to us about actual situation in Germany. There are by count 2,000,000 Displaced Persons already to be cared for in Assembly Centers. It is an enormous job. Already 90 teams of UNRRA are out and there will be 40 to leave next weeks, one of which I will be on. Yesterday, I was told I had been put on a team. After dinner I was given a slip of paper notifying me that I was on Team 104--Director, Mr. Koster. That is all. I was dying of curiosity. In an hour I had duffle bags packed, hauled down stairs. In a truck, and rode over to the School which is the Training School Center. What a place! At present there are about 500 UNRRA people at Granville and at Joulouville. An average of 300 come and go out every week. It is a tremendous movement. Granville (Normandy Hotel) is the receiving center. While training (6 days) the Casino at Joulouville is the residence and then one moves to the School when placed on teams. The teams go out in convoy from the school. The School, an ex-Preventorium, is a series of glass enclosed, very large rooms with cement floors. There are 14 of us in a room. Cold, plumbing and water almost impossible, and no lights. Still worse--Helen and I have remained together throughout, although we have been separated from some of our friends. I met my Director, Mr. Koster, and the administrative officer, Jackie De Garter, both young Dutchmen--very nice. We are scheduled to leave Monday.

Saturday May 5th
My Dutch Director found me in the morning greatly disturbed. He had just been told that he was being sent on a special mission to a concentration camp. He was raising cain because I was not to be his welfare worker. He was going to refuse to go unless I could. Later he had a conference, was ordered to go. I didn't have enough languages. I have a new Director, a Belgian, Mr. del Marmol. Ona told me about it, very apologetically, said they were looking out for me. They have been very nice.

So not only had Team 104's mission changed in the course of two days, but so had my own assignment, from Team 104 to Team 108, under del Marmol. I had been rushed through, with very little of the training we were supposed to get. However, it worked out to the good, as I was lucky with my teammates. The Belgian Director, Charles del Marmol, a professor of law at the University of Liege, had studied law and economics at Columbia University in New York and traveled some in the United States. He spoke very good English. *A tall, lanky Belgian who is slow talking, a humanitarian, but can't say much for his organizational ability. I like him very much. The first thing he did was to show me a picture of his wife and two children.* Jack Atkins, an elderly Englishman, the Supply Officer--*he was too old for the job, but pleasant.* Philippe Malleret, a Parisian, about thirty years old but quite boyish, had been with the Maquis underground in Southern France for the last two years. Yvonne Moerch, *the little French nurse is blond, red cheeked, and spoke no English.* Roger and Jean, both French, were the two drivers.

Monday, May 7th
On the way to supper someone casually remarked that peace had been declared, just like that! No one seemed terribly excited. After supper, went from one cafe to another--everyone listened at eight o'clock to the broadcast, drank white wine, sang songs. At about eleven the jeep came to take several of us Americans to the Villa. The atmosphere there was tense (the Captain glued to the radio, with headphones on). No one knew whether the Channel Islands had surrendered or not.

The actual surrender took place at 2:41 a.m. on May 7th in Rheims, but was repeated for the Russians on May 8th in Berlin--hence May 8th is considered official V-Day.

ON TO GERMANY

May 8th, VE Day, the end of World War II in Europe.
The day of departure. I got up at daybreak, finished packing my duffel
bag, made my bedroll, donned my "limey" (British army issue) slacks,
uniform shirt and G.I. knitted cap, ready to leave. By nine our trucks
were loaded, then we set out. We were to report to the Seventh Army in
Heidelberg. We pulled out, four teams of eight trucks (pre-Dunkirk
British lorries), two trucks per team, one canvas covered and one open. I
sat in the back of our canvas-covered truck on the duffel bags and bed
rolls with Philippe and Mr. del Marmol. Yvonne didn't have slacks so
she rode in the front of one truck with the driver. Jack Atkins, being
rather elderly, rode up front with the other. I was teary at parting from
my friends with whom I had bonded in College Park, London, Granville,
and Joulouville, desolate at the thought that I might never see them
again.

The day was perfect. It was official VE Day so all the country was
celebrating. Every French house had flags out, every village was filled
with flags. The people filled the streets, some very quietly, some very gay;
sometimes we would see long processions marching towards the
cemetery. Everywhere we went, people waved because our trucks were
painted as American trucks and we were in uniforms. The G.I.s we
encountered were jubilant when they found I was American. Some
French towns were tragic--not a house or building standing--Argentan
and Vire, especially. The beautiful, peaceful Normandy countryside was
in such contrast. Many villages were unharmed, however--streets and
cafes full--holiday air everywhere--always flags, flags, flags.

It was a long, hard day, a day of sharp contrasts. We made our
way from the French coast under brilliant blue skies. In every
town or village through which we passed, throngs of people
welcomed us, sometimes offering champagne and wine. Most
were middle-aged, the women wearing dresses with long, black,
bountiful skirts and white lace-trimmed blouses with sleeves
rolled up. We saw few children. Some French towns had been

demolished. It seemed queer to watch as individuals appeared from underground where they had been living in cellars. Signs of recent fighting conjured up all the film shots we had been seeing in the movie houses during recent months. I almost expected to see helmeted G.I.s with guns crouched behind buildings.

We arrived in Chartres at dusk to a celebration so joyous and exuberant that it seemed to be trying, in a single night, to make up for all the suffering of the war years. Champagne corks popped in a kind of giddy civilian artillery.

In the lobby of the small hotel where we were billeted I met an American Captain--he begged us to have champagne with him--he was very lonesome. After we washed up, donned clean uniforms, the group of us joined him and two other captains for champagne. Then Philippe, Yvonne, the captains and I went out on the town. The streets were jammed. We wandered around, went to another cafe--more champagne. There was dancing in the streets--we danced and went to a little carnival in the middle of the town, rode the merry-go-round and the caterpillar, had a marvelous time. At one point a Frenchman ran up and kissed me on both cheeks. It was my true celebration of VE Day.

I was determined to see the famous Chartres Cathedral. Just before dawn, I left the still noisy square and entered the silent church. The fabled stained glass windows had been removed for their protection early in the war. *It was beyond description. Pure Norman architecture, white stone inside.* I stood completely alone in the ethereal atmosphere, under the whiteness of the arched ceiling supported by the majestic white pillars; lit only by the rays of early dawn. It is difficult to describe the flow of emotions on that memorable morning. With a deep sense of humility, I walked back to the noisy street just beginning to tone down from the night's revelry. Locating my teammates, we set out in our trucks on the next day's journey.

May 9th we made it to Troye. We had crossed through increasingly devastated countryside. Undoubtedly we were following the route of the American army on its push to Germany. The roads could barely be navigated because of bomb craters and dust. The Loire and Champagne regions were nearly deserted, ghostly.

Thursday, May 10th, Nancy.
Another day in the back of the truck. The land gets poorer--the villages sometimes completely deserted. Another UNRRA truck broke down so that a Belgian doctor, and a French social worker rode most of the day with us. The conversation was entirely in French--my French is improving. I had lost my voice the first day and by now could hardly croak.

In Nancy, Philippe was determined that I would have a real French meal, my last night in France. He scurried around, finally arranged a "black market" meal at a cafe. It was an interesting place. We were the only people there. We had red wine, hors d'oeuvres, steak, potatoes, green salad, pastry and liqueur. It was very good.

This meal seemed to have special significance for Philippe. He was so eager for me, the non-European, to have a real French meal, cuisine being justifiably the pride of France. Also, he knew it would be his last good French meal in the foreseeable future. The restaurant was small, with white undecorated walls and dark wood trim, simple white tablecloths tended by a waiter in a dark coat over white trousers. The hors d'oeuvres were the specialty of the region, paté de fois gras, the steak a rare treat at a time of still severe shortages.

Friday, May 11th, Nancy to Heidelberg. Into Germany!
A long, hard day's trip. We crossed the Rhine and went into Germany. Now, everywhere were signs of recent fighting. The roads were terrible, crowded with war vehicles. All along the sides were wrecked tanks, machine guns, German cars. The German cities were completely leveled. There were few people around. What a contrast between the joyous French and the furtive Germans.

Sometimes we had to pull over to let long lines of American troops pass, slogging along. When they discovered an American girl in the back of the truck there was much shouting passed along the line. "Where you from?

Hey fellars. Look who's here, an American girl!" The G.I.s looked dirty and weary. It was very hot and dry. By the end of the day my arm ached from waving. The first day out I had attempted to keep my hair combed, to put powder and lipstick in place. By the third day on the road, it was all I could do to tie a red bandana around my head and wipe the dust and sweat off my face.

Months later, Charley del Marmol recalled our journey in a toast on my birthday. Though the English was a little awkward, the sentiment was moving. *"It was a funny mixture of all sorts of people, talking different languages but united by the same ideal and optimism,"* he said of Team 108.

And amongst these people there was a girl. There was a girl that nobody had met before. She had a pair of pants on, and she was rubbing her nose once in a while with a mixture of dust and beauty powder. There was a girl who did behave herself as a real soldier. Flat tires, shortage of gasoline, the lack of a ladies' room every ten miles, nothing could impair her morale. There was a girl, cut short and sharp from all her friends from overseas, completely lost with a strange continental people, speaking many funny languages with an Oxford or a Paris accent.

Already the team was growing closer. Charley, our Director, was so lanky as to be Lincolnesque; he had been too old to fight in the war. Charley's English was excellent, as were his interpersonal skills. Good-humored and sensitive at the same time, he had a remarkable knack for maintaining authority while never actually appearing to do so. Elderly, white-haired Jack seemed almost stereotypically British. Essentially genial, he nonetheless spoke only English and would all but scream at anyone who didn't. I was surprised to observe that more often than not he managed to get his point across. Philippe was a Parisian whose boyish looks belied his age of about 30 years. Though married and the father of a young child, Philippe had spent the last two years fighting with the French resistance in the southern part of the country. Philippe spoke no English, so while riding atop our baggage in the back of the truck we entered a contest to see who could learn more English/French first. Needless to say, my high school French improved markedly during those days with Philippe and Charley. Her curly blond hair tucked under a French army beret, Yvonne too spoke only French, but as the only two women in the group, we quickly became friendly and somehow learned to understand each other. Though shy, Yvonne was a hard worker.

The team's various personalities and work patterns quickly emerged. For instance, on the first day out, at lunchtime, Jean and Roger pulled the trucks to the side of the road and unloaded a box of rations. They put it on the ground in the adjacent field and everyone sat down, picnic style. Soon it became evident that they were waiting for me, the Welfare Officer, to take over. I let them know then and there on that dusty first day that it was not their welfare I was responsible for.

In her own UNRRA memoir, *The Wild Place*, Kathryn Hulme calls the UNRRA teams "the United Nations test tube",

> [S]mall groups, representing five or six different countries, not sitting in diplomatic politeness around some international round table with earphones at each place to give simultaneous translation, but thrown into the wilderness of World War II's destruction like small wandering tribes from Babel, to live together all twenty-four hours around the clock with no escape in any direction, to break bread together three times daily and to do a work that had never been done before.[7]

I now realize that our journey was somewhat hazardous, but at the time I was largely oblivious of the fact. For instance , whenever we had the occasion to stop by the roadside, the men simply walked around the truck to relieve themselves, while Yvonne and I had to locate a suitably substantial clump of bushes. One time, she and I were crossing a field on our way to such an improvised ladies room when we were startled by an uproar behind us. Turning around, we saw Charley, Jack, Philippe, and a

---

7 Kathryn Hulme, *The Wild Place*, Boston: Little,Brown, 1953, pp.x-xi.

couple of peasants jumping up and down and waving their arms wildly, shouting,

"Stop! Halte-là!"

"Pourquoi?" Yvonne called out.

"Land mines!"

"Oh, the hell with them," I muttered to Yvonne. We headed for the bushes and returned to the trucks a few minutes later, unharmed.

On this fourth day, May 11th, we crossed a part of Germany that had fallen only the week before. Here, the countryside was magnificent. The rolling hills were neatly covered by walled vineyards and punctuated at intervals by masses of yellow mustard plants. The trees were sapins, dark evergreens-- Christmas trees. Though many villages had been wiped out completely, and white flags and sheets still hung from windows, some of the smaller villages were untouched, clean and picturesque. "Germany is the most beautiful country I have ever seen," I wrote my mother. I couldn't help wondering why a country with all this wanted more, enough to go to war for it.

We were getting close. In the middle of the day, one of our two trucks broke down and had to be abandoned. We all clambered aboard the other truck and rode through dinner without stopping, eating our army issue K-rations among the stacked and bouncing bags and bedrolls.

There was a dramatic contrast between the jubilation of the VE Day celebrations in France and the sight of the furtive, frightened appearance of the few old men, women and children scurrying along the streets in the German towns.

We reached Heidelberg about nine that night, filthy, dirty and dead tired, and finally located the UNRRA headquarters. The first person I saw was my good friend, Helen! Her team had come via Verdun, Rheims and Metz. We changed our clothes and set out to see the city. It was after curfew (7:30) so the streets were deserted except for a few American soldiers. We didn't go far as it was getting dark and an eerie feeling to walk the empty streets. We had on uniforms but were cautious. A jeep drew up, however, and a very nice American officer asked if he could ride us around. He picked up another officer and they took us up a mountain and into a tower from which we could see the whole valley. Heidelberg was hardly damaged at all. It was picturesque and charming. The two officers took us to their hotel and showed us the Ratskeller that Goering used to frequent.

When we returned to our billet, I found a note to saying to be ready to leave the next morning at 5 a.m.

THE WORK BEGINS

Saturday, May 12th
It was a hard day! The road had been beautiful but was bombed and dusty. There was a continuous line of army vehicles--tanks, convoys, machine gun carriers--all filled with weary, grimy American boys. We gave up on any conversation. It was hot, dusty and we went very fast when we had an opening.

We pulled into Munich, weary and dirty, about ten that night. An MP (Military Police) jeep picked us up on the outskirts, leading us through the rubble of the dark bombed-out city to the Rathaus (City Hall). This magnificent gothic building faced on the square, Marienplatz, which even at this late hour bustled with soldiers.

The entire US Military Government staff was working as if it was 12 noon. We were greeted by an officer, taken to the basement restaurant, the Ratskeller, for a late dinner. Then Yvonne and I were escorted to a room across the street in what was left of the Excelsior Hotel. The door wouldn't shut and the windows were missing but there were beds and running water. The men put bedrolls on the Rathaus floor and slept there. We had arrived.

The arrival of our UNRRA Team was the beginning of the beginning. While the shooting had stopped and the war was officially over, the task of picking up the pieces had hardly begun. Human lives, as well as countries, had been thrown into chaos, so the debris of both had to be cleared up and reconstruction started. Nothing would ever be the same again. The challenge to overcome obstacles usually evokes limitless depths of human capacity and resourcefulness, and this was the case in 1945. The next few weeks in Germany were marked by an almost unbelievable drive to return to a so-called "normal life."

What made this even more remarkable is that it was accomplished without any kind of official German participation. The Nazi regime had collapsed completely and Germany was without a government, either at the national or the local level. In anticipation of war's end, Roosevelt, Stalin and Churchill had met in Yalta, in southern Russia, to map out terms for the surrender of the German Army and the subsequent occupation and reconstruction of the country. The agreement reached, known as the Yalta Agreement, was signed by the three on February 11th, 1945, three months before the surrender. One of the terms of the Agreement established the basis for the occupation of Germany, dividing the country into four zones to be under control of French, British, American and Soviet military forces. In each zone, the respective military was to govern temporarily until some kind of denazified German government could be created. Just what it would look like, or when it would happen, no one knew. The Americans had planned ahead and as soon as territory was liberated by American forces, the US Military Government moved in. Its purpose was to bring order out of chaos and to rebuild civilian life in the parts of Germany for which it was responsible, as did the military forces in all three zones. It meant dealing with everything from food supplies to housing shortages, to providing policing and a system of justice, medical care and social services at a time when German civil society had disintegrated. It was also to these zonal military forces that the responsibility for supplying and supporting UNRRA fell, when teams were finally called forward. It was an odd relationship. UNRRA was an independent, international body. However, it only operated in an occupied zone on the invitation and suffrance of the military occupation authority. This would ultimately seriously constrain UNRRA's operations. Success depended on the American military's largess, or at a minimum, on its indifference.

One of the first actions taken by the Allied forces after defeating the Nazis was to deal with the masses of foreign forced laborers and concentration camp victims found in Germany, the "displaced persons" or DPs, as they came to be known. Sketching a picture of this wretched population is mind boggling. As the conquering armies pushed forward to Germany, a mass movement was set off. Roads in all directions became clogged with streams of horse-drawn wagons, trucks, vehicles of all sorts bulging with humanity--families, ragged individuals, freed prisoners of war--Germans and non-Germans, many with nothing, many barely discernable under piles of belongings of all shapes and sizes. It seemed that all of Germany was on the move. In Germany, the armies of occupation were aggressive in taking over almost any habitable structure in which to collect those displaced. Estimates vary; the best guess is that there were six to seven million DPs in Germany in the summer of 1945, of various nationalities and ages.[8] They were homeless, sick and desperately needed food, shelter and medical care. It did not take long for military units in the field to call for UNRRA to take over the administration and care of these millions, something which the military was not especially well prepared or willing to take on.

Thus, as soon as Munich had fallen to the US Army, the Military Government had taken over the city which had been bombed to moonscape. The entire core of the city had been flattened. In the midst of this devastation, the military had established itself and begun the arduous task of bringing order to the rubble-strewn area. The first visible signs of its presence were checkpoints set up every few blocks and at road intersections on the outskirts of the town. These checkpoints served a number of purposes, one of which was to direct the flow of humanity. Military personnel at checkpoints were instructed to direct any DPs to special camps established by Military Government to collect them and provide shelter, housing, and basic necessities of life. For those DPs who were some distance from camps, the military provided transportation. And so began a massive humanitarian effort to feed and house, sort and register, and ultimately repatriate or resettle the millions. This task ultimately fell to UNRRA, which soon took over the camps' daily administration. It was a

---

[8] Malcolm Proudfoot cites the SHAEF figure of 6.75 million United Nations displaced persons being cared for or repatriated in September 1945. M. Proudfoot, *European Refugees, 1939-1952: A Study in Forced Population Movement*, Evanston, Ill: Northwestern University Press, 1956, p.158.

formidable undertaking, and while the founders of UNRRA had understood the task at an intellectual level, no one was prepared for the reality of the situation and the enormity of the task.

Sunday, May 13th
In front of the Rathaus the next morning, we piled into our one remaining truck for the last time. Philippe was missing at first, but just as we were about to pull out, he ran toward the truck clutching a small table lamp and grinning broadly. I was puzzled by his glee until I realized that the little German lamp, confiscated from somewhere, must have represented some sense of victory over the Germans--a reparation, a symbol of revenge for what they had done to Philippe and his country. I felt my values jolted. It was the beginning of a two year period during which I would constantly be faced with the dilemma of distinguishing between stealing, capturing, confiscating, and appropriating enemy material.

There were two large assembly centers for DPs in Munich. We were assigned to Center 17. On arrival we saw an enormous camouflaged building, formerly the one great quartermaster and supply depot for the Nazi troops in Bavaria. Across the street was a row of apartment buildings which had been taken over for the DP Center. The whole complex for the center consisted of about three city blocks of these modern buildings. All had been badly looted. In some apartments there were no beds, others were completely furnished. We dumped our bags in a bare apartment on the floor above several apartments which had been designated as the Office, and started in.

Captain Templeton (head of the US Military Government DP Team) explained that there were 2,000 people there and a thousand expected that day. The Army DP Team was pulling out at four that afternoon, turning the Center over to us. I was told to take over the feeding--just like that! I was completely floored. Charley wandered around all day in a daze. I'm sure he had no realization that the Army was really leaving. I went to the kitchen, a huge, beautiful modern one--nicely arranged and adequate for the purpose. All the workers were volunteers (they got extra food), mostly Dutch. I tried to find out as much as I could about running the place. Yvonne stayed to watch our baggage and make plans for our sleeping. Jack Atkins took to bed, weary from the trip. Philippe had nothing to work with, not even a band-aid. So that left Charley and me to cope. That night, still dead tired, I slept on a spring on four wooden legs with my bedroll spread on it. I had a very sinking feeling in my stomach.

The complex which was to be our DP camp resembled the permanent military bases in the United States with their combination of administrative buildings and troop barracks. The big five-story office building covered a whole block and was completely honeycombed underneath with stock rooms for supplies. These had been ruthlessly vandalized and looted but still were a source of some supplies for us--paper, ink, et cetera. We had been sent out without so much as a pencil. An American ordinance unit was occupying the building since there were facilities for vehicle repair, gasoline, et cetera. The apartments across the street apparently had been officer and troop quarters. They had electricity and water--two precious utilities at that time. The fact that General Patton would take over the site within two weeks for his headquarters gives an idea of its size and condition.[9]

The next day, Monday, the Army DP Team moved back in at eight in the morning. It was decided to make it a huge camp, using the big building as well as the apartment section. (I have always figured that the Army Team took one look at us and decided they had better stick around). Trucks began to arrive almost immediately, loaded with people of all nationalities. They came so fast that the people were just unloaded in the street; the trucks took off for another load leaving the new arrivals to find their way haphazardly into any apartment. I now had no definite

---

9 "From Munich.. Patton and Gray drove 30 miles to Bad Tolz. There Patton had his headquarters in a structure that formed a huge quadrangle.....Built by the Nazis in 1936, the building passed into American hands two days after the Nazis fled..... displaced persons, 'their habits being absolutely filthy' occupied it and did a lot of damage." After Patton took it over, the area went by the designation "Bad Tolz," the name of the Munich suburb where it was located. Stanley P. Hirshon, *General Patton: A Soldier's Life,* New York: Harper Collins Publishers, 2002),p. 648.

assignment. I really wasn't needed in the kitchen. I found that there were five French social workers attached to the Army Team doing a good job. The worst part of the operation was the reception and placing of the new arrivals. I talked with the Captain and he agreed that I start on that with Sergeant Berge. We figured out a way to use the enormous garage in the courtyard behind the row of apartment buildings and planned to put our system into effect the next day, registering and dusting the newcomers with DDT. We tried it out for a while in the afternoon, taking individuals from each incoming group to help. It worked very well. All afternoon Poles, Russians, and other nationalities poured in.

This setting for handling arrivals turned out to be ideal. The large courtyard had probably been a huge parking lot for German personnel and was entered through a gate from the street running between the large central building, now dubbed the "Big Building," and the row of apartment buildings. At the rear of the open space was a mammoth garage. To see how it worked, we co-opted a DP to wave trucks from the street to the gate where I stopped them, jumped on the running board or in the front seat and directed the driver to the reception tables we had set up at the garage entrance. Before the truck occupants unloaded, I would call out "Wo ist ihrer 'Fuhrer'?" At first I hesitated to use that term, but soon found it was immediately recognizable and accepted. To my surprise, I found there was always an acknowledged "Fuhrer" or leader, who was then made responsible for conveying instructions, assisting the receptionist and serving as liaison with the truck's occupants. It facilitated matters considerably.

By the end of the day, Sergeant Berge, a smallish, wiry dynamo, and I thought the system might work and were ready the next morning to set it in motion.

Tuesday, May 15th
In my wildest dreams, I could never have conjured up any conception of such a day. By nine o'clock people were coming in by the truckload. Sergeant Berge and I set up a desk at the entrance to the garage, found an interpreter to ask questions, disseminate information about the Center

organization and direct the DPs to lines waiting to be dusted with DDT. All day we dusted newcomers, registered them, gave them meal tickets stamped with the date and "DDT" (confirming they had been dusted). The meal tickets were pieces of cardboard cut into squares from material we had scrounged from the basement of the building across the street. We stamped them "official" and made them as we went along. (To make the stamps we cut a piece of an old automobile tire and carved the words, found some ink pads in the stock rooms. Germans used "Schtempels" for everything so there was an ample supply of ink pads.) I had a Russian girl helping at the desk. Sergeant Berge had two Dutch teams dusting and two boys registering. We had a Dutch nurse dusting the women.[10]

This dusting was a military requirement intended to prevent epidemics, in particular the threat of louse-borne typhus which had killed thousands across Europe after World War I. It was accomplished by the use of a contraption, a so-called "gun," which was shaped like an elongated coca-cola can with a long handle protruding from the top which held a plunger which, when worked up and down, produced a spray of powder, or "dust." The procedure could be performed in two minutes and the effects lasted two weeks. It didn't even require the subject to disrobe. The women often rebelled against the indignity of being sprayed under their skirts. Most hated it. Some few, however, took to calling the DDT "sleeping powder," as it killed lice and therefore allowed them to rest comfortably.

All day stragglers and whole truckloads of people arrived. Over 100 French political prisoners came in--sunken cheeks, wounded, sick people. But mostly there were weary, hopeless, shifty-eyed individuals--very few women and children. The actual count for the day was a total of 1322:

Yugoslav--75	*Polish--188*	*Russian--210*	*Greek--13*
French--347	*Ukrainian--60*	*Belgian--27*	*Austrian--3*

---

[10] During the Nazi occupation of the Netherlands, Germans had picked up Dutch boys too young for the army and brought them into Germany to handle baggage in railroad stations.

Hungarian--66	Czech--32	Turkish--42	Misc.--57
Danish--3	Spanish--3	Lithuanian--3	
Roumanian 14	Italian--4	Latvian--11	

We had no time to wonder who they were, or find out why they were in Germany.

My sense of geography and European politics was not too astute at the time. Except for the obvious groups from the Dachau Concentration Camp, I presume most of the others were those brought into Germany for forced labor. Mark Wyman, in *DPs: Europe's Displaced Persons 1945-1951*, graphically describes these.

> Paralleling the concentration and extermination camps' legacy of horror was the Nazis' exploitation of some 8 million foreign workers, who comprised 29 percent of the... labor force... by May 1944. The term *slave labor* widely used in referring to these workers, is perhaps inaccurate when applied to all 8 million, but it was wretchedly true for many.[11]

Everything else seemed to be chaos, but somehow things got done. Now, all the apartments were full. The men were placed in the Big Building-- no beds, no cover, only rooms which had been looted and cleared out--but with electric lights, running water and toilet facilities. It is estimated the Center now holds 5,000 people. The most pathetic group I have seen is the 80 Hungarian boys, all fourteen years or younger--clad in dirty clothing and dragging their feet in wooden-soled shoes.[12]

---

[11] Mark Wyman, *DPs: Europe's Displaced Persons, 1945-1951*, Ithaca: Cornell University Press, 1989, p.22.

[12] Wyman mentioned that, included in this mass of forced labor, were groups of very young workers--teenagers, children as young as 10. As an example, he referred to "a group of Hungarian orphans who had worked in a Nazi labor gang: their ages ranged from 10 to 14." Wyman, pp.23-24.

The two French doctors are most ineffective as they have nothing to work with--no medicine, no dispensary. No medical examinations can be given. They never seem to be around when needed. It was found, in a visit by one of the G.I.s this morning, that there are many bedridden people in the apartments--many who appear to have T.B. Nothing is being done for them.

The feeding and what welfare there is, is being done by the French girls who are doing a terrific job, especially the feeding. Three meals a day are cooked in the large kitchen with DP labor and supervision. Breakfast is bread with butter and cheese, and coffee; dinner (in the middle of the day) is soup, coffee and bread; supper, stew. At least three thousand are fed every day. There is another kitchen on the outskirts of the town where large amounts are cooked and hauled to the Big Building for the men. Most families have their own eating equipment. There was a very large supply of paper cartons found in the supply depot and are used. The US Army provides all the rations, of course.

As for our living arrangements, they are terrible. Yvonne looks after them with the help of a Russian woman.

My own apartment was becoming livable. I had spent the first night on my trusty bedroll, but a few nights later when I returned to the room a proper mattress was on the bedsprings. The next day there was a proper bed for the spring and mattress, then a chair, and finally a chest of drawers. Just as with Philippe's lamp, I didn't know for sure where they came from, and I didn't ask. I knew only that one of the team's drivers was very busy during the day.

Jean and Roger (the drivers) are marvelous--have scrounged all sorts of furnishings. We eat in a restaurant nearby, where we have food issued by the army, for their preparation. It is good--not very balanced.

I found the walks to and from the restaurant very amusing. It was necessary to pass along the building where an Army Ordinance Company's personnel were living and as soon as Yvonne and I turned the corner the whistles began. It was like a chain reaction, with grinning faces popping out of windows in turn as we moved along. Nowadays, such behavior no doubt would be considered offensive, but at the time it seemed like a game, entertainment for all of us in a situation where entertainment was hard to come by.

Tonight we are rather discouraged. The Army seems to be piling more and more people in--no moves being made to get them out. We have reached saturation point. The French, Dutch, Belgians are wonderful. The Poles and Russians are unmanageable. Food will not last forever. Looting is unbelievable--c'est terrible!

The next day, Wednesday, was another unbelievable day. The morning was not too heavy--stragglers coming in to be dusted and get meal tickets. The greatest problem arose from DPs living in Munich, satisfied with living arrangements, but who had no food. There is no food available for civilians except bread rations.

The afternoon was more hectic. Within an hour 20 or 30 trucks of people arrived--mostly Polish, being evacuated from other camps. In a bureaucratic mixup a truckload of former inmates of the Dachau Concentration Camp, which is located in the US Zone, not far from Munich, were dumped--all had been picked up from the concentration camp (only liberated two weeks beforehand), taken to a hospital, from the hospital here, by mistake, still wearing their pajama-like blue and grey striped camp uniforms. I have never seen such stark misery. One boy could not eat he was in such condition. All had diarrhea, were dreadfully ill. We finally sent ten to a hospital--put ten or twenty up for the night. God bless the American soldiers--the war hasn't dulled their sensitiveness to human need at all--they are so kind and thoughtful.

I also had a Polish child so frightened at the dusting that he was hysterical. His parents made matters worse by trying to force him, shouting at him. Suzanne and I found him huddled in a corner. After keeping his family away, and much soothing talk we finally got him to relax--wiped his face--with much coaxing persuaded him to accept a piece of chocolate which I happened to have. We omitted his dusting, gave a card to his family. I also saw a mentally retarded child in a group today. In all, however, there were very few children.

Our food holds out. The French girls located and, with much effort, "procured" two mobile kitchens to supplement the present kitchen equipment. A total of 1187 DPs arrived today, ten nationalities (the largest number, Polish). The Center now holds about 6,000. We worked until about eight-thirty as usual.

The night at the Center is an amazing sight--just like Mardi Gras in Mobile.[13] Everyone wandering up and down the street between the apartments and big building--women and men--singing, dancing, radios blasting. All kinds of languages going at once. What a conglomeration! Freedom!

Thursday, May 17th
Reception going rather well, thanks to Suzanne, a "White" Russian, now my full time assistant who speaks many languages. For reward, she and her mother have an apartment and we share rations with them. We have no money to pay and even if we had, there is nowhere to spend it. I have over 100 dollars in German marks and haven't spent a one--there is not a store open in Munich. In the evening, just as I was about to go up to my apartment I heard shouts for a doctor, so returned with Philippe. One of our interpreters had found a man stumbling up from the basement of the big building. Evidently he had been hiding out or was ill there. He was a living corpse, looked like a mummy. He couldn't talk, was blind, and the stench was terrific, you couldn't get near him. We put him on a stretcher and took him to the hospital immediately. Later learned he died.

Friday
Rumors. Seventh Army leaving and Third Army taking over (General Patton). A detachment of guards moved in.

Another truckload of people who had been at Dachau came in--terrible looking. Lt. Hill had told me of coming by Dachau. He saw many boxcar loads of bodies of people who had been transported from another camp,

---

[13] This celebration of Shrove Tuesday, the day before Lent fasting begins, brings out the whole populace into the streets, some in costume, most with some loud or musical toy, all in a festive mood.

with two days rations. The trip took 17 days, so only one person was alive when it arrived.

Our second Sunday in Munich was the first day of Pentecost. Some Poles had made an altar at one end of the garage--a most remarkable accomplishment. They cut large boughs from trees for background, and somehow located large candlesticks, a picture of the Virgin Mary which they framed in electric lights, and white lace to adorn the altar--all the religious equipment for mass. A priest had been brought from Dachau, a former inmate. I attended the church service along with Poles, Russians, Dutch--Catholics, Protestants, Jews--in the very simple setting of the garage, crowded with everybody focusing on the altar. It was most moving, sharing in this simple, yet profoundly meaningful ceremony.

We had new arrivals all day--15 trucks arrived at one time, over 300 people. We dusted, registered, and housed them in less than an hour. That day we received a total of 1336. The Camp (we seem now to refer to the Center as the "Camp"), now has about 8,000 residents. The Big Building is full--six or seven in a room, not half of them on mattresses. Then on Monday, beginnings of lots of things. The Russians were loaded and sent to another camp. (We understood that orders were for all Russians to be returned to Russia, forthwith.)

We hadn't realized at the time that an agreement had been reached between Roosevelt, Churchill and Stalin at the famous, or infamous, summit meeting in Yalta in February 1945. In addition to decisions as to the establishment of the United Nations, the creation of Allied zones of occupation in Germany after victory and other post-war matters, a small section was included regarding repatriation of liberated prisoners of war and civilians. This was a particular concern for Stalin, who was insistent that all Soviet prisoners of war and citizens be returned to their homeland. The British and Americans were not in a position to object. At the time there was a deep need for a show of cooperation and friendship between the three powers as the last push of the war was transpiring. The Western Allies were also keen to cooperate as they feared that, if they failed to turn over liberated Soviet citizens, the Russians might be reluctant to do the same regarding American and British prisoners of war in Nazi installations liberated by the Soviet armies.

Subsequent to this Yalta meeting it was revealed that a secret US-Soviet agreement, known as the Crimea Agreement, had been signed at Yalta, with a parallel agreement between the Soviets and the British, providing for the immediate repatriation of Soviet citizens and prisoners of war without regard to their personal wishes. Just fourteen days after VE Day, a follow-up agreement was signed at Halle, Germany, on May 23rd, with more specific details, but not altering the basic agreement.

At first, there was positive reaction to these repatriation provisions as it was assumed that the citizens and freed prisoners of war would be eager to get home. In fact, in the early days the departures were full of fanfare--flags waving, music, et cetera. "In nineteen days after the Halle agreement more than 1 million Soviet nationals were brought into the reception centers and began heading eastward at a daily rate exceeding 50,000."[14]

I attempted to set up an information bureau in connection with the reception and dusting. The DPs were eager for information which might relieve their anxieties about their future, advise ways to get in touch with relatives, etc. My Dutch boys and girls were wonderful. I also have a Yugoslav girl, her father was an architect. After the war started he was brought to Germany, later put in a concentration camp at Dresden. When Dresden was bombed, Helena's mother, father and sister were killed. She alone was left, nineteen years old. She speaks six languages, a very pretty blonde. I found a room for her in an apartment above us.

Helena's story illustrated the complexity of the political situation and the inner conflicts suffered by many of those individuals displaced by war. It also illustrated my own lack of

---

[14]Wyman, p.64.

comprehension of the intricacies of European history and geography. Helena's last name was "Smidiger," which should have told me something. It is not a Yugoslav name, but German. It later surfaced that she was born in that section of Yugoslavia adjacent to Germany which once had been German. Even when the boundary was shifted after World War I, when Yugoslavia was created, the population remained culturally and politically loyal to Germany. They were called *Volksdeutsche*.[15] It was through this region that the Germans invaded Yugoslavia. Helena's father was an engineer, not an architect, and like others in the population with skills needed by the Germans, was brought to Germany to work. When the devastating bombing of Dresden started, Helena, who was at work in a factory, managed to escape on a bicycle, certain her family had perished.

On the next day, Tuesday, orders came to have the camp evacuated by Saturday! Trucks leaving all day. Our team's fate hung in the balance.

We were notified in the afternoon that 3,000 Poles were to leave the next morning. Went to the kitchen, planned with the French social workers for each truck to be supplied with a box containing butter, cheese and one-third loaf of bread per person; also, three Red Cross packages in which were canned milk for babies. These supplies were to be put in large cardboard boxes we had scrounged from the Big Building. Everyone alerted, ready to go. The Camp to be cleared in 72 hours.

Amazingly, such a task no longer seemed insurmountable. Though he had seemed almost shell-shocked upon arrival in Munich, Charley had soon swung into action. Immediately he had summoned representatives of each national group in turn. Charley had nothing to do with their selection, the DPs' leadership had simply emerged from among their ranks. Although some groups had obviously been together for a period, there was never any apparent, formal organization. Presumably an individual with a presence of authority was recognized,

---

[15] *Volksdeutsche* were people of Germanic origin who had been identified as such by the Nazis. They were to be part of the Nazi effort to rebuild the Aryan race.

perhaps one with language ability. However it happened, and the process was not clear to us, no one questioned their leadership. We were just grateful they existed. They made our task much simpler. Charley worked with them to keep order, handle crises, and get the necessary work done. In this instance, they functioned brilliantly, assuming responsibility for almost all the preparations. Without them, our job would have been impossible.

After supper, the streets were seething restlessly--several dances in progress as usual. There was one murder--a Pole, stabbed, shot, hit over the head and stuffed in a chimney. I saw the man who did it shortly afterwards. He was smiling, a very nice, clean looking man. He said the man was a SS officer. (Many of the SS troops and Nazi officers did try to disguise themselves as DPs in order to escape.)

It was too early in my new experience among multinationals to comprehend the subtle, and sometimes the not so subtle, feuding and tensions between certain ethnic and national groups. Only later did I gain knowledge of the reasons for the tensions between the Russians and the Poles, for instance. It was often just a gut feeling that there were differences, often unexpressed, of which we needed to be aware.

Thursday, May 24th
By seven-thirty in the morning the streets were lined on both sides with people and piles of baggage--mattresses, suitcases, huge bundles tied up in a blanket or sheet, everything imaginable. The individuals seemed happy, didn't get restless at the long wait until the trucks finally arrived, 86 of them. Then everyone piled in--flags on every truck. They pulled out for a 15 hour ride to Aschaffenburg. I felt a little sad. They were just going from one camp to another, at least it was a step towards home. There were some early signs that many did not want to go home at all. However, as the loaded trucks pulled out flags of nearly every group fluttered in the breeze, a stirring scene.

By Saturday, May 26th, Center 17 was completely vacant and ready for General Patton's arrival. In the fortnight since we had arrived, the facility's population had grown from 2,000 Displaced

Persons to 8,000; then almost literally overnight, the center had emptied out altogether.

In the afternoon I went through some of the vacated apartments. It was shocking. The furniture was broken, everything was filthy, the stench terrible. The emptiness was like the silence following the last chords of a symphony. And I shall always have a sound effect in my mind for this experience, the clacking of wooden shoes on pavement under my window at night, and all day long I hear it.

So ended the first stage of my UNRRA experience. VE Day had marked the end of the shooting and the beginning of reconstruction. It had also been the milestone marking the end of my grooming for the overseas assignment, and the start of work itself. A life had quite literally been left behind and new experiences, new perceptions crowded in at a surreal pace. A scant two weeks had elapsed since my arrival in Munich and yet everything seemed different now, irreversibly changed. I could handle anything, or so I was beginning to believe. The team seemed to believe it too, and deferred to me constantly as a result. As a woman in a man's world, I was sensing a power hitherto unknown to me.

Even in retrospect, it is not easy to measure the impact, or to delineate the strongest impressions of that particular period, as they meld with those which continued to build during the next two years. For instance, as Americans, I believe we failed to understand the depth and importance of the differences in culture and behavior of the various nationality groups, and often we failed to detect the undercurrent of hostility and distrust that run deep between them. As an example, at first I couldn't understand why the Army and UNRRA almost immediately set up different camps for Poles, Ukrainians, Jews, Western Europeans, et cetera Imbued with the idealistic sense of the goal of "one world," I felt disillusioned when that unity didn't materialize right away. I soon realized, however, that for both psychological and practical reasons, national grouping was best during this insecure and traumatic time in the lives of the displaced.

One of the most striking revelations to me was the degree of resilience in human beings--not only to survive, but to throw off repression, hunger, inhuman treatment in a relatively short time (at least outwardly). As an American social worker, I had anticipated signs of mental breakdown, depression, hopelessness, anger. I was therefore surprised and heartened by the ability of the DPs in those early days to dance, laugh, work with joy and for no pay. Of course the fragile and the vulnerable hadn't made it this far, having been "screened out" in a brutal fashion, so to speak, so those I saw were the most resilient.

Still, I was shocked by certain parts of their value system that collided with mine. I'd already run into this with Philippe's table lamp, but I was not prepared for the loose interpretation of "right" and "wrong," "proper" and "improper" behavior. When was stealing or "scrounging" acceptable? Manipulating truth or plain lying under some circumstances was acceptable and sometimes not. Most restrictive regulations were to be laughed at and, in fact, pride taken in breaking them. Status was achieved among DPs, G.I.s and UNRRA personnel alike by how much you could put over on a "dummy." No questions were asked as to where material had been acquired, from what source new clothing had appeared, how a pass into the city had been produced. For instance, as I observed the DPs lined up waiting to get on the trucks I couldn't help wondering about the massive bundles of possessions which must have been acquired under circumstances where no money was exchanged, even if it was available. At liberation, starting from scratch, individuals must have resorted to some unaccountable methods to assemble that amount of personal effects. Despite recognizing the turbulence of the times, a Southern Presbyterian lady found it difficult to come to grips with this ambiguity.

I had to remind myself that war ends with victors and the defeated--roles which carry both material and psychological distinctions. Terms of surrender ordinarily grant privileges and rewards to the victor, the "spoils of war," as well as demands, penalties and retribution from the defeated, particularly when the defeated were the perpetrators of the hostilities which had produced acute deprivation and suffering on the part of the antagonist. This instinctively creates a sense or "right" for acts of revenge to make up for hardships endured. The DPs had not only been deprived of their individual freedom and their dignity assaulted. They were appalled by tales of how their countries had been ravaged under German fighting and occupation. It is understandable, therefore, that there would be some satisfaction from even slight actions to "get even," or so I told myself. This "getting even" often manifested itself in procuring items to make life more livable at the time. Presumably, such things as material, furniture, articles of clothing were fair game if from the conquered enemy. Even confiscated goods from UNRRA or the military could be rationalized as easily replaceable by those who had so much. Carrying out these actions of manipulation or acquisition seemed to give a sense of power; the principle of "anything goes" implied freedom. Thus the word "scrounge" or "organize" took on a special meaning. The use of the terms were often expressed by a motion of the hand, a kind of reverse grab, no words needed. In general, under the circumstances, to pilfer, to steal, was acceptable as "getting even," obtaining something that was "due" or that you "gotta have."

For us, the need to scrounge was exacerbated by the fact that UNRRA teams were sent in with no equipment whatsoever--not a pencil, no medicines, no transportation, nothing. To handle the crises facing us, means had to be found to acquire even the basics. There was no way to purchase anything on the open market, even if the necessities were available there, which they weren't. The military authorities were supposed to provide us with the necessary supplies, but their own resources were limited and the paperwork involved when requisitioning goods was overwhelming. It was much easier to scrounge, and we were more certain of getting what we needed that way and quickly. For instance it was immediately apparent that Helena, my interpreter, had to be identified as a part of UNRRA, as well as be provided with much needed clothing, so I sought out an officer in charge of a military supply depot, presenting the story of our need, with a smile, of course. He responded with some material, "off the books," with which we were able to have a uniform made for her.

And yet I was thrilled to be functioning in a completely unstructured situation with near-total freedom from authority and restrictions, and to be able to draw to the fullest on my creativity and imagination. I found that almost nothing was impossible if I put my mind to it--that regulations were made by people and could be changed by people too, if they posed obstacles. Being one of just a handful of American women there also gave me a powerful weapon--my femininity. Those in command were all men, mostly Americans, and it was a new and exciting game to get their acquiescence to what I needed to get the job done. My Belgian Director learned early to send me to the Army for negotiations and requests of any kind.

And I suppose that, during those early days, the headiest part of this remarkable experience was the result of finding myself in the center of a large number of American men, the only American woman those soldiers had seen in a long time. Once I was walking along the street when a soldier driving by in a jeep slammed on the brakes and whirled around. "My God, an American girl!" he yelled. I was one of the first in Munich, there even before the Red Cross girls arrived. I thrived on the male attention. It was cathartic and a balm to a bruised ego and soul after a disastrous marriage. Yet I was also spared dealing with the complexities of deep relationships. In our bull sessions at College Park, we UNRRA women from the US and Canada had established basic ground rules. Start out with the premise that all guys are married and learn to say "no" in all languages. A serious affair wasn't in the cards. After all, transfers were so common that it was unrealistic to believe anyone would be around very long. There was a certain safety that came with the rapid turnover and large numbers of men vying for my attention. No relationship could be more than a light flirtation, which suited me fine.

I had learned a lot, but was ready for a break from the frenetic pace. I had a few days' respite after the camp's evacuation, and it was welcome. On one of those days, to my delight, the Captain of the Ordinance Company occupying the Big Building had turned up, asking if I would like to take a ride. It seemed that in the tunneled area underneath the building a civilian car had been found, a brand new BMW. It was a dream car--shiny black, red leather seats, white-walled tires and a canvas convertible top. As he was ranking officer it became his property; in military jargon, "confiscated enemy material." A couple of days later, he turned up at my door again. "Susan, would you take care of the car for me? I'm being transferred and I'm not allowed to keep a civilian car. You could let me use it now and then. When I get located, I will come and get it." He took me to have it authorized in my name; later, had his men work over it until it drove like silk. A few days afterwards, he was transferred. I never heard from him again. I was the absolute envy of everyone in UNRRA as there was no provision for transportation for teams. For the next two years I managed, with a lot of smiling, fast talk, and some flirting, to get proper registrations and stickers to keep the car.

One day during the interval between camp assignments, an officer requested I go to the big general hospital in Munich to distribute some Red Cross packages still in stock, but no longer needed by the Military. They were to be given to non-German patients as the American Red Cross was obligated to have them go to Allied personnel only. At first it seemed a straightforward assignment, but it turned out to be very distasteful. Entering a ward with a young German woman doctor and going from bed to bed, asking the nationality of the patients, then turning away from the sick Germans who looked longingly at the packages made me most uncomfortable. There, I encountered some concentration camp survivors. They were a distressful sight--heads like skulls with a bit of flesh, faces the color of putty, sunken eyes. Some were still in their striped pajama outfits. I was embarrassed to have to play the role of an American benefactor, a "lady of charity," so to speak.

It was not easy, still so close to the end of hostilities, to view the German population objectively. They were the enemy. In fact, it was rather remarkable to me that the guys there in the American zone, the battle troops, showed so little anger or bitterness as many had seen their buddies killed and had feared being killed themselves. Generally, there was just an attitude of disdain, a perception that the Germans were second-class people, but to my knowledge there were no overt acts of revenge. It was more like, "OK, the war is over, let's get on with it." From the beginning, German refugees were kept separate from non-Germans, taken care of by the German Red Cross. More importantly, they fell outside of UNRRA's jurisdiction. Nonetheless, the situation in the hospital where there was a distinction between German and non-German, grated. It went against all I had been taught as a social worker. All were sick and hungry, no matter what their nationality. And, as a social worker, I believed that services and goods should be dispensed on the basis of need.

The second experience was as uncomfortable. Since General Patton was taking over our premises, we had to find new billeting and I had been assigned the task. Accompanied by an American officer, we set out to find a suitable house.

It was an unusual experience to walk into a German house, look it over, and walk away again. We finally located one we liked. We gave the German family until the next morning to move. I can't say I enjoyed the experience. The house is a large one, 3 stories, in good repair and built in good taste. The people took all the furniture but we have enough to be very comfortable.

Under terms of the surrender, the US Army had the right to requisition dwellings for Army use, even if it meant displacing a German family. In this instance, the Army exercised this right on behalf of UNRRA which was functioning under its auspices. The house was located at Number 2 Galilei Platz and remained occupied by Team 108 for the next two years.

DEUTSCHES MUSEUM

Thursday, May 31ˢᵗ, new job. The Deutsches Museum.
The Deutsches Museum is located in the center of Munich and was once
a beautiful building. Most of it is in shambles. The part we use opens on
a huge court. The whole front is bombed. By walking through the debris
at the entrance we can get to a part of the building which is not too bad.
There were at present 200 Polish DPs there, and offices of the Polish
National Committee.

We went through it--found a good kitchen, only seven toilets working,
electricity only partially in operation. We made an estimate of beds,
mattresses and repairs needed. It can be quite a good thing.

This famous scientific museum was located on a narrow island
around which the Isar river swirled. A giant clock atop a tower
looked down on the courtyard. It was not a usual clock. Instead of
numerals, it had signs of the zodiac in shiny gilt bas-relief
porcelain against a blue background. Though an object of great
renown, the clock was still now, stopped, symbolic of the status of
the museum it crowned. It was said that Henry Ford had lingered
there for six weeks at one time, fascinated by the exhibits
including whole trains and a reproduction of a coal mine in the
basement. I never saw any of these exhibits. My concentration
was on the flow of life which soon commenced.

The Museum was to be a Transient Center--a place to collect,
register and sort DPs before quickly moving them on to camps
where they would remain until finally repatriated or resettled.
The idea was that they would not stay with us for long, but move
in and out rapidly. Evidently a bomb had been aimed at the
entrance to the building, leaving a big jagged hole at the top of the
steps leading up from the courtyard to where the doors had been.
One walked in under a huge chunk of concrete dangling from
twisted iron concrete-reinforcement rods. It was a bit frightening.
Rubble was everywhere. Lathe hung from the ceiling through

which could be seen patches of sky, the same deep blue of the clock's face. Corridors ended abruptly in blank walls of naked brick.

Palmer Bovie, a reporter for *The Stars and Stripes*, wrote:

> The Museum had been bombed haphazardly: Fallen ceilings, broken glass, stone and plaster dust shrouded the display rooms. The history of metallurgy exhibits were still visible, with their cross-sections of mines and models of smelting processes. "Alchemy" was dust-covered and petrified, the figures more like mummies than models. In the yard behind the metallurgy room Amundsen's plane which had flown to the Pole was a skeleton of burnt metal. It had received a direct hit.... The sky-lighted two-story airplane room was badly caved-in, sprinkled with glass, and the early planes were either dangling eccentrically by cables or had crashed into heaps at the corners of the room. After stepping across improvised planks, into puddles, and crunching on glass for an hour, we gave up.[16]

The section behind the museum's entrance hall was in comparatively better condition, however, and included a large beautiful white-tiled kitchen (the reason above all why the museum had been chosen for a DP Center). The long, wide corridor leading to the kitchen must have been an exhibit area but had been partitioned into large rooms which could be sub-divided into small cubicle-like rooms by beaver boarding. These would become the sleeping quarters for the travelers. Some bits of furniture had been scrounged from other sections of the museum, now off limits.

---

[16] Palmer Bovie, a Lieutenant in a Signal Corps unit located near Munich, and a journalist in real life, was assigned to cover DP activities. He spent eight weeks at the Museum interviewing residents and recording the general atmosphere--something for which UNRRA had neither the time nor talent. His report was never published, but he did give me a copy of it, from which this quote is extracted.

Entrance to the Deutsches Museum

We found twenty Poles who want to stay and who will run the whole Center for us.

This was fortunate for us, since, because of the small size of our spearhead UNRRA team, it was essential to recruit assistance from the DPs themselves for running things. Though perhaps unforeseen, this development also had its advantages. As my friend, Bill Rogers, a member of another UNRRA team pointed out,

> ...(we) were aiding their rehabilitation much more than if we had attempted to do everything for them. Gradually our role became what we wanted it to be; that of advising, helping, supervising and providing supplies for people who were interested in helping themselves.

Thus twenty members of the Polish National Committee, all ex-Dachau inmates, agreed to stay and took on the responsibility of much of the day-to-day operations. The Deutsches Museum had

71

become a gathering point for Poles after VE Day, and the Polish National Committee had been created to represent them. A leader emerged almost instantly, Walter Hnaupek. Blond, like many Poles, his long narrow face was exaggerated by sunken cheeks which testified to years of near starvation. Walter at first appeared deceptively mild-mannered, low key. Alert blue eyes betrayed his razor-sharp sensibility, one that had certainly been honed during his years spent behind concentration camp barbed wire. He quickly gathered around him some of his Polish compatriots from Dachau and these formed the nucleus of the Center staff. Stephan was in the kitchen day and night to see that food was always available for the DPs arriving and departing. Janach set up a warehouse for the driblets of supplies that were obtained through initiative and ingenuity. Mr. Debocki looked after the sick. Tarteusz worked with the distribution and storage of food. Gerard Dyla and Josef Proch just did everything. A Polish priest from Dachau almost immediately began to hold services in an improvised chapel. Others came, worked, departed. There was no money, only prestige, the joy of authority and work, perhaps a bit of extra food. A group of Belgian boys who had worked for the German army came in and were put to work as cleaners. "Nothing was impossible to accomplish," the staff mantra.

One of the key figures in this start-up was Alfred, a Polish boy who spoke very good English. He became our primary interpreter. Although most of the DPs spoke German, having been forced to learn it to survive, we had to depend on interpreters a great deal of the time. Alfred became indispensable. Alfred Mrowiec was a blond, robustly built boy of seventeen, full of energy, resourcefulness, and ingenuity. Those are general terms to describe someone who could scrounge anything, "organize" whatever and perform tasks like quicksilver when it was in his favor. I was never really sure of his background, but he told of having come from Katowice, Poland in April 1945. The Germans occupying Poland were eyeing him as a prospect for military duty so he made up a story that he wanted to go to a SS Training School, talked his way across the Polish/German border and trekked slowly towards Munich. It was warm and he slept in haystacks or with German families who often fed him. He arrived in Munich on April 23rd, dawdling efficiently until the American troops entered. Then he mingled with the thousands of liberated Polish persons milling through the city in the ecstasy of the chaos of freedom. He soon found the Polish National Committee at the Museum and attached himself to Walter. They became a team, Alfred serving as the interpreter for Walter, who spoke no English and was rather shy.

Almost immediately, the Deutsches Museum Transient Center was in business.

Saturday, June 2nd
One hundred and ten Hungarian women had arrived the previous night. We sent them by truck to another camp. They were clean, well organized--had been in Dachau. In the afternoon we took in about fifty people of various nationalities.

Soon trucks began pouring in, loaded with DPs. Apparently word had gotten around that all DPs should go to the Deutsches Museum. The Center acted as a sort of a clearing house. It was a transit center, meant to feed and house DPs very temporarily-- overnight or a few days, at most, until they moved on to the Assembly Centers, where they would be cared for until being repatriated. Typically, two or three hundred DPs would arrive at once--the old courtyard would be filled with trucks. There never seemed to be any shortage of trucks coming into the courtyard to unload, but it was a challenge requiring creative tactics to arrange for trucks to transport residents on to their next destination. Sometimes we could persuade a driver to do a turn-around with outgoing passengers. Beer and joviality helped. There was no time for bureaucracy. It was essential to maintain this turnover as the capacity of facilities was limited. Soon groups of seven or eight hundred people in transit were being fed and housed for the night. Though initially short on beds, double-decker bunks were gradually constructed of unpainted rough wood and mattresses procured. There was a story going around that Jean, one of our drivers, had located a woman running a factory making straw mattresses. He began sleeping with her and returned to the Museum every morning with a truckload of mattresses.

We were so engrossed with internal pressures at the Museum that we were hardly conscious of our surroundings, the city of Munich. It had been one of the last holdouts as the Allied armies moved through Germany, and had fallen only ten days before we arrived. It was in shambles, ninety percent bombed. There was only one street open through the ruins. Klaus Mann, the son of the author, Thomas Mann, described the scene in an article in *The Stars and Stripes.*

> Approaching Munich, I expected to find a mutilated, half-destroyed town; reality turned out to be much worse. Munich is dead, it does not exist. What used to be the fairest town in Germany, one of the most attractive European cities, has been transformed into a vast cemetery. Throughout the whole center not one--literally not one--building has been spared. There is nothing left but heaps of rubble and some seemingly undamaged, or little damaged, fronts behind which is rubble again. I could hardly find my way through the once familiar streets.

At first there were no signs of German life whatsoever. Windows were boarded. White sheets still hung from others. There was nothing to buy and no one to buy it from. The only vehicles to be seen were US Army trucks, jeeps and command cars.[17] After the sun fell, it was gloomy as there was only a glimmer of electricity here and there. No people were on the streets after dark, as curfew was nine o'clock. However, life gradually appeared. By the end of the first week in June,

Munich is beginning to awaken. There are more people on the streets all the time. Streetcars are now running feebly--bread lines get longer. The

---

[17] Large, open, canvas-topped cars used by officers and their drivers.

first newspaper was printed the other day. Food is very scarce--beginning to pinch.

Bakeries began to open, still with lines. Gradually other shops began to appear: butcher shops, small grocery stores, and then beauty parlors, in that order. The food situation was acute--bread cost $8 per loaf--so the population was existing primarily on hoarded food. The black market sprang up, cigarettes being the major medium of exchange. But breweries and restaurants were not reopened yet, that came later. Some factories resumed operations under the Military Government. German prisoners of war were seen cleaning the streets of debris, in uniform and under guard.Each day in this awakening city was unique; sometimes fast-paced, sometimes boring. Work at the Museum was sporadic. Everything was still an adventure, unpredictable. For instance, on 7 June, Helena and I went in my little car on an errand and found ourselves caught up in a crowd lining a street waiting for a parade. Soon we saw columns of American soldiers in dress uniforms, brightened by their brilliant yellow scarves and matching yellow insignia patches on their arms--all spit and polish. A Scottish Regiment which followed was in full regalia, their kilts swinging in the sunshine to the tune of their bagpipes. Tanks lined a square, standing in formation, bands played, flags flew. It was quite a sight. A ceremony then took place in the same square where Hitler had reviewed his Nazi troops, returning a drum lost at the abortive landing at Dieppe by a Scottish Regiment and later recovered by the 42nd Division of the US Seventh Army. The American soldiers were such clean, handsome and confident-looking boys. I was so proud to be an American that I literally choked up with emotion.

Friday, June 8th
The Deutsches Museum is fast becoming the Waldorf Astoria of Munich. In spite of the crumbling front, the Polish staff keep it spotless, have organized the Center so it runs like clockwork.

Walter, a former engineer, managed to find German carpenters, plumbers and other workers for reconstruction of the building. Panes of glass began to appear in the windows. Electric fixtures were installed, plumbing put in order. We scrounged medical equipment and clothing, paper, pencils, even a typewriter. Charley was requested to provide organizational help to several other camps in the vicinity, so I was essentially left in charge of the Museum.

For the DPs, one of the most creative services we established was a canteen. The American Red Cross still had a sizable stock of Red Cross Packages (originally intended for the US fighting troops) stored in warehouses. At the end of hostilities, one of their plans for disposal was to donate them to DP camps. At the Museum, instead of just passing them out to residents intact, we decided to open them, stock the items on shelves with value numbers for each item. Then each DP was given a voucher for an amount which could be "spent" as she or he chose. It was quite popular. It had occurred to me that the luxury of "shopping," of making decisions, would far outweigh the value of the goods, and so it did.

And what is life without a party now and then? To celebrate the first week in our new jobs, in our new quarters and with the friends we had made, we set about throwing one on Sunday, June 10th.

All day spent in preparing for a party that night. In the afternoon I worked like a dog making sandwiches and helping in the kitchen. Roger and Jean had made a stage and all sorts of decorations for the living room. When these continentals give a party, they really give one! We had dinner for 27. It was certainly a mixed group. Some DPs from one of the camps had a string orchestra and if it wasn't swing, it could be danced to. Everyone seemed to have fun--about 50 were there, all nationalities and a good many Americans, both enlisted men and officers. I wore civilian clothes for the first time. I danced and danced.

During the evening I had a few serious moments with Captain Bill Harris. He told me something about himself, how he had married a 20 year old girl--had only been with her for 45 days--has not seen her in almost four years. He tries not to think about it. He talked about the troubles his boys have. Some of their wives have had illegitimate babies. Some of their girls have married other boys. It has been rough on these boys, a most abnormal life.

Parties, and soon the opening of officers clubs, added a lot to the social life and were an antidote to the boredom of the troops and a much-needed boost to everyone's morale. Fraternizing with German girls was forbidden by the military powers for servicemen. No doubt this enhanced the popularity of the few of us non-German females around. I must confess I was happiest when I could dance until late at night after working hard and intensively all day.

And the work did continue to intensify. Efforts were made to be of help to the anxious, dislocated individuals filing through the Center. Our British (DP) staff member, Edith Hoven, sat at a desk in the big entrance hall all day answering questions, giving directions, and sometimes advice. We knew it was an inadequate answer to the needs of the DPs, but the best we could do under the circumstances. Before Edith took over the desk, Helena had drawn on her facility with languages to field the questions which came at her in quick succession. She kept tabs at first, recording in a notebook the type of information requested. With some amusement, she had told Palmer Bovie about the type of queries and the answers she gave, comparing the queries of the people by nationalities.

> The Jews asked very few questions; the Lithuanians, Estonians, and Latvians wanted to stay (most of them had come to Germany voluntarily, and didn't want to return to Baltic Russia); the Poles wanted to find national committees or organize political groups, or get married and be assured of a wedding cake from the Deutsches Museum kitchen; the Italians wanted to go

home; the Yugoslavs and Rumanians wanted to stay; everyone wanted to go to America.

It wasn't long, however, before the Military Government asked Team 108 to open a more comprehensive Information Center, as they found they were not equipped to answer such questions or provide needed services. People continued to come in, asking all sorts of questions in a myriad of languages--"Where can I get a travel pass?," "How can I get to the nearest Lithuanian DP Camp?," "Where can I get an identification certificate?," et cetera. There were streams of people looking for a brother, a mother, children. Reunions witnessed brought lumps to my throat. A tracing section had been set up almost immediately, initially only a primitive arrangement on a huge bulletin board where names and messages could be posted. Then a legal section was established; a translation service added. We also attempted to attend to the smaller needs of the DPs and had available a tailor, a watchmaker, a barber and a photographer. These shops met a double need, providing both goods and services as well as vocational training. There was also a secure area for left baggage, a place to wash clothes, space for children to play, even a multilingual lending library. Meanwhile, visible changes continued in the city around us.

June 28th
Munich is changing daily, both from the civilian point of view and from the military. As far as the civilians are concerned, there are more and more on the streets. They are seen smiling now and then--sometimes even arrogant. The streetcars are packed. Small shops are beginning to at least take the boards off the windows. I learned that there are about one hundred small restaurants opening for the Germans. The food situation is rather acute--everything is rationed, an average per person:

> *1 liter of milk, per week*
> *1/4 pound of butter, per month*
> *200 grams of meat, per week*
> *10 eggs, per month*
> *500 grams of bread, per week*

Black market is rife--with prices such as cigarettes 50 cents each (the preferred medium of exchange). The Third Army won't allow further requisitioning of civilian property so people are moving back into their own homes. The newspaper and radio are functioning, under Military Government auspices.

As for the army, law and order are emphasized since the Third Army came to town. There are MPs everywhere. Social life is beginning to pick up. Several Officers Clubs are about to open. I understand that even a movie might open soon. Rumor has it that the Red Cross is to open a club and that 150 WACs (Women's Army Corps) are coming to town. An Officers' clothing store opened this weekend.

At the Museum we now have a capacity (beds and mattresses) for over 500. We have good food, over 2,000 calories per person a day, a lounge with a radio. Everything is running smoothly. The DP situation in general is not too good. They are trying to close out all small camps. It is rumored that Patton wants all Munich cleared of DPs by July 16th-- maybe we will go, too. It looks as if most of the DPs would be home before long--except the stateless persons and Poles.

I went out to our old camp, Tergenseer Landstrasse, found it completely occupied by the Third Army Rear Headquarters. It is all polished, completely changed. I rather resented being stopped by the guard--even had my car taken when I parked it in front of the building.

UNRRA has finally located us. I met Grace Sewell, Marion Hutton, and Lillian Robbins in their new headquarters in Munich, recently arrived senior welfare supervisors. They were all freshly dressed in strict uniform. I had no tie, was without cap and had my coat unbuttoned. I felt like the combat troops do when a desk officer turns up.

Our UNRRA team has begun to expand. There are now twelve of us, four French, four Russian, one Yugoslav, one English, one Belgian, and me, the American. I have a bedroom of my own! Our house at #2 Galilei Platz is well located, convenient to the Museum, a couple of blocks from the Munich Opera House and across the street from a house occupied by an American officers' group. The latter arrangement resulted in an instant linkage. The Americans enjoy the contact with the international group and vice-versa. There is a lot of backing and forthing between our houses, sharing of parties, etc.

Our life was so intensely centered in our small circumscribed arena that we seemed disconnected with the outside world. There were only the German local newspapers, rarely a radio and little time to search for either. It was only through shreds of gossip, rumors, news from passing contacts with the occasional UNRRA team member, army personnel or a DP did we have any idea what was going on. Only gradually, for instance, did we even get a hazy picture of the broader DP situation. It seemed that, although the armies had expected to have to cope with refugees as a part of waging war, the scope and immediacy of the problem was a shock. As the armies moved into Germany it was like a spigot had been opened, spewing out masses of humanity suddenly erupting in a rush for freedom and safety from crossfire from opposing military forces. There was panic on both sides--the refugees fleeing to safety and the armies desperate to be unhindered in their pursuit of the enemy. So it behooved the military to quickly organize shelter, food, safe haven, although temporary, until the situation could settle.

DP camps sprang up in all sorts of accommodations, if you could call them that--bombed-out factories, schools, whole villages were requisitioned. In short order, the makeshift "collection centers" funneled the assembled DPs in the French, British and American zones to these camps. Some camps were established in caserne-type installations, former German military complexes, usually four-story, dark green, stucco clusters of buildings. Others, the more ubiquitous, were brown-colored barracks which had housed labor camps or less important military units. And then there were the camps composed of the dwellings in villages or towns where the residents were dislodged to make way for the DPs. Quickly the pattern of distinct ethnic groups composing the population of each camp became the norm. There was no formal designation of a camp for a special nationality group, it just happened. Usually the first settlers set the pattern. Word got out through the grapevine and DPs of that nationality showed up by all means of transportation, as well as transported by military trucks. These nationality-specific camps became typical, each operated by an UNRRA team with varying degrees of success. They quickly transformed the sites from dirty, ill-repaired accommodations into workable, livable and orderly facilities in most instances. In the US Zone, it was to these camps that the Deutsches Museum residents were transferred.

The camps formed a pattern not unlike a chessboard, with constant but deliberate movements of groups from one square to another, sometimes eliminating a camp, a square, as groups were consolidated or moved off completely. That generally meant repatriation, or return to their homeland. That was UNRRA's mandate, after all, to care for them until they could be repatriated.

As for repatriation of DPs, I had noted on Monday, June 11th,
4,000 Russians are leaving daily to return to Russia. All do not want to go. I hear rather ominous things about Russia.

In fact, hundreds of thousands of Soviet citizens were being repatriated that spring and summer, whether they were willing or not. Rumors were flying that the DPs who returned were being arrested and sent to Siberia; that the women were being raped; that everyone was regarded as a traitor and treated as such. These DPs truly feared what would happen to them when they got to the USSR.

Who were these Russian DPs? One rarely heard of Russians in concentration camps unless they were Jewish. In the early days at the Deutsches Museum, no attempt was made to record nationalities of the transients or to keep accurate statistics. That happened at the next stage, in the Assembly Centers. The count we did was usually for meal tickets issued. The open door and wide entrance was not policed so there was easy coming and going, a general policy of welcome. So I was not conscious of any sizable presence of Russians. It was only later that I gradually became aware of the mass Russian repatriation and some of its controversial issues.   I only subsequently learned, for instance, that the early success of the German Army's march into Russia had resulted in over two million Russian prisoners of war, with approximately 875,000 being put into forced labor to work for the Reich in Germany. Additionally, about a half million disgruntled Red Army defectors were in the Nazi armed forces at the war's end. It was these prisoners of war that the Halle Agreement primarily addressed in its demand that "all prisoners of war and Soviet citizens of the USSR.....will be delivered [to the USSR]." The only exception to this agreement was the refusal of the Western Powers to consider the Baltics (as citizens of the Baltic Republics were known) as citizens of the USSR, although the Soviet had annexed Latvia, Lithuania, and Estonia a year earlier, when the German occupation of those countries ended with the collapse of the Finnish front under Soviet pressure.

After the Soviet DPs were repatriated, it was the Poles who formed the majority of the remaining DP population. They were also sometimes a difficult group to deal with. Most refused to repatriate, although it took us a while to realize that. They refused because they vehemently objected to returning to a Poland under Soviet domination and Polish Communist rule. Until Poland was free and independent, they intended to remain exiled. Meanwhile, the summer was moving on.

Wednesday, July 4th
I worked as usual in the morning until Walter, Joseph and Alfred came for me and very formally escorted me into a room where they had a bouquet of flowers for me. Alfred recited a message of congratulations on our Independence Day and we drank a toast with a Polish drink (some kind of liquor whipped with eggs). I was quite moved by their thoughtfulness and sincerity.

Finally, the DPs were losing their anonymity for me, becoming individuals with faces and stories, rather than just a crowd moving past. There was Ellie, who, on that 4th of July, invited me and Helena to an eighteenth birthday feast in her little cubicle room which was about the size of a large closet, just large enough to hold a double bunk against the wall, a chair and a stool, with stacks of bags and clothing neatly piled in a corner.

As the elder, I was ensconced in the chair, Helena on the stool, and Ellie on the bottom bunk, officiating from a little table loaded with the goodies. She had prepared a meal of meat balls and spaghetti with a delicious cake for dessert, remarkable as she had to rely only on DP camp ingredients. As a Yugoslav, she had connected with Helena immediately due to their shared background and past. In fact, it may have been Helena who had been strategic in arranging for her staff position. Not particularly pretty, Ellie was vivacious, with a lot of personality, and remarkably mature for her eighteen years. This birthday obviously had a lot of meaning for her, in this foreign country, alone, with an extremely uncertain future. The situation seemed even more poignant on learning her story, at least the bare bones of it.

She had been brought into Germany with her parents by the Germans, presumably under the same circumstances as Helena's family. Her parents were shot by the SS, as well as her four brothers, who had refused to go into the German army. She was forced to work in a factory until liberation. She did not want to return to Yugoslavia. She wanted to go to Belgium with one of the Flemish boys working at the Museum. In those early days, I was reluctant to ask for more details, realizing the DPs' suspicion of anyone in authority who might use the information against them in some way. I was well aware of the way facts frequently shifted to either cover something that might be held against a person at a later time, or to present a story that would put a more favorable light on their past. With Ellie, for instance, I would liked to have known more about why her parents were shot and she was spared. She would have been only a young girl when she came to Germany. Where did all this take place? The brothers, how old were they? Such stories were a window into a world to which I was just being introduced, and they helped paint the picture of the circumstances of the times. I wish I could have been more journalistic in my approach, but perhaps it would have alienated me, for prying into habits and tactics which had been a means of survival.

Saturday, July 8th
Much excitement at the Museum--the day of the grand opening of the
NEW YORK ROOM, a coffee and beer lounge. Walter, Alfred and
Joseph had worked very hard for several days decorating what was once a
huge corridor. They hung red cheesecloth material around the top of the
walls. They had gold leaves here and there. There was a stage built at one
end, complete with footlights. There were tables with table-cloths, a bar
with all the trimmings. It was a very high-class room. At four it was
crowded. There was a Polish orchestra from the Polish Officers' camp at
Mulnau (former Polish POW officers)--a marvelous orchestra. It played
classical music. There was a dance team, with colorful costumes, dancing
Polish dances, and an A-one violinist.[18] The concert lasted until seven
and after that there was a dance orchestra. Several army officers had
been invited and a Belgian Director of UNRRA Team 106 was there. We
danced and sang until late at night.

Word had gotten around about the event so, by early afternoon, the place was jumping. There was much greeting, laughter, moving around. This was an occasion to "dress up" so everyone was in their best, the men with clean (uncreased) bland-colored trousers with white shirts open at the neck, as there was no such thing as a tie. The women, in their cool, faded cotton dresses, had put on lipstick and made efforts to curl their hair. Again it was brought home to me that there were no class distinctions among DPs, it was a leveling existence. There were no trappings to signify social, economic or occupational status. Judges, shoemakers, farmers, concert musicians, teachers, lawyers, colonels were all in the same boat. I had already learned that the

---

[18] After my return to New York, I frequented a restaurant where DP Herman Rosner had found work. Inevitably he would come over to my table and serenade me with soulful, romantic tunes. It made a great impression on my dates.

Cafe New York

only way to size up an individual was to look in their eyes. Undoubtedly as populations became stabilized in the nationality-oriented DP camps differences and hierarchies, "classes" emerged, but not at the Deutsches Museum Transit Center. The temporary stay in the Deutsches Museum left little time for socializing. Concentration was on food, shelter and plans for the next move. Of course there was the natural clustering of nationals at social events, in the Cafe for instance, but segregation was never pronounced. There seemed something of a common bond resulting from common experiences and current circumstances, particularly in this temporary state of limbo. The cafe offered a setting for the greatest mingling of nationality groups. When it came to dancing, the women, who were in the minority, were sought after by lonely partners without consideration of background.

The city of Munich was hostile to the DPs and afforded them little outlet for recreation. That being the case, the cafe provided an essential social setting. Far beyond just a place to eat or drink, it was important to the morale of those waiting to return to their homes. For Europeans, after all, sitting around a table and talking is a fundamental activity.

In his book, *The Reawakening*, Auschwitz survivor Primo Levi wrote of his refugee experience.

> Life in the camp...rapid oscillations between hunger and a full belly, between hopes of return and disappointment, expectancy and uncertainty, barrack life and improvisions, almost a spurious form of military life in a temporary and foreign environment, aroused in me discomfort, nostalgia, and above all, boredom.[19]

Discomfort, nostalgia, boredom; Cafe New York (as it was soon dubbed) was designed as an antidote to all three. The Museum staff had organized it all, rushing around for days in a state of excitement. No questions were asked as to where the decor, the tablecloths and trimmings came from. The coffee was made from the popular "ersatz" coffee which was reputed to be mostly sawdust, purchased on the black market; but never mind, it was "coffee," served hot, in a cup. We even had DP volunteers in white jackets waiting on tables.

Thursday, July 12th
A memorable day. Went to Dachau with Walter and Alfred. This was just a little over two months after it was liberated on April 28th, by US Seventh Army troops.

Dachau was the first concentration camp built, in 1933, at the order of Heinrich Himmler, Munich's Chief of Police at the time. Designed to imprison opponents of Hitler's regime, it held communists, socialists, then Jews, Gypsies and anti-Nazi clergymen from all over Europe. By the end of the war, it was notorious and every nationality had its representatives among its

---

[19] Primo Levi, *Survival in Auschwitz and The Reawakening, Two Memoirs*, New York: Summit Books, 1986. (*Survival in Auschwitz* originally published in 1958 (trans. 1960); *The Reawakening* originally published in 1963 (trans. 1965), p. 251.

inmates. Walter had been among that camp's survivors. As we rode through the beautiful countryside, I was buffeted by mixed feelings. On the one hand, I was curious finally to see the scene that had been described to me so often of late. At the same time I wanted to shrink from exposure to something that promised to be so horrifying, and was genuinely afraid that it would prove to be more than I could handle. I felt like someone on her way to a hospital operating room.

We first drove up the road into the camp for which Walter, an engineer, had drawn up the plans. The foundations were human skeletons. A ghastly revelation. We saw the beautiful modern homes and barracks occupied by the SS Troops--their swimming pool, their recreation buildings, even certain barracks reserved for them to house their women. We then went into the barbed wire enclosed area where the prisoners were kept--one thousand in each small barrack or block, as they were called, which had been designed to house three hundred.

On the way to Dachau, Walter had told me his story. He had been a company commander in the Polish People's Army. On the evening of September 14, 1939, he returned from duty to his home in Katowice. About an hour later a German knocked at his door, said he represented the Gestapo and took Walter to the police station. He was held for three days, tortured, and repeatedly asked why he had told his troops that "the war would be over in two weeks and the Polish Army would be in Germany." Walter replied that he had read it in the newspaper. He was then released and he returned to his home, which he found completely empty of all contents. He reported the looting to the German authorities. Shortly, the Gestapo arrested him again and sent him to a prison in Teschen, sixty kilometers away, where he was tortured for eight months. The conditions and abuse were nearly indescribable. Inside a cell intended for one, with a one-foot square window, lived six men. One of these, Walter said, was a Hapsburg prince who had governed a Polish province. He was beaten regularly because he called himself a Pole instead of an Austrian. Once a week, the men were let out into the courtyard to talk freely for half an hour. Like the prince, Walter and the other prisoners were periodically questioned and beaten, usually for unsubstantiated accusations.

From there, he was sent to Sosnowiec, a Lager or work camp from which prisoners were sent into Germany. Here, Roman Catholic priests were singled out for special humiliation, such as cleaning out the latrines. An SS officer once tried to win a theological argument with one of the priests. When it became clear that the priest could not be trapped, the officer shouted in frustration at the rest of the prisoners, "There is no France, there is no England! On earth there is only the German Reich! And in heaven there is only the Luftwaffe!" From Sosnowiec, Walter was put on a train in a small compartment with seven other men. For several days they traveled without food or water. The passengers drew some hope from the belief that they were traveling in the opposite direction from Dachau, but after four days the train pulled into a station displaying a sign that read DACHAU.

After parking the car Walter, Alfred and I went all over the Camp, Alfred along to interpret. At times, Walter became quite emotional, but it seemed to mean something for him to show it to me.

Walter described the first day which was really a test of endurance--those who could make it moved into the everyday pattern of work, meals, work, meals. Those who showed weakness were flogged or killed. The old men were killed at once. The test was to run with a heavy stone from one corner of the camp to another, time after time. Walter passed his test and over the next five years, was confined to a space just over a few hundred yards square, constantly watched by guards. He managed to live by his wits, making himself useful to the guards by "organizing" everything from designing cards for them to send to their girlfriends to arranging a symphony orchestra. I later learned that, as leader of Block 16, Walter was credited with saving thousands of lives.

Walter took me to the crematorium. I could see stains on the walls, showing the line up to which the bodies had been piled. The stench was still there. I saw the gas chambers, the room where injections were administered, the room where they were suffocated by gas, the ovens for cremation. I saw the place out front for lynching, and at the side, where they were shot. Walter said that over a period of six years there was an average of 300 killed a day. I saw where the ferocious dogs were kept.

Although years of emotional constraint inhibited any display of emotion, it was clear to me that Walter was having difficulty controlling his feelings as we went through the buildings. Sometimes he was just silent. Sometimes he cut short his explanation of places, or he paused as if reflecting. As for me, I was speechless, inwardly revolted by the horrors, and I found it hard not to just turn and run away. But here I was, walking along with this man, dressed in his tan, unpressed trousers and open-collared shirt describing almost as a tour guide, the scenes and facilities with details that no tour guide could have known. In my mind's eye, I could visualize Walter in the ubiquitous blue- and grey-striped camp uniform which made me again marvel at the resilience of human beings.

As we walked through the camp, Walter told me about liberation day. It was known that Himmler had ordered that no prisoners were to fall into enemy hands alive. Walter reached into his pocket and pulled out a cloth tape bearing his prisoner number, 12518, and a "P" on a small red shield patch indicating he was a block leader of Polish nationality. He also produced a piece of paper which he still carried, the order typed by an SS officer and dated April 14, 1945.

> Die Ubergabe kommt nicht in Frage das Lager ist sofort zu evakuirn, Kein Haftling darf lebendig in die Hande des Faintest caiman.

> (There is no question of evacuating the camp. No prisoner can fall into enemy hands alive.)

When shooting was heard on the outskirts of the camp, the PA system ordered all inmates to march out to the guards' machine guns.

Just then, American soldiers began showing up on the other side of the barbed wire fence, and almost immediately the eight SS guards in the tower nearest Walter's block showed a white flag and descended. As they approached the Americans, one of the guards pulled a pistol from his belt, at which the Americans shot all eight of them. Then, one of the soldiers picked up the guard's pistol, waved it in the air and threw it away. The inmates burst out of the barracks and went wild--freedom!

The camp was now under the control of the US Army, which had arranged for some of the former inmates to stay and work, maintaining the buildings, the grounds, and the warehouses still full of goods, until a decision could be reached about its disposition.

We went into the big warehouse and Walter took great pleasure in loading our trucks with everything imaginable. Everywhere we went he met friends who were working around the place. There was much hugging, slapping of backs, indications of the bonding which had taken place in sharing life and experiences through the turbulent days at the camp. Walter took me to the room of one of his friends for a quick lunch. They treated me like a queen although they spoke no English and I spoke no Polish. It was most interesting to watch their faces-- see how easily they laughed. They were fine-looking men. None wanted to return to Poland because of the Russian domination of their country.

Now, almost 60 years later, Dachau's images in my mind have not faded. They all seem colored gray. The dingy buildings, the stained once-white walls, the wooden floors indistinguishable from the earth outside, colored by the dirt ground into them by the thousand of boots trampling over them. Dirty windows let only gray light into the rooms. Stark bunks lined the barrack walls, only a broken chair now and then gave evidence of furniture. Although it was hard for me to take at the time, I'm grateful to have been exposed to the reality of the extent to which the evil in men was expressed in that place. I'm also glad I saw it in the raw, not later, when it had become a tourist attraction. Ruth Kluger, in *Still Alive*, expressed her distaste.

> I once visited Dachau with some American friends. It was a clean, proper place. Today a fresh wind blows across the square where the infamous roll calls took place, and the simple barracks of stone and wood suggest a youth hostel more easily than a setting for tortured lives.[20]

---

[20] Ruth Kluger, *Still Alive*, New York: Feminist Press at the City University of New York, 2001, p.67.

ON THE MOVE

The days became faster-paced and more demanding. As Bill Rogers wrote about the times, "The kaleidoscope of the next few weeks turned so rapidly that coherent narrative is difficult. There was no time for a daily record of events. It is difficult to live history and write it at the same time."

July 13th
Our Museum is now a regular hotel. We rarely get large groups of people except those waiting for transport. We have steady streams of people all day long--about 300 a day coming and going. The Lithuanians are the biggest problem at the moment. They won't go back to Lithuania. Most are well educated, intelligent people.

The Lithuanians didn't want to go home? Such emerging sentiments began to shatter the concept that, at the end of the war, there would be a mad rush of DPs eager to get back to their countries of origin. Then, why wouldn't the Lithuanians want to hit the road? A look at the history of that little country during the twentieth century gives some basis for understanding the decision facing those nationals who found themselves in Germany in that summer of 1945.

Lithuania, a little country about the size of the state of West Virginia, is bordered on the south by Poland and on the north by Latvia. Geographically, it is often lumped with Latvia and Estonia under the rubric of "the Baltic States," as all three face on the Baltic Sea. Throughout the century, Lithuania was buffeted between the countries of Poland, Germany and Russia. The perpetual goal of independence was a mirage, only sighted for short spans during the period. The first was when, at the end of World War I, it was proclaimed an independent kingdom under the protection of Germany in February 1918 and later, in November of that year, became an independent republic. Real independence, however, was elusive, threatened by ongoing hostilities with Poland which only ended with a non-aggression pact agreed upon by the two countries in 1938. Then came World War II. That was the end of the pact and the beginning of a see-sawing era of occupations by the Soviet and German armies.

Hitler, prior to his invasion of Poland on September 1, 1939, sought to forestall any distractions from Eastern Europe by an agreement with Stalin, then an ally, to divide Poland between the two and grant Russia eventual sovereignty over the Baltic States. The German invasion of Poland was Stalin's signal to claim the Baltic Republics and the eastern half of Poland for the USSR. In October 1940, he sent troops into Lithuania, Latvia and Estonia, incorporating them as constituent republics of the USSR. Schools and church properties were taken over; factories, rural cooperatives and farms were nationalized; and complete control of the governments assumed. The real horrors began, however, when on 14 June 1941, the secret police rounded up and deported thousands of individuals, including intellectuals and many in leadership positions, to Siberia, Kazakhstan and other remote areas. It has been estimated that the Soviets deported or killed 131,500 Balts during a period of less than 18 months.[21] Reeling from this situation, it is not surprising that most Balts welcomed the German invasion on June 22, 1941.

At first the situation seemed bright. Considered Aryans, the German policy was that the Balts should not be "enslaved" but accorded privileges such as ration cards. The countries became part of the Third Reich, as the "Ostland" provinces. However, soon there were ominous signs of tougher times to come. Two hundred thousand Lithuanian Jews were killed or deported. Thousands were recruited for work in Germany. Forty thousand Balts were sent into concentration camps. Nor was that the end of the suffering. In 1944, after their successes against the Germans in battle, the Russians returned to take over the three countries again and there followed more mass deportations, particularly of intellectuals and farmers. After liberation, it was understandable,

---

[21] Wyman, p. 31.

then, that the option for Lithuanians in Germany to return to their homeland, now under the Soviet heel, was not an attractive choice.[22]

Monday, July 16th
Busy day at the Museum--lots of Jews now. Poles are being moved out. While I was at the Military Government news came in that the Karlsfeldt Camp was to be evacuated. It is the best camp in Munich, a Polish camp. It is very discouraging to see camp after camp closing and the people being moved from place to place like cattle.

Tuesday, July 17th
Two nice Norwegian Liaison Officers were in for lunch, they were making arrangements for return of DPs to Scandinavia. Had dinner at Military Government where I heard interesting discussions about the food situation in Bavaria. The Germans are receiving 1500 calories a day--the DPs 2000. It is expected to be 30% better next winter. There will be no fuel, however.

The Deutsches Museum played a significant role for the Jewish movements in Germany from the time of liberation until the end of UNRRA. As a transit camp, with a steady flow of displaced persons passing through its gates, the Museum was a key source of information about the possible whereabouts of relatives and friends, and an important point of contact with the authorities. This was true for all displaced persons, Jewish or not. But the Jewish survivors of the camps around Munich soon organized themselves into what they called "the Federation." It was led by Dr. Zalmon Grinberg of Kovno, a concentration camp survivor himself. The Federation had moved into the Deutsches Museum, setting up office on the ground floor. It became a leading force in the Jewish population, at first regionally, ultimately for the whole US Zone. Interestingly, only the Jews and the Poles had organized themselves at this point. The presence of the Federation (later known as the Central Committee of Jews in the US Zone of Occupation) didn't have any significant impact on the day-to-day

---

[22] Only in 1990 did Lithuania gain its independence from the USSR.

operations in the Museum, but it was apparent that there was an increasing number of Jews coming and going. It became increasingly clear, too, that the Jews considered themselves a separate and special group among the DPs, and deserving of special treatment.

As well, from time to time, conflicts between Germans and DPs began to surface. At first it was just rumors of an undercurrent of bitterness among Germans over the difference in the food allocations between the German population and the DPs. The DPs' rations were more generous than those of the Germans, although only moderately so. Also, there were reports of sporadic physical violence between the two groups. I witnessed just such an incident once. It shook me badly.

On Wednesday, July 18th, I witnessed a horrible sight. While I was parked in front of a mental hospital I saw a crowd coming, beating a man. I had never seen anything like it, except perhaps in the movies. I cringed in my little car appalled not only at the sight but at the sound of blows on flesh and bone, with screams of hate by the attackers. I was terrified and horrified. An American army jeep rescued the victim. He was bleeding, was in terrible shape. Civilians were beating him, saying he was a former German SS soldier. I never found out the identity of the civilians.

Generally, however, caught up in our work at the Museum, we were insulated from events and changing moods on the outside. National groups were increasingly using the center as a collection point for repatriation. The Norwegian Liaison Officers finalized plans for assembling all Scandinavians from around the Munich area for repatriation. On another day there was a movement of Dutch children who had a remarkable story.

Friday, July 20th
Was very moved by the sight of 22 Dutch children (boys, all about ten years old) drinking their milk together. There were 1,000 Dutch boys taken from Holland into Germany. This group was used to carry luggage in the railway station in Plzen, Czechoslovakia. They were in a camp and

there was a Dutchman, a teacher, with them. He had been with them throughout. He had taught them and cared for them. After the surrender he appealed by radio for homes with Czech families and placed them all. Every day they came to him for school and for play. The children are now in fairly good health. One is epileptic. They sang songs for me--so well that I suggested a concert that night. They did sing and were so proud. I shall always think of them on hearing "Happy Days Are Here Again."

Even sadder is the memory of another song they sang. As I was leaving the Museum, I heard a plaintive melody, in two-part harmony with harmonica accompaniment, and found the boys sitting on the steps in the moonlight under the zodiac clock. I was deeply moved by the sight of the rows of tow-headed kids, bound together by their song as if lost in dreams of home.

> Holland is our country, where we fish and swim,
> I want to play all day, and never go to school.

Saturday, July 21st
Belgium Independence Day. A big day for us because of Charley del Marmol. Went to work early--at nine o'clock Alfred and Josef presented flowers and drank a toast to Belgium in Charley's office which they had decorated beautifully. After supper the party began. We had an orchestra, the house was decorated. There were lots of French and Belgians, and a good many DP girls. The party lasted all night--we danced until six in the morning when curfew was lifted and the orchestra could go home.

Very little work had been done that day because guards were busy keeping DPs off the streets. All troops were confined to their quarters and none could come to the party.

Monday, July 23rd
On arriving at work I found large numbers of DPs standing around waiting for "registration." For two days there had been a security check and so all DPs decided they had to be registered. A lieutenant arrived, asked us to register. We decided that if it would help the DPs we would give them small white cards with their names, signed by us. After several

hours I decided it was useless--went to the 3rd Army Headquarters and told them so. They agreed, so we quit.

This was a tense time in Munich. It was common knowledge that General Patton was not sympathetic about the presence or situation of the displaced persons. He was used to order and to giving orders. He was of the opinion that the country should be cleared of DPs and that they should all be repatriated forthwith. Eisenhower was much more considerate. Patton, to carry out his policy, had issued an order on July 10th that all liberated persons in Munich should be transferred to repatriation centers. Presumably this order was the cause of the security measures in late July, as well as the DPs' unease. However, our insulation from outside currents didn't completely remove us from rumors, complaints, threats from the outside world and we were aware that inevitably we would be caught up in some way. It finally touched me by July 22nd.

Had news of lots of changes in UNRRA which had been under considerable criticism.

It seems that complaints of maltreatment and intolerable conditions in the camps in which DPs were living, especially the situation of Jewish displaced persons, had reached the White House. An appeal, July 21st, by the World Jewish Congress had been transmitted to the Allied leadership meeting in Potsdam. President Truman promptly dispatched an envoy, Earl A. Harrison, the United States representative on the Intergovernmental Committee for Refugees, to study the situation. His report, although it was not made public until early August, clarified several issues, particularly the definition of "displaced persons"; and whether Jews should be classified by nationality or ethnicity. The distinction between ethnicity and nationality can be complex and confusing. Ethnic groups are often racially and historically related with a common culture, speech, and sometimes religion. Their population frequently cut across national borders or formed a minority within a larger population, like the Hispanics in America. In Africa, tribal groupings are considered ethnic segments of nations. Nationality, on the other hand, is determined by one's place of birth and/or citizenship. One of the most convincing arguments for the classification of Jews based on ethnicity was that they had not been sent to the crematoria as nationals or citizens of a particular country, but as "Jews," a racial category. It was therefore concluded that separate camps should be set up for that group, just as camps were being set up on a nationality basis.

Meanwhile, the pace at the Museum never slowed. At one point, I thought it would be edifying to record a typical day. It was exhausting, but exhilarating at the same time.

Saturday, July 26th (typical work day)
Very busy day. First had to check about gasoline as we hadn't gotten any--sent Roger, our driver, for our ration. Had to talk with Yugoslav girl (Ellie) about working in the kitchen. She had no family--had returned to Yugoslavia but had seen and heard so much on the way about the Russian occupation that she did not even leave the station in Belgrade. She left all her clothing, everything, to catch the next train back. She will again work in the kitchen, just to stay and to eat. I checked the kitchen to see if food was there--what the menu was, if everything was O.K. Talked with a committee of DPs from Ebersberg who wanted food and transportation for 600 DPs in that vicinity. Called Military Government to discuss the matter. 16 Italians arrived, sent by Military Government. Made arrangement for their billeting. Sent some DPs to Funk Caserne by truck, arranged to get DDT powder from there. Sergeant from 220th Battalion arrived with two DDT spray guns we had requisitioned. The officer in charge of our P.X. supplies arrived to bring posters and collect for P.X. An officer from CIC (Central Intelligenced Corps) came to get information about the camp, to check rumors of mistreatment of DPs. Mr. Smith, from Public Relations Department of UNRRA, arrived to say that the press would probably visit our Museum the following week. He wanted to see our place and to get interesting details. Captain Coblenz came by to find four Yugoslavs to go to Coberg to do a special job in archives department. Two Hungarian women came to say they had made plans to move in to town and thank us for their stay at the Museum. Captain Bonavie, the Norwegian Liaison Officer,

was in to say he had completed plans for the Scandinavians to fly home, leaving at two o'clock. The Swedish opera singer discussed this and bade farewell. Talked with Lieutenant Klausner[23] about the Jewish situation. We agreed that from now on all Jewish people would be accepted in the Museum on the same basis as anyone else. A Colonel came by after lunch to bring authorization for continuing to print the DP Express (the Museum newspaper). This was a thrilling piece of news for us. I had a beer with him and worked out a plan to distribute a Polish paper for USFAT (US Forces, Atlantic Theater). A Czechoslovakian girl who works in the Radio Office came in to ask for trucks to move baggage. Talked with Roger, went by the Radio Station later to tell her plans were completed--talked with boys about radio publicity, made appointment for an interview on Monday. Talked on the phone with Military Government about seven Polish girls who were being evicted from an apartment, agreed to accept them at our center. At lunch discussed food with our cook. Found gasoline had not been delivered. Returned to the Museum. Gave special order for clothes for Hungarian woman who had been in Dachau. Discussed with Rumanian woman the possibility of having a story hour for older children. She agreed. Talked with a Russian woman who wanted to work with UNRRA--a Lithuanian boy who wanted to join the American army. Signed papers for Walter to get German food rations. At the end of the day, before going to Augsberg, stopped at the Museum to leave authorization for gasoline. Found Sir George Reid of the London UNRRA office there on an inspection tour. Had to talk with him. Wound up the day at two parties in Augsberg with my friend Helen Zilka and friends, arriving home about three in the morning. What a day, a Saturday at that.

I also learned more of Helena's story. In many ways, her story exemplified that of all DPs. Helena, who was my interpreter, was also now my assistant and friend. I didn't realize that she had relatives in the United States, but it seems that shortly after she arrived in Munich, she had written to an aunt in California. An

---

[23] Abraham J. Klausner, Lieutenant in the US Amy and Jewish Chaplain, helped with the Central Committee of Liberated Jews and later was elected its Honorary President. As chaplain at the 24th General Hospital in the heart of Munich, he was in a unique position to help with problems. Schwartz, p. 324.

answer came on Tuesday, July 25th, telling her that her parents were living and were in Freiberg, in the Russian Zone of occupation; and that her sister was in Italy, just across the German border, not far from us. Of course, Helena was excited beyond words. They were alive! I immediately promised to take her to Italy the following Sunday to find her sister. But on Saturday, just as I was leaving for Augsberg I learned that Helena had received word that her parents were in Nuremberg, instead of Freiberg. So we quickly switched plans and agreed to go the next day to Nuremberg instead of Italy.

Sunday, July 29th
Up at six. Helena and I drove to Augsberg to pick up Helen Zilka, then on to Nuremberg. It was a beautiful summer day, cool and delightful. We drove along narrow winding roads, going through sweet little villages-- pastel painted houses set directly on the streets--flowers in the windows, geese walking along streets, even a shepherd with sheep. The countryside was rolling, green with rye cut and stacked in even rows of sheaths. There was a castle or two--beautiful estates.

Arrived at Nuremberg about one. Nuremberg was nothing but a rubble heap. There were only a few streets cleared. It was tragic. We located Helena's family living in the basement of the Railroad Ministry. Their meeting brought a lump in my throat.

Helen Zilka and I went to the 116th General Hospital where we found a friend of Helen's waiting for us with a chicken dinner. He is the C.O. (Commanding Officer) of the hospital. He took us all over it. I took a nap. Went to the officers' club for a picnic supper out in the yard under bright-colored umbrellas. Picked up Helena and drove home in the evening,

Helena was quite emotionally upset. She had learned that her father had taken out German citizenship papers, thought maybe that made her a German, too. Had a long serious talk on the way home.

On finding the address where her parents were living, Helena had gone in and shortly afterwards brought them out to be introduced, a middle-aged couple who seemed rather stiff and distant. Recognizing that there was obvious tension, Helen and I had departed, arranging a time later that night for a pick up to get back to Munich. Helena told me that her parents had been shocked to see her wearing an American uniform. I suppose to them America was still the enemy, and here was their daughter, identified with the enemy. There was strain in the air, in spite of their joy of finding each other and sharing tales of what had happened to each in the intervening time since the bombing of Dresden. The visit had left Helena quite torn and sad. Several days later, Palmer Bovie told me of a conversation he had with her. On congratulating her about the reunion, she thanked him and when he commented that she didn't seem much happier, she had said "Well, you see, it's still so hopeless. What can I do? I'm working for UNRRA here, and want to go on, wherever they will send me. I can't bring my parents to Munich--there is no place to live and food would be a great problem. In the future they will depend on me; and I don't know what to do about them. I want to get an education, and a job. I already know some languages and I'd like to study them more. I have an aunt in Berkeley, California, who has written me two letters. I want to go there and study. Of course, we all want to go to America." Helena eventually did go to America, by the way, as the bride of an American serviceman, and when I last heard of her several years later she was working towards a Ph.D. at an American university.

I was beginning to comprehend some of the complexities of relationships distorted even more by the events of the war. In the meantime, Munich continued to show more signs of recovery, albeit slowly. The economy was still in shambles, but the essentials of life were coming on the market. The Germans were developing creative ways to reach out to potential customers among the foreign population, mostly the armed forces and DPs. The barter system was in place to underwrite their efforts.

Wednesday, August 8th
Found, for the first time some few shops beginning to open--was able to buy some hand-painted Tyrolean cards, attractive but expensive. Went to

have my typewriter fixed, taking gasoline for payment. Went also for cards to use for meal tickets, paying five packages of cigarettes for a thousand printed cards. An Estonian girl took me to a German woman who makes beautifully embroidered things in the Bavarian style. I will have to bring material and food for pay. It is an amazing system in effect.

Some of the DPs were getting restless in camps and sought out living arrangements in the city, but ran into the difficulty of overcoming rationing limitations for purchasing food. In order to learn the process for a DP to obtain a ration card, I took off time one day to see how it worked. I wound up spending most of the day going from place to place, finding it frustrating and difficult. And all I wanted was information. Perhaps it was made purposely difficult for non-Germans, although it was not forbidden. Walter and Josef eventually arranged with the widow of a German soldier to rent part of her house to them, and with patience and shrewd negotiations, finally did get their cards. Increasingly, Walter was developing a leadership role, not only in the Museum, but in the larger family of DPs. For instance, he had enthusiastically supported the initiation of our newspaper, *The DP Express*, which was a great success. I noted,

Walter and Alfred returned from Heidelberg bearing fruit, gifts and a story of success. Walter had been able to make arrangements for about 50 Polish students to go to Heidelberg.

This was quite a coup. Young DPs had been deprived of higher education during their years of forced labor, so there was a real thirst for opportunities to catch up. Heidelberg was the headquarters of the US Zone Occupation Forces and undoubtedly their support was brought to bear on the request for permission for these students to be admitted to the famous Heidelberg University.

Speaking of the US armed forces, as time moved along I found myself included in the nightlife at officers' clubs and other military facilities. The clubs were usually former German mansions or elegant restaurants with excellent German orchestras and floor shows. Costs of drinks and other refreshments were minimal. I was included, as well, in the audiences of some of the American-sponsored entertainment for the troops. I saw Jack Benny, for instance, and later Paul Robson and Eugene List who performed in Munich's Stadt Stadium. The incomparable Bob Hope appeared at a show in Füstenfeldbrük, a former Luftwaffe airfield which had been turned into a US Air Force base. He brought the house down with his gag, "First in war, first in peace and Fürstenfeldbrük."

As days passed, news began to seep in that there just might be an end to the war with Japan. First, only rumors, then more rumors. Could it really be surrender? Suspense. Then,

Wednesday, August 15th
V-J Day!! At breakfast I heard the news. Shivers went up and down my spine. At last, peace. It was also St. Mary's Day, a Catholic holiday, so a chapel had been prepared in the Deutsches Museum for a service. It was very interestingly and tastefully done by our Estonian girl. I attended mass, appropriate for the day and a moving experience.

Though, of course, we learned of the bomb and its use in Hiroshima and Nagasaki, it is worth noting in retrospect that the weapon's implications weren't much discussed at the time. Rather than nuclear war's potential for mass destruction, we focused on peace and the end of World War II. At last the guys could return to the States, settle down with their families. All in all, however, the celebration in Germany was rather low key. Its greatest impact was on the servicemen who were scheduled to transfer to the Pacific. Maybe, just maybe, they could go home instead. Soon there was a popular refrain among them to the tune of *Lilly Marlene*,

> Please, Mr. Truman, can't we go home.
> We have taken Berlin, we have conquered Rome,
> Please, Mr. Truman, can't we go home.

Although the end of World War II signaled the shift of the

military's focus from war zones to the American homeland, the shipment of thousands of troops to those shores could only be accomplished over time. But movement was in the air. Our UNRRA focus didn't change, however. Perhaps it placed even more emphasis on the need for solutions for the throngs of DPs in Germany, still shuffling from camp to camp, waiting for the repatriation trains, or settling in with dreams of a new life in a new country. The day-to-day operations didn't noticeably change. For instance, August 17th was another typical day.

The day was a legal holiday, but not for us. There was lots of work. Getting a convoy of 50 Brazilians off, with some difficulty.

A Dutch boy and his sister had been with us for quite a while. He had found her after much searching in Germany after liberation. In the meantime it was found he had T.B. and I had arranged for care for him at a local hospital. Today he came to say that he was better, could fly home (on a special flight for the disabled) but his sister couldn't go with him. I took them back to the hospital, talked with the US captain in charge, persuaded him to say the sister had a fever, therefore needed the special flight, also. We helped her get her luggage from the Museum and back to the hospital.

About 20 Austrians from Belgium arrived, among whom there were several priests. We had to take care of them.

A group of 30 Hungarian Jews arrived, were redirected but were given a noon meal.

I had to check the supplies in the canteen and discuss a new method of distribution.

Went to the children's play room with the camp leader, Walter, and Yvonne. We decided it was too small, selected another one with windows; arranged for an adjoining room for beds for naps. Discussed the decoration of the rooms with Mrs. Picoya, an Estonian.

Arranged for transportation of 14 Stateless persons to the Karlsfeldt Camp [clearly it hadn't closed]. *The 10 Greek Jewish boys were put on a truck for the Feldafing Jewish Camp. They presented me with a picture of themselves as they left.*

Talked with UNRRA Headquarters in Pasing, trying to get through by phone to the UNRRA Indersdorf Children's Center. I wanted to arrange to take a child there on Monday. (On the next day, Monday, I took the little Swedish boy, first to see his mother, then to the Children' Home. His mother had been in an accident the Sunday before, his brother killed. He was left alone in our Museum).

Two Americans arrived from the Landshut Camp with information that a whole truckload of DPs were arriving. Had to clear with the 220th AAA (Military) Group.

Went with Walter and Alfred to negotiate for a typewriter for me. Walter is so paternal, he is sure I let people take advantage of me.

Visited the kitchen, discussed food, planned menu for the next three days.

There was movement within UNRRA, too. A Bavarian Area Headquarters had been established in Pasing, a suburb--really a small town on the outskirts of Munich. New departments and services were developing. One of them was headed by Dorothy Lally, an UNRRA Welfare Supervisor who was putting together a plan for a children's project. In early August, she and I met and she had casually inquired if I would be interested in a special job with children. Later, after her plans became firm, she offered me a position in a Child Search operation. The job would mean visiting the countryside looking for unaccompanied DP children. I would be on the staff at the Area Headquarters in Pasing, but would have to travel. It was agreed that I could take Helena with me. It would mean a promotion and raise.

I thought about it, discussed it with Charley, and although I felt desolate about leaving him and Team 108, I decided to accept. After all, child welfare was my specialty, and I was intrigued with the challenge of this new venture. They wanted me to start immediately, part-time, but agreed that I could continue to live at "home" for the next two weeks. Charley and I decided not to say anything about it until I moved. This wasn't easy, but we managed. We did have one last fling, though.

Friday
I came in late, to find Charley in his room. We talked quite late about the future of the Deutsches Museum, my successor, etc. He looked tired. I suggested that we go to Salzburg the next day. He said "You are crazy," just laughed.

The next day, soon after getting to work, I called my Mobile friend, Colonel Demouy Spottswood, in Salzburg, asked if it would be possible to get tickets for the famous Salzburg Festival that night. He said "You are crazy." It was the first Festival since the beginning of the war, and its last night. Tickets were sold out weeks ago and finding a place to stay would be next to impossible. I told him we would come anyway. At least he might take us to dinner.

We had a busy day at the Museum. I told Charley we were going to Salzburg, to pack his bag. He wouldn't believe it, but finally did pack his bag. As we were leaving, Philippe told us we had better take K-rations as it would be difficult to get food. We laughed at him. It was a beautiful summer day. We put the top back in my little car and went down the autobahn (highway) to Salzburg in wonderful spirits. Although we had none of the passes required for travel, with a lot of kidding the MPs at the check points along the road we arrived in Salzburg about five-thirty. Stopped first to see the Mozart Gardens. Found them beautiful but with cabbages growing there instead of flowers. Met Demouy at his hotel, had drinks and dinner. He had managed to procure tickets for us after all, so we went to the opera, a Mozart opera in a lovely little opera house with red velvet seats, white walls--excellent voices and music. Afterwards we went around to an officers' hotel looking for rooms. Asked if we had orders we said "no." OK, we were given rooms. Said we were hungry, persuaded a mess sergeant to fix us sandwiches, were joined by some UNRRA colleagues. When we were ready to go to our rooms, a colonel acted as a bell-boy, carrying our bags.

The trip finished off the next day with a walk for an hour around Salzburg, poking into courtyards, around the narrow winding streets, into churches. It is a charming place, completely untouched by war. It was again a beautiful day, drove with the top down through the Austrian Alps to St. Wolfgang which is on a beautiful lake in the mountains. King Leopold, the Belgian king, was still there where he had been confined during the war. We drove up in front of the famous "White Horse Inn" just at twelve. A sergeant at the door said, "Just in time for lunch." We were ushered into the Officers' Mess which overlooked the lake. After a walk around the village we drove back, getting to the UNRRA Headquarters in Pasing in time for dinner. An incredible weekend.

I realized more than ever that leaving Charley would be difficult. Though never romantically involved, we shared a close friendship at this stage. He had been so great to work with, a man with whom equality was never an issue, integrity could be taken for granted and affection was openly given. Some of the military, and yes, some UNRRA personnel tended to look down on the DPs, treating them almost as second-class citizens. Not Charley. Additionally he was full of praise for the success of all of the team members, while quick to assume responsibility when things went wrong. I never saw him angry.

Nor was it any easier to leave the rest of the Museum staff, either DP or UNRRA. They had taught me a lot, about myself, my limits, but more importantly, about my capabilities. I had grown tremendously, in such a short time, no small thanks to them. I had come to greatly respect the DPs especially, who worked hard for little tangible compensation and took great joy in it. It was a hard leave-taking.

Monday, August 27th
Went with "the family" to a staff party at the Museum which started at nine. It was a very thrilling experience for me. It was in the Cafe--only staff members and their girl- or boy-friends. They were all so well dressed--so happy looking. There were about a hundred. They were so different in appearance from the sad displaced persons who had come to our Museum three months ago. There were sandwiches, cake, wine and

beer. Walter was master of ceremonies. It was informal, good music, singing, lots of dancing. I thoroughly enjoyed it. There was good comradeship. Charley and I were both choked up. If we had done no other good, this was satisfaction enough.

Summer's end has always been marked for me by my birthday, August 30th. For days beforehand, there had been sly looks, whispering and interrupted conversations, leaving me suspicious.

Thursday, August 30th
My birthday! And what a birthday. Everybody seemed to know it was my birthday, thanks to Charley. I was dressing when there was a knock at my door. It was Charley. "Aren't you hungry?," he asked. When I went down to breakfast the door was locked so I had to go around the house, enter the dining room by way of the garden. I found a huge American flag on a flagpole in front of the house (borrowed from the Military Government). At breakfast the whole team was assembled, much kissing of my hand, congratulations. My place at the table was decorated with a bouquet of red carnations, and my chair entwined with greens--all from Roger, one of our drivers. For breakfast we had hot biscuits and fresh eggs, a very rare treat.

When I arrived at the Museum I was escorted to the office. On the door was a huge sign, "HAPPY BIRTHDAY." There was a little doll dressed like me hanging on the door. The inside of the office was completely decorated--draperies, a huge American flag on the wall, flowers everywhere. On a table were spread gifts. Walter, Alfred and Josef stood there, grinning. Alfred made a speech, presenting me with a beautiful bunch of roses. The gifts included a pair of real silk stockings from Poland from Walter, a lovely stein and bottle of perfume from Charley, a porcelain piece from Suzanne, a blouse from my Estonian girl, and best of all two books, one of water-colored painted caricatures of staff members with their greetings[24] the other from our team. Each member had done a

---

[24] The paintings were by Walter, and in the upper corner of each page with a picture of a veteran of Dachau was a red triangle with his Dachau number. To them it was a kind of badge of honor, courage and survival, in which they took great pride.

page. Very touching. Then people began coming in, bringing me flowers. First, two Lithuanian students, then the Flemish boys, two G.I. sergeants, Victor and Anatonie who work at our house, the Hungarian doctor, and one or two members of the staff. All morning they came with huge bouquets. I've never seen so many flowers. I finally got away long enough to go to the hospital to see Mrs. Hoven, our English noblewoman who works in our Information Center. She had a baby girl the day before, named Susan. A special birthday present for me!

We had lunch at the Museum in the office, with the whole DP staff--a lovely lunch ending with a big birthday cake from the chief cook, and champagne that Walter had brought back from Heidelberg. Charley made a speech, humorous and quite sentimental. No one else knew I was leaving so there was a subtlety only I caught. He was almost in tears, and I was, by the time he finished. I was not allowed to go home until late in the afternoon. On arriving I found everyone had been working all day. There were more flowers--a beautiful bouquet from Yvonne, one from my Roumanian woman. The whole of the downstairs of the house was decorated--garlands, flowers, and hundreds of little red pennants with "A" (for Alabama) sewn on them. The girls had been sewing for days. On the walls was another huge American flag, with British, Belgian and French flags. More gifts--a scarf and a lovely old silver Yugoslavian pin from Helena, and a new beautiful ping pong table in the garden. We had supper--ice cream and a lemon pie made by two G.I.s who live back of us. After a while, guests began arriving for our party, about fifty or more. Many of my military friends, UNRRA colleagues, etc. The orchestra played, we danced, had refreshments galore. A famous Polish dancer had been brought by Walter to dance for us. A very fitting end to one of the happiest years of my life, although it had started out with so many heartaches and difficulties.

CHILD SEARCH

Just as the season changed, summer breezing into fall, so my job shifted from the Deutsches Museum to a Child Search operation. It meant a physical transfer from Galilei Platz to Starnberg, a lakeside suburb about a half-hour away from Munich by BMW. The blue, usually mirror-like lake was beautiful, and famous as the one in which the mad Bavarian King Ludwig II had drowned. It was ringed with handsome, tree-shaded villas most of which were occupied by American Army officers. The large, rambling house selected for the UNRRA Regional staff belonged to a Baron and was sufficiently spacious to accommodate six of us, mostly Americans. Helen Zilka, now Regional Child Welfare Officer, and I were delighted to be reunited again, sharing the master bedroom. The living room had red damask walls and a crystal chandelier with heavy, dark, uncomfortable looking furniture, so it was dubbed "the chamber of horrors." We tended to congregate in the den in the center of which was a wonderful, elaborately decorated, typical German porcelain stove giving off a cozy warmth. It became the center of our life, particularly as the days grew shorter and colder.

My new assignment was a sharp swing from the Deutsches Museum. The one similarity was unprecedented activity demanding innovation on a day-by-day basis. The objective was to locate non-German children of Allied nationality who were alone or with unrelated caretakers, and start the process for their return to family and/or country. We called them "unaccompanied children."

I thought I had already been exposed to the maximum extent of the diabolic treatment of human beings by the Nazis but found that there was no end. Stories continued to emerge which I found shattering. As inconceivable as were the tales I had heard about death and abuse forced on adult DPs, the cruel treatment of children was beyond the pale. At first, dealing with individual cases or small numbers obscured comprehension of the depth of the atrocities. However, as time went on, the magnitude of the problem of unaccompanied children wandering and lost in liberated Germany began to surface. Much has subsequently been written about these children. These were children, innocent children. Tales of their inhuman treatment have been subsequently documented by Mark Wyman, by Dorothy Macardle in her book, *Children of Europe, A Study of the Children of Liberated Countries*[25], and by others. Thousands of children were imprisoned in concentration camps, many saw their parents killed. Wyman described some of their mind-boggling tasks in the camps.

> Labor assignments varied. Some children were harnessed to a hearse at Auschwitz, carrying bodies one way, returning with ashes; others were forced to cut down bodies from gallows, or they stoked fires for the crematoria, buried victims in pits, or laid out the dead in swastika patterns in fields.[26]

So Helena and I started our search, revealing bit by bit what turned out to be just the tip of the iceberg.

The Nazis had a clear policy in regard to these children snatched from their families, homes and countries. One, if they could be useful to the war machine or fill a labor need they survived, forced to work on farms, in factories--and some even fought in the German army. They took children between the ages of ten and eighteen, but even as young as five. There was another reason for kidnapping these children, however, that went beyond the immediate needs of war. The Nazi regime sought to reunite and then nazify the entire Germanic population of Europe, including those who had been living in the east for centuries. The purpose was to create an Aryan nation. These people would be part of

---

[25] Dorothy Macardle, *Children of Europe--A Study of the Children of Liberated Countries: Their War-Time Experiences, Their Reactions, and Their Needs, with a Note on Germany*, Boston: Beacon Press, 1951.
[26] Wyman, pp.90-91.

building the new and greater Reich that would stretch from the English Channel to the Ural Mountains in Russia. To do this, Germany needed to cull the European population for those of Germanic stock. Children were especially desired, as they were the future and also more amenable to being re-educated and nazified. Children with a Nordic appearance, then, were singled out by the Nazis. Blond hair and blue eyes was sufficient to mark a child as Germanic. These children were kidnapped, either individually or in groups (even whole orphanages), and placed in German foster homes. Poland and Czechoslovakia were prime sources for such children.

After liberation, inquiries from frantic parents and relatives began to mount. At the same time, various east European governments, especially Poland, were bringing pressure to bear on UNRRA to find these children. Estimates of how many had been taken varied widely, from thousands to tens of thousands. We would never know exactly how many. UNRRA had already established the Central Tracing Bureau to facilitate the reunification of families, but something more proactive had to be done. In response, UNRRA created a new special program, Child Search, which was first launched in Bavaria.

Helena and I were a team of two, the first team to set out in Bavaria. We designed our own pattern of work. Helena's facility with language was essential. We would travel to a Kreis (a geographic/administrative area somewhat similar to an American county), check in with the Military Government in charge. We would be referred to the German Jugendamt, the local child welfare agency. From the Jugendamt we obtained the names of German children's institutions in the Kreis and any information they had on hand about DP children who might be in the area. We then visited each of the institutions, reviewed their list of inmates, looking for non-Germanic names, as well as to request information on any non-German children who might be in the facility. To complete our coverage, we visited DP camps in the area, talking with the UNRRA welfare officers to learn of any unaccompanied children in their centers. Children identified or found in our search were immediately reported to UNRRA Headquarters and to their national Liaison Officers for action.[27] In this process we located children in displaced persons camps, orphanages, jails, hospitals, convents and in German homes. They included youngsters who had no idea where they had come from or where they belonged. Our search procedure was sketchily illustrated in a three-day trip, October 8th through 10th.

Started out on a three day trip, in a jeep, having put on all the warm clothing I could find. Tied a scarf around my head and left. Went first to Pasing to get Helena, then we first stopped at Chersberg. Talked with the (UNRRA) Welfare Officer, Miss Isgrid. She has several small DP camps under her supervision. There were two Czech boys, unaccompanied, and one Polish child in a German family. We made arrangements for them to go to Indersdorf.

Next stop at Steinhoring, a German Children's Home. There were two French babies brought in from Belgium. Next to Bad Aibling. There was a Russian baby whose mother was in an Insane Hospital. On to Traunheim. They have a problem in that they have 35 Austrian children.

At Rosenheim there was a Polish boy whose mother was in jail--hadn't properly cared for the child. Drove on to Salzberg. When the sun went down it was a cold drive. Went to the Hotel Pitter about dinner time, begged a room from the sergeant at the desk, had dinner.

October 9th, continued our jeep trip to Laufen, arrived at the Jewish camp, Lebenau, just about dinner time, ate dinner with the DPs--a huge meal of meat and potatoes served in a barrack-like, very crude dining room. Talked later with some boys and girls, registered them. All had been in concentration camps, completely separated from their families

---

[27] Each government that was a member of UNRRA appointed staff to liaise with the Administration. They acted as the government's representative when decisions had to be made about a DP's status. The Liaison Officers were key in deciding the children's fate, as they acted as the children's legal guardians, once the child's nationality had been determined.

with no knowledge of their fate. Most had the same story. Taken by the Gestapo, sent from one concentration camp to another, released on liberation. No word from families. All wanted to go to England, anywhere out of Germany. One boy had TB.

Drove to Berchtesgaden. Snow on the mountains, indescribably beautiful in the sunset. Berschtesgaden is the loveliest village I have seen in Germany. One could understand why Hitler had chosen it for his hideout. Every house is freshly painted, with interesting architecture. The DP camp is a former SS camp, good cement barracks so ideal for a DP camp. We found 22 Yugoslav boys there, ages 10 to 16. All were wearing remnants of G.I. uniforms. They each had been picked up by Germans about a year ago, brought into Germany, worked on farms or in villages. They are now together with a Yugoslav professor. They don't want to go back to Yugoslavia.

On the next day, October 10th, left Helena to register all the Yugoslav boys and went on alone in the jeep. About noon, near Bad Toltz, my jeep puttered out. Two G.I.s came along and worked on it for me for about an hour, finally found two friends to tow me. I arrived home at Starnberg in a weapons carrier, towing my jeep.

So it went. In the next few days, Helena and I also located two Canadian children and one American who were living with German relatives as their families had gone to the States to escape the war threats. In a baby nursery which we had previously visited we found that one of "our" babies had died and, since four others were not in good condition, we removed them immediately to the UNRRA children's center at Indersdorf. We found two Jewish boys in Tannhausen whom we registered and for whom we arranged a transfer to Wohlfratshausen, and on to England. At a German Children's Home in Bashenegg we located two children, one Polish and one Russian, in the care of a jolly, kindly nun. The Russian child's mother was in an Insane Hospital in Kaufbeuren. Then, on October 17th, we went on to Kaufbeuren.

Visited the Insane Hospital, found that a Russian woman doctor had been sent out--had removed all Russian patients and sent them back to

Russia, including the mother of our baby. In Kaufbeuren we had gone first to the Military Government. Then to a German children's home. At first the nun in charge said there were no DP children there. Then, well, yes, there was one. It finally came out that there was a group of children who had been brought by the Germans from Poland. It seems that very suddenly a whole orphanage in Oppeln, near Breslau, Silesia, was put on a train and brought to Germany. There were 300 children which were broken into five groups and sent different places. They had heard that one of the groups wound up in Schongau but didn't know whereabouts of the others. Helena and I had noted that the nun was wearing an unusual blue colored veil with her black nun's habit.

Went by Markt-Oberdorf--visited the Military Government there. On to Schongau. Found the Children's Institution with the other group of children from Poland. The nuns were very reluctant to give information.

Helena and I were struck immediately that the nuns were wearing the same color blue veils that we had noticed in the Children's Institution in Kaufbeuren. With careful and patient questioning Helena was able to draw out the story of the children. It seems that the German troops came suddenly to the orphanage in Oppeln[28], which is in the Silesian part of Poland, and ordered all the children and nuns to immediately board a train taking them into Germany. They were put in five cars and from time to time when the train stopped a car was dropped off, or sent on another track to a different destination. In some instances, brothers and sisters were thus separated. The nuns were not given information as to the final location of the groups. The group in Shongau didn't seem to know about the group in Kaufbeuren and appeared delighted to hear about them. Of course, this story was reported to UNRRA and presumably, to the Polish Liaison Officer.

In retrospect, the history of Silesia, which was unknown to me then, might throw some light on the actions of the Germans at the time. The geographic area known as Silesia, as in many parts of Europe, has mixed national affiliations. It is that piece of land in

---

[28] The town is now known as Oppole.

the southern section of Poland, bounded by Czechoslovakia and Germany. In modern times it was politically divided between Czechoslovakia and Poland. The Polish part was in the former Prussian provinces, therefore culturally and politically Germanic-leaning. After WWI, the peace settlement called for a plebiscite to determine whether Upper Silesia would remain German or pass to Poland. The results favored Germany, but the Poles in the region found this unacceptable. To resolve the problem, the League of Nations partitioned the area with the largest section ceded by Germany to Poland, which also happened to be an important industrial region. However, after Germany invaded Poland in 1939, it annexed all of Silesia. It was not until the Potsdam Conference at the end of WWII, in 1945, that Silesia was ceded back to Poland. The orphanage, located near Breslau was in this disputed territory and at the time it was taken, it was considered, at least by the Germans, "German annexed territory." One wonders what nationality the children or their parents considered themselves--probably Polish as they were represented to us. It certainly must have been an awkward, confused position in which the nuns found themselves. Were they Polish or German? Had I known this intricate history of the area from which the group came, I would certainly have pursued answers to some of the unanswered questions.

Another politically tainted saga, that of the Yugoslav boys, continued to play itself out over the next few weeks. Helena and I had contacted the Yugoslav Liaison Officer in Munich, Captain Sloboden, telling him the story of the boys, officially reporting their history. He wanted to immediately make arrangements for their return to Yugoslavia, but we put him off, at least temporarily. The children were adamant they did not want to return to Yugoslavia.

October 29th
Helena and I went to Berschtesgaden to talk to the 22 Yugoslav children in their rooms. Helena spoke to them in Yugoslav. It was a moving sight to see the 12 and 13 year old kids stand at attention and say they refused to return to their homes until King Peter was back on the throne. It was

117

almost incomprehensible that children so young could reject home and family for political belief. It is true, however, that they have many fears-- have been subjected to propaganda. We could not make any headway in persuading them, did not want to force them, decided to have the Liaison Officer come down.

Friday, November 16th
Up early to go to Berschtesgaden. After difficulty getting the car started, got off. Helena and two Yugoslav Liaison Officers accompanied me. The weather was cold, snow on the ground in most places. It was foggy so we could not really see the mountains to their best advantage. Arrived about twelve. The Yugoslav officers talked to the 22 Yugoslav children. The boys still don't want to return. They fired questions at the officers who handled them very well. It is still amazing to me how emotional children of 14 or 15 can get over politics. It was obvious they were being propagandized.

The boys had gathered in one of their two rooms at the camp that day, sitting on their double-decker bunks and on the floor. The conversation, of course, was in Yugoslav, so I couldn't follow it, but soon it was apparent that there was hostility in the air, some kind of confrontation pitting the boys and the teacher against the Liaison Officers. Finally, Helena tugged on my arm lightly, telling me with her eyes that it was time to leave. As we drove out of the courtyard, several boys threw rocks at us, presumably meant for the officers who represented the current hated regime which had dislodged their King. As far as we were concerned the matter was now in the hands of the country's officials.[29]

Mascots attached to US Army groups and outfitted in American uniforms posed another and unforeseen problem. They were taught to speak English, and of course to curse. They had been taught to smoke. The G.I.s spoiled them and often made empty promises about taking them to the States some day. When the Army units did leave for the US, these boys were abandoned, often at dockside, or turned over to UNRRA, who took them to

---

[29] These children were ultimately resettled elsewhere.

the center at Indersdorf. After the status and freedom of the G.I. company, however, the children found it difficult to adjust to an environment where a certain amount of discipline was enforced.[30] I wrote about one such case on November 26th.

Went by the Company B Battalion Headquarters of the 69th Signal Corps near Starnberg to talk to them about two youngsters that they had picked up and more or less adopted. One was a boy 16, who was born in America--his mother was South American, his father a naturalized French American. They came to France to live before the war. His parents had been picked up and taken to an internment camp. He heard no more from them. He was taken by an American unit coming through France and had been with them since. The other was a 17 year old Polish boy, rather undersized, who had been brought into Germany with other boys to work in an airplane factory. His parents are dead and he doesn't want to go back to Poland. Boys who have been with the army are usually spoiled, have been made promises of going to the United States which is unrealistic. UNRRA has a hard time convincing them that anything they have to offer can compete with what they have with the army.

Recognizing the symbolism of a bolted exit, UNRRA never locked doors or gates; the children were always free to leave. Many of the mascots took advantage of the situation and walked out. One of them, a Polish boy named Josef who was at Indersdorf, took off, looking for me and eventually turned up at my billet in Pasing one night. He said he had "taken the day off." Still wearing his cut-down G.I. clothes, he had a defiant bravado that had melted in the face of the alternatives to the children's center. I took him back with an explanation to those in charge.

There seemed no end to the variety of situations which Helena and I encountered as we pursued our search. There was the

---

[30] The stories of the mascots was vividly exemplified in the film, *The Search*, directed by Fred Zinnemann, with Montgomery Clift playing the lead role of the soldier and a Czech boy, the mascot. It was released in the US in 1948.

experience with the English boy, for instance. My first mention of it was on October 31st.

Went to inform the German foster family that the English boy must go back to England. Quite upsetting to me. He had been with them for seven years. A week later--went with the British Consul to get the English boy to go back to England. The German foster mother refused to let him go. Four days later Helena and I again visited the boy. A very difficult case. The Germans do not want to give him up.

The Germans were a middle-class couple living in a simple, but comfortably furnished home in Munich. There was an obvious attachment to the child, who never left the mother's side, often standing by the chair in which she was seated, clinging to the chair arm. He looked about age 9 or 10, very blond, blue-eyed, and never spoke, frightened. I don't recollect the circumstances for his being with the family but they must have been together before the war started. Whatever the reasons, policy required that he be removed and returned to his homeland. No Allied child was to remain with a German family, whether they wanted to stay with them or not. I have to confess that I was relieved when, on our final visit, we found the house closed and no one around. We dropped the case. It seemed to have been a matter of an allied child being in the home of an enemy family with a decision being made about the future of a child irrespective of the child's welfare and wishes.

In fact, unbeknownst to those of us in the field, a debate was developing over what to do with these children. UNRRA's mandate was clear, all unaccompanied children of non-German nationality were to be returned to their families, and if their families could not be found, to their homeland. This did not necessarily mean that it was in the child's best interests, as in this case. Increasingly, the US administration preferred to leave the children where they were, if they were receiving adequate care.[31] This would ultimately put UNRRA's child welfare workers in an

---

[31] Proudfoot, p.268.

awkward predicament and stall the whole search and settlement process, but that was something in the future.

As the days and months passed, cold rains and shortened days signaled the coming of winter. The snow began. Having passed my own childhood in Mobile, Alabama without seeing snow, I never ceased to be fascinated by it. The snow in Bavaria was deep and soft and a clean white-white. It covered trees and I thrilled at the sparkle of sun on its surface, the glistening drifts. Jeeps were not heated, not even enclosed, and we were navigating more and more in our more maneuverable jeep than in my car. Often it was only the thought of those hot Tom and Jerries[32] waiting on the porcelain stove, made by our thoughtful colleague, Roger, that got Helena and me over the last miles to "home."

As the days and weeks passed, I began to feel restless for a variety of reasons. The emergency phase of the displaced persons work was giving way to increased bureaucracy and I felt growing impatience with staff meetings, reports to be prepared and other administrative details.

September 11th
Another conference--child welfare workers. I am getting very discouraged over the amount of talk and lack of action.

October 2nd
Meeting all day, with field supervisors, welfare workers, trying to determine who is a DP. The nationalities are so confused. Welfare meeting. We discussed policy all morning, reached no conclusion--very discouraging.

October 16th
Meeting of welfare workers (my meeting) to organize and set up a reporting system.

---

[32] A drink made from egg yoke, sugar, allspice, rum beaten together and blended with beaten white of egg and brandy, sprinkled with nutmeg.

October 24th
Meeting all day at Pasing. Nothing reached as far as decisions.

November 5th
Staff meeting all morning. UNRRA is now organizing on a regional basis. The organization is becoming more effective but still leaves much to be desired.

November 8th
We had a meeting of welfare officers in the district (Muldorf), about 30 in all. It was the first meeting of its kind. Information about employment, education, tracing and child welfare was disseminated. I was disappointed in the child welfare program, was determined to ask for reassignment.

Life with UNRRA had become a string of meetings. The Administration was trying to impose order and uniformity to our rather ad hoc operations. In the process, it meant UNRRA was becoming increasingly policy- and regulation-bound, and very bureaucratic. At the same time, things were becoming very politicized. It was not necessarily an improvement, at least from my perspective.

On the 29th of October I wrote a letter to Aunt Katie, summarizing my thoughts about the early administrative developments in UNRRA, tracing this evolution.

Dear Aunt Katie,
There are many changes in UNRRA now. Morale is at a very low ebb. In many cases it is justified, in many it is not. There are not many of us who came here in the beginning who cannot testify to some pretty bad experiences as far as UNRRA administration is concerned. We were badly outfitted, poorly equipped! We had to 'scrounge' for what we got. Scruples played no part in it. There were almost insurmountable obstacles everywhere we turned. The Military to which we were attached were not always sympathetic, cooperative, or even civil. Fortunately I have not had as much to complain about as the rest of them. I happened to get a good director, and because I had a Southern accent and blue eyes,

we got lots more from the military than many teams. On the other hand, UNRRA did a very poor job of recruiting on the continent. There is good personnel from Belgium, Holland, and a few good English. The French are notoriously bad. Some few UNRRA personnel can do more harm as far as prestige is concerned than a dozen good people. It has taken a long time to weed out the incompetent personnel but that has been done now. The top administrators in Washington, London, Paris, and even in Frankfort have at times appeared to be doing more to block the situation than anything else. That is the reason for the low morale. I will say that the teams which are in the field actually doing the job are magnificent. They get little credit, they work like dogs, and are accomplishing a lot. If some of these congresswomen and men just spent a few days in the camps instead of interviewing the desk-sitters they might get a different idea about the whole situation! I have no idea about how long the job will last here in Germany. I believe if we can take care of things this winter the greater part of our job will be over. There will just be a few tag ends to tie together after that...

Whereas I was caught up in the immediacy of Starnberg and the Child Search operation, the Deutsches Museum and No.2 Galilei Platz were like magnets with a continuous pull for me. When in Munich, I often found reason to drop by for lunch, or to accept an invitation to parties or events involving all my old colleagues. I felt welcomed, didn't sense any fading of bonds with my former teammates. As the outside world was changing, however, so was that intimate world. Charley was leaving.

October 2nd
On returning to the office I met Charley, found he had just resigned. He was so happy, now that he had made the decision. His wife was going to have a baby soon. He felt UNRRA could now replace him. Basically, I think he was a little fed up with the 'channels', red tape, and rules being laid down by UNRRA. It was a blow to think that Charley would not be around. UNRRA will lose a marvelous person.

Charley's leaving elicited many expressions of gratitude for his service and contributions to the reordering of lives after the end of hostilities. The number of parties given in his honor was testimony to the degree of affection and respect held by all who had come in contact with him. One of the most memorable was on Thursday, October 18th.

Party was at Walter Knopek's house on the outskirts of Munich. It was a farewell party for Charley del Marmol. Present were Mr. Atkins, (English), Charley (Belgian), Helena (Yugoslav), Alice (French), Walter (Polish), and me (American).[33] *The conversation was a jargon mixture of French, English and German with a little Polish here and there. It was a hilarious meal--good fellowship with very deep feeling about Charley's leaving. The food was delicious--hors d'oeuvres, soup, pastries, meat and vegetables, dessert and pastries, coffee and cake followed by fruit punch with wine in it. Cognac had been served throughout the meal. It was a sincerely happy, international evening. Walter announced his engagement to Alice.*

And on October 25th, the finale--the real dissolution of the original Team 108.

Had dinner at 2 Galilei Platz, the last night. Charley, Jean, Roger and Philippe were to leave early the next morning. We tried to laugh, to be gay. They offered me the job as Deputy Director, or even the Director of the Deutsches Museum. After I said goodbye to Charley I drove back to Starnberg, unabashedly sobbing the whole way. I felt deeply the loss of a dear friend.

Meantime, experiences in the search program continued to build. Immediately following liberation of the DP population in Germany word began to seep out, first to the European countries closely connected to events in Germany, about the plight of the children victimized by the Nazi regime. The shock and horror gave way to an urgency to do something, immediately; to rescue the victims; to reach out with compassion and relief. Doors opened in many countries, many of which were still reeling from the war's devastation. The most needy children were considered

---

[33] Just a few days before Charley left, I learned that he was a Belgian baron. He was so unassuming, so un-royal, that it was hard to believe.

to be the survivors of concentration camps and several countries offered them temporary care in sanitoria, so that they might recover their health while awaiting final disposition. Three hundred were flown from the Theresienstadt Camp to England in August 1945, 150 from Bergen-Belsen. Sweden sent a Red Cross ship to bring other former Belsen inmates to Sweden. Three hundred and fifty children found in Buchenwald were taken by the Swiss. There was an outpouring of services and programs from European countries for these devastated children still in Germany.[34] England had been particularly generous in offering refuge to unaccompanied Jewish DP children. I had been involved in the selection and preparation of a group planning to go.

Thursday, Oct. 4th
Meeting in Passing to review cases of children selected to go to England. Jewish, mostly boys under 16, all having been in concentration camps, with no parents.

It seemed like a perfect short-term solution. It would remove the children from the inadequate facilities we could offer and speed their healing, while waiting for the final decision on their ultimate settlement. But this, too, soon became a political issue that pitted political interests against the children's best interests.

On November 6th,
I drove over to Wohlfratshausen with the field supervisor, a Czech/American Jewish woman. We discussed with the Director of the camp the question of the Jewish children going to England. One hundred children have already gone. About 300 more are ready to go, the next group to leave on Monday. Now, the Jewish people in Germany have made a resolution saying that no more children can go. They have made a political issue of it. They feel that these unaccompanied children are theirs--that because they survived the ordeal of persecution their lives should be used for a purpose. In this case it is to try to force England to open Palestine. It is shocking that no consideration can be given the individual child, all of whom want to go to England--anything to get out

---

[34] Wyman, p.98.

of Germany. We finally had to admit defeat, admit that to risk having the children undergo any other physical or emotional violence or strain, it would be best to postpone plans for sending them to England.

As the days and months passed, I was becoming more aware of the profiles of the different national and ethnic groups, their characteristics, their "personalities," their culture. The Jewish DPs seem to be more and more in my central vision. I wrote in my letter of October 29th to Aunt Katie:

There are several matters that we get a slant on that might interest you. The Jewish problem is the most complicated, the most evident one that faces this continent; and really, the world. There are definitely two sides to it. The suffering of the Jews has been beyond any stretch of the imagination. Millions killed in brutal, inhuman ways. Millions of children done away with. We find no Jewish babies--no children under twelve or thirteen. The suffering endured in the concentration camps, the continuous shifting and mixing of the people, which separated families to such an extent that it is almost a hopeless task to unite them. The whole ethnic group is left without any property, any country, almost without hope. The TB rate is terrific. The American soldiers who came in and rescued them from their concentration camps thought they would never forget.

After their liberation they were left stunned. They went into DP Camps that were overcrowded, run as best they could under the strain of the times. At first there was an attempt to make no difference in nationalities or different ethnic groups for fear of discrimination. That didn't work. The Jews demanded to be segregated. They have been terribly difficult to help. They have been demanding, arrogant, have played upon their concentration camp experience to obtain ends. I saw rooms in our camp after they left--filthy dirty, furniture broken, such a mess as no other group ever left. They are divided into factions among themselves. One of our camps has to have six synagogues to keep the peace. They refuse to do any work, have had to be forced by gun to go out and cut wood to heat their own camps. American soldiers have developed bitter attitudes in many cases.

I am still sympathetic, believe that only with great tolerance and patience can the problem even come near a solution. The Jewish agencies have some excellent workers trying to do the job. It will take a long time for them to heal, to gain self respect, to believe in anything. Now they are living by their wits, as they had to do for many years. They are the biggest black market operators. The children have tales to tell that make my spine crawl. We are trying to evacuate as many children (when I say children, I mean ages 12 to 20) to England and Switzerland. Their idea of heaven is Palestine. The stories of Jewish people coming back from Poland are true. We recently had 150 children from an orphanage in Poland seep back into this territory. It is very discouraging to think there is no solution, even temporarily, for the future.

All of this is tied in with Patton's removal. There are three big Jewish camps in our area. One is just across the lake from here, in Feldafing. Another is a children's center under my supervision, Wohlfratshausen--a huge capacity of three thousand, one thousand of which are for our children. The other camp in this area, Landsberg, is not far from here, also one of 'my' camps. The Jewish people raised so much Cain about conditions that Truman sent a special investigator [Earl Harrison, author of the Harrison Report], *as result of which Patton was called on the carpet. The conditions in the camps were admittedly bad--no worse, no better than a lot of other camps. Patton has never been interested in the DP problem. It was a good thing for him to be removed. But too bad under the circumstances. Almost to a man, any of the boys here who have been under his command have nothing but praise for him. To them he is a great soldier.*

Stanley P. Hirshon, in *General Patton: A Soldier's Life*, discussed the Harrison report and Patton's reaction.

> Earl G. Harrison, the former Commissioner of Immigration and Naturalization Service, who was sent by Truman to investigate the conditions of displaced persons, stressed Patton's disdain for Jews.....The Harrison report objected to DPs, 'particularly Jews' being kept in unsanitary camps, fenced in by barbed wire and forced to wear either concentration camp

clothes or discarded German uniforms. "As matters stand," Harrison reported, "we appear to be treating the Jews as the Nazis treated them, except we do not exterminate them." "If the camps were not enclosed," Patton responded, " the DPs would spread over the country like locusts .....Harrison and his ilk believe that a displaced person is a human being which he is not, and this applies particularly to the Jews, who are lower than animals.[35]

General Eisenhower vigorously defended the American Military Government's performance to President Truman, in the face of Harrison's accusations.

Since Mr. Harrison's visit in July many changes have taken place with respect to the conditions of Jewish and other displaced persons. Except for temporary crowded conditions..., housing is on a reasonable basis....

The housing problem must be seen in full perspective. This winter the villages and towns in the US Zone of Germany will be required to house more than twice their normal population.... The resulting housing shortage is... desperate.... At the time of Mr. Harrison's report there was perhaps 1,000 Jews still in their former concentration camps. These were too sick to be moved at that time. No Jewish or other displaced persons have been housed in these places longer than was absolutely necessary for medical quarantine and recovery from acute illness.

The assertion that our military guards are now substituting for SS troops is... misleading. One reason for limiting the numbers permitted to leave our assembly centers was... banditry by displaced persons.... Despite all precautions, more than 2,000 of them died from drinking... poisonous liquor. Many others died by violence or were injured while circulating outside our

---

[35] Hirshon, p.659.

assembly centers. Perhaps we were overzealous in our surveillance....

In certain instances we have fallen below standard, but I should like to point out that a whole army has been faced with the intricate problems of readjusting from combat to mass repatriation, and then due to the present static phase with its unique welfare problems. Anticipating this phase, I have fostered since before D-Day the development of UNRRA so that persons of professional competence in that organization might take over greater responsibilities.[36]

The Jewish DPs were not the only group who posed a challenge. As I wrote Aunt Katie,

...as for the Russians, they deserve a whole chapter. Most of us here are not a little alarmed. We have no idea of what is actually going on in the Russian Zone. They see to that. We hear that trainloads of furniture, clothing, everything they can lay their hands on are going into Russia, returning loaded with guns and ammunition. We hear that a woman is not safe from rape, that Anti-Semitism is rampant, that freedom of political belief is impossible. We know that many Poles, Czechs, Yugoslavs are fleeing and coming into Germany. I have talked to several. I know that Russia forced every Russian DP to return to Russia regardless of their wishes. I know of one case where they even went to a Mental Hospital and took the Russians and returned them to Russia. We have no Russian DPs in the American occupied zone.

It was not unusual to encounter or hear of numbers of ragged, malnourished children and youth wandering roads and the countryside--often begging or stealing, using their wits to survive. These were children who chose not to enter the DP camps, for whatever reason. They balked at the camps' structure and rules, after practically a lifetime of evading regulation and authority. Many just couldn't settle into a life designed for children. Sometimes they landed in jail. In the case of Russian youth the

---

[36] Proudfoot, pp.332-334.

option of going to a DP camp was even less appealing, as it was feared it would lead to prompt, forceful return to Russia. :

September 17th
Had made arrangements for a Russian boy, age 11, to be released from jail. Visited the jail, took the boy to the Freiman DP Camp.

And on October 30th
In Munich, went to the jail where two Russian boys were being held. One was age 10, had been in a foster home in Munich. We had him released and took him to his foster home. The other, an older, more delinquent, was left until we could report it to the Liaison Officer. I had a long talk with Lt. Shaw about planning for DP children who get into the Munich jail.

It had only been six months since the war's end, but it seemed years. If work was getting increasingly frustrating, the social life continued to provide excitement and new friends. The shifting military personnel always produced replacements for the "goodbyes," so that there was never any lack of dates, dinners and dances. Life in Starnberg introduced an infusion of more UNRRA social contacts, but Munich was close enough for access to military clubs and newly opening German facilities. With time, restrictions on fraternization with the Germans had loosened and increasingly German women began to appear at social events. I don't ever recollect seeing any German men in social situations. These women were dubbed "Frauleins." It was a German designation for "Miss," but carried a special and derogatory meaning under the circumstances. Until recently they had been the enemy and it was still awkward to be socializing with them. My first mention of it was on Saturday, October 13th.

Went to a house warming at a new house just moved into by six colonels. There were four frauleins, one Red Cross girl and me. One of the frauleins was a very interesting girl from Berlin. Not much fun--very strained....

And then, *on November 1st*
After dinner (at 3rd Army Mess) with two officers we went to the new officers club, The Seehaus. It is a very nice club, resembling our country clubs at home. It had a fair floor show. There were lots of German frauleins there--rather nice looking, most of them. Some American girls refuse to go out where there are German girls. I don't feel that way. There are so few American girls here and the boys naturally want female companionship.

The Red Cross Clubs were becoming more ubiquitous. Numerous Red Cross snack bars were opened along the autobahns or major highways, offering coffee and doughnuts. Then there was the Red Cross Officers' Club opening in Munich.

November 15th
Went over to the Red Cross Officers Club. The Club is an elegant former restaurant, crystal chandelier, et cetera There is a good orchestra playing semi-classical music, soothing and pleasant. We ate doughnuts, drank coffee, spent a pleasant evening.

Even UNRRA had contrived to come up with a formal arrangement for official entertaining by taking over an old, rather famous Munich restaurant, Schwartzwalder's. It was closed to the public, had excellent food and wine, so provided a convivial spot for UNRRA personnel and guests. Meanwhile, the city continued to come alive, like a sleeping giant gradually awakening. As it did, I found myself shedding some of the official military-oriented restraints trying to emerge as a civilian. Often in the evenings I was getting out of uniform for "civvies." There were even forays into beauty parlors, usually bartering PX-issue soap for shampoos.

November 15th
My friend Lillian Dick and I went into Munich. My pet beauty shop didn't have enough electricity to operate the dryers. Then we went to the Elizabeth Arden shop. Lillian couldn't get over finding an Elizabeth Arden beauty parlor in the midst of bombed-out Munich.

Meanwhile, my Search operations were punctuated with conferences, foreboding winter weather and my growing inclination for a change of job. On November 11th, I formally requested reassignment.

I feel that the job of seeking unaccompanied children in the area is about over, the responsibility from now on should rest with the UNRRA Team Welfare Workers. Also, I am eager to get back on a team--would like to go back to the Deutsches Museum as Deputy Director or Principal Welfare Officer. To me the Deutsches Museum is the focal point of the DP program operations in Munich, the largest city in Bavaria, and will be the biggest problem this winter. I don't believe Mr. Atkins can handle the job.

Even in those last days on the Search job, stories of kidnapped or escapee children were still emerging. I regret that I was rarely able to get the whole story of each child, of each group, leaving frustration and a sense of half-knowledge. Language, of course, was a barrier. Helena's interpretation had to be limited because of time pressures. In some instances, I was sure the whole story was not given to us, but had the assurance that once we had confirmed the identity and status of a child, there would be intensive follow-up and planning. Our job was just to locate the unaccompanied children and report them. As time moved along, I was more and more horrified at the inhuman measures carried out against these thousands of innocent children. As the stories piled up, it became evident that each was different and a discernable pattern was emerging. One of the last encountered was about a group of Czech children.

November 16th
After lunch, went to investigate the living conditions of 16 Czech children in Berchtesgaden. These were what was left of a group of about a hundred children who had been evacuated from cities during the bombing. There was a Czech woman in charge--had brought them (on foot) in front of the Russian armies. They came to Bad Reichenhall. Some had been found by their parents, others were sure their parents were killed. The group was living in a large house in Bad Reichenhall under

very poor conditions. Will recommend they be removed to Indersdorf until they can be screened and repatriated.

We had previously talked with the Czech Liaison Officer who advised that he had a list of 300 unaccompanied Czech children in Bavaria who had been brought in by the Germans.

In a letter to Aunt Katie on November 11th, I wrote,

I have about finished the initial part of my job, anyway. I have covered the whole territory, interpreting to the UNRRA teams in the Landkreis what we were looking for, how to seek the children, what information we wanted about them, how the children were to be admitted to our children's centers. Where there are no UNRRA teams I have done the same thing with the Military Government. I think we have located most of the large groups and it will be only individual cases that will turn up from now on. That being the case I will talk this morning about reassignment. I will let you know about the decision.
Then, *on November 14th,*

It is an actual fact, with details to be worked out, I shall return to the Deutsches Museum, to Team 108, as Principal Welfare Officer!

By a strange twist of fate it turned out that Polly Bakeman, my former *Kota Gede* bunkmate, was to replace me. She had been reassigned to our Regional center two or three weeks before. We had a warm reunion. Her early experience had not been too happy--an assignment up near Bremen, poor Director, all-French team. She was delighted to be back in child welfare and in the US Zone.

Thursday, November 22nd
Thanksgiving Day, 1945!! It began with a knock on the door, telling us to get to breakfast in ten minutes. Fresh eggs! The first time in several weeks. We had two fried eggs each. We all sat around, dressed in bathrobes, over coffee. It was a rather gray day, cold enough for us to be glad of our fires. The whole family gathered for dinner. We had eggnog first, then adjourned to the dining room. The table was decorated with

fall leaves and flowers. Nuts, candies, fruit cakes were around, contributed by members from things sent from home. A very American dinner followed--fruit cocktail, roast turkey with dressing, ending with pumpkin and apple pies. We ate from two-thirty until five o'clock with much lively conversation and singing. Charity Grant (our other Kota Gede bunkmate) came in, has been in Wiesbaden doing administrative work for voluntary agencies. It was a very happy Thanksgiving.

DEUTSCHES MUSEUM REDUX

On Tuesday, November 27th, I had moved into Munich, bag and baggage, to rejoin my teammates at Galilei Platz.

I went down to the Museum, spent the afternoon roaming around. It struck me with a bang! What a gruesome, bloody cold place. It was horribly depressing. Spent the rest of the afternoon at the reception desk to see who the people were who were coming in. The majority were Jewish, Polish chiefly. Many were what we called "infiltrees." People who were just now coming into Germany from Poland, Czechoslovakia, or other countries because of anti-Semitism. A trainload of 55 came in that day from Czechoslovakia. Also, there were many Ukrainians, many students coming to the University. Most people were seeking relatives, going to another camp, or just traveling. The situation was rather discouraging.

It seemed as if the Museum was serving two functions now, the entry point for Jews returning to or seeking haven in the US Zone of Germany; and as a hotel for individual DPs in Munich for brief periods to get information and assistance with registration and documentation, to seek relatives or friends, and those in transit to and from other camps. Whereas initially the staff had been reliably stable the turnover had picked up with repatriation, movement into nationality-oriented DP camps; and in some cases, to lodgings in the city. There was still a segment of "old hands," however, including Walter, Josef, Alfred among them.

Wednesday, November 28th
I made the rounds with Walter. It was almost the most depressing experience I have ever had. The courtyard in front of the Museum was milling with people, mostly Jewish, openly selling black market stuff. The entrance to the Museum had been bricked up except for a narrow door on account of the cold. Here stands a guard examining papers. Beer barrels were all around. The big hall was brutally cold and gloomy. People wandered aimlessly around. The information section was cold. There is

no electricity in Munich in the morning from seven until ten for three days out of the week. The other days it is off from one until five in the afternoons. This made the narrow hallways caverns of blackness. The rooms were cold, bare--maybe it was the cold that made everything appear bleak and dismal. There were many disturbing features--money being charged for services, dirt, food not too good. The whole spirit of the place seemed different. I was sick at heart by the time I finished and realized what a tremendous job was ahead.

After lunch Marion Gallagher, a new team member, and I went to the beauty parlor. For the first time we found a hostile attitude towards us. They made us wait, did not wash or set our hair well, were impatient and indifferent.... After dinner tried a movie in the area, found it closed so sat around talking until midnight when word came that there were 300 people coming to the Deutsches Museum. They did arrive. Our Supply Officer, Harold Cook, Mr. Atkins and I went to the Museum, found things well organized. Soup and bread were ready. We had cots waiting as the place was already filled to capacity. The people started arriving about one o'clock in three trucks which we had sent to the station. They were given meal tickets, DDT'd and helped settle themselves on cots with blankets which we had set up in one big hall. Some women and children were placed in rooms. There were many women and children in the group as it was composed chiefly of families.

The story of this group was amazing. They were Polish Jews who had been put on a train near Nuremberg to return to Poland. For four weeks they remained on the train, going to Poland, to Russia, to Czechoslovakia, and to Munich. The people were in a daze. They accepted calmly the food, the beds and blankets. In spite of the hour of the morning they did not appear sleepy, took a long time to settle down. It was three-thirty before we left the Museum.

Thursday, November 29th
Spent a hectic morning attempting to find out where to send the people and make some order out of chaos. Found everyone was going their own way, doing in many cases the same thing someone else was doing. Spent much time in the information center. Discussed medical things with Yvonne who had more responsibility.

Friday, November 30th
In the afternoon went with Mr. Atkins to a Directors' meeting. It was
very interesting. All the Directors of camps in the Munich area were
there. Present also was the doctor in the Military Government who was
responsible for the Munich area. He made some very forthright
statements about the control of VD (venereal disease) and contagious
diseases. The VD rate in Munich is greater than in Paris, Marseille, any
city in the American zone of occupation. I had my first chance to observe
Ed Broughton (the new team Deputy Director) in action. I think we will
get along.

Saturday, December 1st
Ed Broughton, Yvonne and I went through the Museum with the
UNRRA doctor and nurse. I had requested this service in analyzing the
whole situation. There was no heat in the Museum--some trouble getting
the right kind of coal. The sanitary conditions were frightful. We got sick
and sicker as we went through. It was Ed's first trip throughout. We
found liquor, silver fox furs, food, rats, dirty dishes, bad ventilation,
unsanitary conditions. By the time we finished I was about ready to give
up. Ed found P.X. candy being sold in the black market in the courtyard.

The black market. Since all traditional means of exchange and
purchase of goods were disrupted at war's end, almost
immediately there sprang up an alternative system. In some
instances, barter arrangements flourished. The cigarette became
the most popular medium of exchange, a veritable alternate
currency, usually originating in the Military P.X.s. And, of course,
the black market flourished. Rationing had been continued after
the war's end. The shortages of food, fuel and other necessities of
life had only worsened. As a result, the black market flourished,
as people sought some way to augment and supplement their
rations. It became ubiquitous. In Munich, there were no shops
open at first, so articles "for sale" were traded outside usual
commercial channels, facilitating the trade in stolen or looted
goods. There were no price controls, no taxes, no accounting, no
restriction on deals in illicit products. However, as shops
reopened and normal business reinstated, the black market was
declared illegal. Both German law enforcement and the American

military authorities aggressively sought to shut down the black market. The transition from the initial era of "anything goes" to "law and order" was gradual, but nevertheless seemed incomprehensible to many in those complex times, coming as an unanticipated shock.

Monday, December 3rd
Went to the Museum, found that there had been 1500 people there the day before. There are beds for only 1000 and cooking utilities for about 800. Went to a meeting where the definition of "DP" was discussed. The screening procedure is a very complicated one. At lunch a CIC (Central Intelligence) man was at the house to discuss the screening of University students for the possibility of subversive groups.

The screening procedure had become a symbol of the intertwined nature of the relationship between UNRRA and the American military authorities, which had evolved since the original Agreement between the two was signed. At the end of hostilities, the original Agreement had rolled over into separate agreements within each of the three western zones of occupation in Germany. Although there were some negotiated differences in each agreement, all continued the initial subordinate role of UNRRA to the military and the basic division of responsibilities. The military maintained responsibility for law and order, for provision of food, clothing, medicines, essential materials, as well as transportation and accommodation in DP centers. One of the challenges to the UNRRA/military partnership was the job of determining the eligibility of DPs for UNRRA and military assistance.

Needless to say, the complexities posed by any attempt to define "Displaced Persons" was daunting. It was important, however, to establish one which could become the basis for determining whether an individual qualified for assistance from UNRRA and the Military. During the early post-liberation days, terms such as "eligibility" seemed irrelevant. Human need was the basis for care. As time went on, however, with costs rising, food growing scarcer and repatriation efforts stalling, attention began to be focused on who is a DP and who is not. By the end of 1945, emphasis began to be put on a determination by a "screening" process. The Deutsches Museum was one of the early centers for experimentation, in its Information Section. Immediate obstacles emerged. Few DPs had authentic "papers" showing country of origin, birthdates, their immediate past history. Language was another barrier to productive interviews. So was a lack of coordination on our part. If turned down in one place, the DP could go to another, having learned some better answers. The screening procedure was later outlined in a directive describing categories of those recognized as eligible by the US Army. It also suggested measures for its implementation:

> UNRRA teams will immediately review the status of Displaced Persons under UNRRA care by becoming familiar with histories of such persons and ... review ... by checking each DP record and by personal interview, reporting any possible ineligibles to the District Office for referral to the military authorities.[37]

Although military-driven, since they were footing the bill, UNRRA usually carried out the screening process, with the military making the decision in doubtful cases. However, UNRRA and the military had a clear understanding that UNRRA did not expel DPs from camps, even if their status was found to be questionable. That was the responsibility of the military. The screening process was modified occasionally and used, in some instances, for repatriation planning, as well as to detect individuals involved in subversive activities.

Tuesday, December 4th
What a day! Beginning with Anatole, the Polish boy servant, announcing he would not work with the new housekeeper. It was cold, snowing lightly, slippery streets. Went by Military Government to see about the problem of providing passes to DPs traveling. At the Museum

---

[37] UNRRA US Zone Headquarters Administrative Order 146, dated 31 August 1946, subject: Screening of Displaced Persons - Eligibility.

it was one problem after another. A question of 76 Royalist Yugoslavs living in a camp drawing food from us, selling it on the black market, so had to be stopped. Seven boys brought in by the police for change of clothing. They were wearing G.I. uniforms. On arriving back at the Museum I had found a group of 113 Jews had arrived after traveling for eight days, tired, cold and hungry. Every bed and room at the Museum was filled. No one at the Jewish Committee was available. Finally arranged for disinfection, setting up cots in a hall, feeding with Kosher food. For the first time it was necessary to say we could take no more people. It was one of the most heart-rending things I ever had to do--on a cold, wet night. (This still haunts me.) *Fortunately, there were not many people turned away.*

Still reeling from the trauma of these first few days back at the Museum, I tried to summarize the events and my reaction in a letter of December 4th to Aunt Katie.

I wish I could pull a few pages from my diary, which I have tried to keep. It might be able to give a better picture of life in Munich. I will say that winter has set in grimly, the stark reality of a war-torn world is upon us. Of course it didn't all happen here at once. It just hit me because of my change in jobs. Sometimes I wonder if my head does not need examining, and I'm sure a lot of other people are wondering the same thing. Here I was--had a nice interesting job, with the prestige of being on the Regional staff as a consultant, my own car, could plan my own work, travel all over Bavaria, live in a luxurious house with a group of grand, interesting, mostly American people. I asked for a transfer back to a job on a team, and whereas it is certainly not a demotion, it may appear to be so.

And the Deutsches Museum! The first afternoon I was rather glad to see all my old friends who were so warmly welcoming. The next day I went all over the place with the Camp Leader. I was heart sick. When we first built it out of a bombed out building, with nothing to do it with except imagination, pure initiative and resourcefulness (which is a poor substitute for material goods) we did imbue it with a spirit of something that seemed to reach the DPs. It was summer and things seemed somewhat easier. Perhaps in the light of warm weather we did not think of bodily needs as much. Now it is all closed in to make it winterized. Not having glass in many cases, it is boarded up or bricked in, cutting out light and air. The effect is one of gloom, bleakness and depression. It is beastly cold--or rather, was last week , as there was some difficulty about heating. There are cement floors so by the time I got home for lunch my feet were numb in spite of wool socks over cotton stockings and walking all the time. The electricity in Munich is off three hours in the morning and three hours in the afternoon on alternate days. We go around with flashlights, to say nothing of the difficulties encountered because of the inability to use the sterilizer in the doctor's office, and all the kitchen equipment is electric. It means that often the kitchen has to cook all night to have next day's noon meal ready. The leadership in the camp has been lacking so there is not the same enthusiasm there was. The place was filthy, the straw mattresses coming to pieces, smoke filled the rooms, toilets were stopped up, the kitchen was dirty, the whole place seethed with people. The most depressing thing, however, was the creepy feeling caused by the implication of all sorts of underground maneuvering. The place is filled now with Jews and stateless people who will not go back to their own countries. They have learned to live by their wits, have learned all the answers so that we find it difficult to know who is a DP and who is not. We have the most famous black market in the area. It is all over the place. From what they tell me, you can buy anything from a fur coat to a ticket to Kalamazoo in our courtyard.

The Jewish situation here is acute. All the Jews in Europe seem to be coming to Munich and to this part of the American Occupation Zone. All the camps are filled to capacity--others can't be opened fast enough. This is an entirely unforeseen emergency as they are not DPs. Most are coming into Germany for the first time, or have been to their countries and returned with their families because of fear for their lives, especially in Poland and Russian-occupied countries. Fortunately, I do have some grand help in the way of the new team member, Ed Broughton. We sat down tonight and worked out our plan of action.

Wednesday, December 5th
One degree below freezing, but not too cold. The Jewish refugee situation is getting worse. Discussed it at lunch with an AJDC (American Joint Distribution Committee) friend, found that thousands expected. The

houses vacated the previous day (to accommodate Jewish refugee) had been so looted by Germans and G.I.s that they were uninhabitable.

Thursday, December 6th
The situation at the Museum is snowballing on us. We had 1660 people at breakfast. Our capacity is for 800. There were 1,000 Jewish refugees. One hundred eighty had come in the night before from Czechoslovakia and Berlin--Polish. No relief in sight for at least two weeks. We have to take drastic steps.

Friday, December 7th
The situation at the Museum seems to get more confused all the time. The Jewish refugee problem more acute. We had 1400 people in the Museum, capacity 1,000. I went through the rooms; in one room there were 200 people. It was sickening. There were two people in every bed. I watched people eat. One man actually held out his hat for his biscuits. Just as I was about to leave at twelve o'clock we got word that 150 people, Polish Jews, had arrived from Berlin. Ed Broughton and I went to the Jewish Committee representative and advised we couldn't accept them. As we were discussing it we looked out of the window, saw two truckloads of Jews arriving--52 people from Salzburg, Austria. We were talking with the leader when we found another man standing by. He had brought a group of 37 boys and girls in from Czechoslovakia. They were in one corner, bag and baggage. At that time we saw the representative from AJDC come in. We arranged for those from the trucks to get back in, go to the Funk Caserne. The boys and girls were put in one part of the Cafe and fed. The 150 were put in another corner. I went to the Military Government and wangled trucks and transported them to Funk Caserne.

Faced with the handicaps of language and time, I found myself frustrated by the inability to learn more about these desperate refugees descending upon us. The war was over. Traveling under the circumstances couldn't be easy. The uncertainly of food, shelter, and the anticipated frightful accommodations which would only realistically be available had to be forbidding impediments to those choosing to leave their homes and countries. One had to believe that those now coming into

Germany must have had compelling reasons and courage to leave their native lands for such a precarious future.

In 1945, when I first encountered the surge of Jewish DPs' desperate quest for a haven in Palestine, my knowledge of Palestine and it's history was almost non-existent. The name conjured up Sunday School stories from the Bible with images of palm trees, camels, villages with cream-colored block-like houses, and people in long flowing robes, the men wearing strangely draped headgear. It was the "Holy Land," with names like Bethlehem and Jerusalem scrambled in my consciousness. Since Jesus was a Jew undoubtedly there was some connection with Jews. It was only when the stateless Jewish DPs in the Deutsches Museum began demanding help in getting to Palestine that I began to understand the complexities of the situation. First it was important for me to put into perspective their rationale for selecting Palestine as their goal. I needed a better understanding of the country and its history, at least since the 20th century. I wish I had known then what I know now.

It was at the end of the nineteenth century that the idea of Palestine as a Jewish homeland was first proposed by an early Zionist Movement. The British, who had an interest in that part of the world, in 1917 expressed receptivity to the idea in the form of a declaration, known as the Balfour Declaration.[38] When, several years later at the end of World War I (1922), the League of Nations approved a British Mandate granting governance by Great Britain over Palestine, elements of that Declaration were incorporated,

---

[38] Arthur James Balfour, Earl of Balfour, the Foreign Secretary under Prime Minister David Lloyd George, produced a declaration for the Government which was incorporated in a letter of November 2, 1917 to Lord Rothschild, leader of British Jewry, pledging support to the Zionist hopes for a Jewish national home in Palestine, with the condition that the rights of non-Jewish communities would be respected. It also promised Arab leaders support for creation of an independent Arab State. These elements were embodied in the Mandate formally approved by the League of Nations in 1922, with Arab agreement, giving Great Britain administrative power over Palestine. "Balfour, Arthur James" entry, *The Columbia Encyclopedia*, 5th edition, New York: Columbia University Press, 1993.

supporting hopes for the establishment of a national homeland for Jews within Palestine and providing that rights of the non-Jewish population would be respected. From the outset, the immigration of Jews to Palestine was a burning issue. The steady increase prompted the British to produce a series of White Papers (1922, 1930, 1937) addressing the issue by setting limits, based on the economic capacity of the country to absorb newcomers. In fact, the British appointed a commission in 1937, the Peel Commission, to assess the situation. Its report concluded that the promises to the Zionists and Arabs were irreconcilable and declared the British Mandate unworkable; recommending partition of the country. That recommendation didn't get anywhere. The last White Paper, in 1939, granted permission for immigration of 15,000 Jews during the next five years, which met with opposition from both Arabs and Jews. As the war escalated, so did the degree of persecution of Jews by the Germans. Therefore, increasingly desperate measures for escape from Europe were sought by those able to get away. The movement into Palestine entered a period of blockade-running, illegal entry of ships, often with tragic results.

For those of us working on the ground in 1945 and 1946 with limited access to the news media, we were in the dark as to these momentous happenings, as well as the maneuvering going on at high levels in the background. Whereas we had rumors of the Harrison Report to President Truman on the intolerable circumstances of the Jewish camps in the US Zone, we were not privy to the fact that the Report had included the comments:

...the issue of Palestine must be faced. Some reasonable extension or modification of the British White Paper of 1939 ought to be possible....

It is my understanding ... that certificates of immigration to Palestine will be practically exhausted by the end of the current month (August, 1945).... The Jewish Agency for Palestine has submitted to the British Government a petition that one hundred thousand additional immigration certificates be made available.

It would not be inappropriate for the United States ... to express its ... support of some equitable solution ... for some reasonable number of Europe's persecuted Jews to resettle in Palestine.[39]

Subsequently, the Anglo-American Committee of Inquiry, established by President Truman and British Prime Minister Atlee in November 1945, called for the admission of 100,000 Jewish immigrants according to the above recommendation. Most of the Jewish infiltrees were Polish. This was not surprising as the Jews had comprised about one-third of the population of central Poland before the war. When the Nazis occupied Poland and began their campaign to eliminate all Jews, they had immediately incarcerated those living in major cities into ghettos. The Warsaw Ghetto impounded half a million Jews; the Kracow Ghetto, 68,000.[40] Poland became the center for the Final Solution.

The Nazis located one of the largest extermination camps, designated exclusively for the murdering of Jews from the Warsaw Ghetto, the ghettos of other cities, as well as thousands of Jews from nine other European nations, a few dozen miles outside of Warsaw at Treblinka. People were unloaded onto specially designed ramps, poisoned using zyklon or exhaust fumes and burned in piles or pits because the through-put of the crematories was insufficient. About 800,000 Jews lost their lives at Treblinka. And Auschwitz is considered to have been the largest factory of death in the history of humanity. Many millions lost their lives there.[41]

All but approximately 100,000 of the pre-war Polish Jewish population of 3,113,900 were exterminated.[42] After the country was liberated in January 1944, survivors, who had been in Russia or who had managed to hide during the war years, returned to

---

[39] Proudfoot, p.328.

[40] *LNT Poland,* www.cyberroad.com/Poland/jews.

[41] *LNT Poland.*

[42] "Poland" entry ,*The Columbia Encyclopedia,* 5th edition, New York: Columbia University Press, 1993, p. 2179.

their former homes in Poland only to find their property stolen, work opportunities non-existent and terrifying anti-Semitism. There seemed no option but to escape. With few alternatives, the American occupation zone in Germany was an attractive sanctuary. Not only was it safe, but it offered the best opportunities for resettlement, ideally overseas.

Saturday, December 8th
Very cold. Has snowed for two days steadily. We had 1700 in the museum. Conditions are frightful but people are out of the snow and warm, with something to eat. A Russian boy was brought in half frozen, had not eaten for three days. Went begging for more transportation at the Military Government.

Monday, December 10th
Hi Wachtell in about the Jewish groups. He is Director of a team taking over a Seidlung (group of houses) for occupation by Jewish refugees. He will take 250 from us, family groups, in two days. Has to be organized.

Tuesday, December 11th
Groups pouring in from all directions. Fed 1900. Things beginning to improve at the Museum, however. Worked most of the day selecting families for the Seidlung. Helena and I went to the Museum at night, went to each room to select families--much wailing, holding up wailing babies, begging to go. It was no fun to say "no." Worked until midnight, compiled the list after seeing each man, woman and child. Rode to the Seidlung to take a copy of the list to Hi--snow and ice everywhere.

Wednesday, December 12th
All day long loading families on trucks, each having to be identified, all crying that they had "Bruder", uncle, cousin, etc. "Nicht", "nein", "keine," "gar nichts" favorite words. Was out in the snow most of the day, from seven in the morning.

Thursday, December 13th
Two huge groups of Jewish people came in--housed and fed them. Population is going up and up. A new Welfare Officer, Kay Tillman

arrived--a swell gal. Another large group of people came in--no trucks. Drove out to the Seidlung, brought the trucks back.

Friday, December 14th
Tried to orient Kay to the Center. She will head the Information Section. Received news we would ship out a large number of Jews on Sunday and Monday. However, large groups kept pouring in, we are sending them on to S.S. Caserne, Funk Caserne, two other large DP camps in Munich. Had the very sad experience of sending out 100 to Funk--they heard a rumor that all were going to Romania. They all came back to the Museum, plus a new group of 63.

Saturday, December 15th
Work began in earnest. We were notified that we would send out 450 Jews at six o'clock the next morning, to go by train to Bamberg. Tried to organize the shipment...At eight o'clock at night Ed, Helena, Kay and I went to the Museum, were met by four members of the JRC (Jewish Refugee Committee) who helped orient the people. We split up, going into each room explaining to the Jews that the transport was going the next morning. We were met with unreceptive response. None wanted to go. Worked until about twelve.

Sunday, December 16th
Got up at four in the morning--went to the Museum without breakfast. Went through the rooms waking people, cajoling, pleading, commanding. Had breakfast brought to their rooms, took up blankets, used "control" men (our guards) to help urge people out. Everyone was sick, had a brother at Landsberg, children in hospitals. A harrowing experience. By eight o'clock we had managed to send out 360 people.

Then heard we were to send out 290 the next morning at the same time. The trucks would arrive at eight o'clock for them. Worked all day regrouping the remainder in rooms together. Conference with AJDC and the Military. Just sitting down to supper when we learned that a trainload of 360 children were somewhere near Munich--could we take them? After telephoning, looking for trucks, went to the Museum, prepared rooms, had lots of cereal cooked. The children arrived. DDT'd them, put them in rooms, fed them. There were two groups. One group of

150 from Budapest had been hidden out by a doctor during the war. There were 50 children ages 2 to 10. The Regional Child Welfare Workers from UNRRA came around. The Military was there. The kids were finally settled. We then had to go back through the rooms telling the people about the transport the next morning.

Monday, December 17th
Up again at five--at the Museum by five-thirty. Same procedure, going through the rooms waking, trying to persuade people to go, unsuccessfully. Lots of AJDC personnel around, and lots of Military, UNRRA, all waving arms, getting in the way. Only 60 people rounded up, part of whom were a group who had just arrived. Very sloppy. The Military were criticized. We missed getting food on the train, spent half the day chasing the train with it.

Had hardly settled down when we were notified that the children and up to 250 would go by truck the following morning. More cleaning of rooms, regrouping. Again work at night. Kay, Helena and I went to the Museum. We were so tired we were silly. We had tried everything on the people so that this time we tried teasing, laughing--even made up a song "Nach Bamberg"--"Gehen wir nach Bamberg"--to the tune of "A tisket, a tasket." I packed boxes of food for the children to go on the trucks.

Tuesday, December 18th
Again at the Museum at six. Waked people, saw that hot cereal was made. Hot milk in thermos jugs for small children. Milk and water for older children. Red Cross packages for trucks, blankets available.

This time things went smoothly, the children were well organized. Had trouble with people in rooms--all were forced out. The Museum emptied. Eleven trucks with 140 people left. As the last truck pulled out of one gate we looked up and droves of people were coming in the other.

We didn't have the luxury of time to ask the obvious questions: "Who are these refugees now flooding in on us? Where are they coming from? How are they managing to get here? Why doesn't someone tell us how many are coming? How long is this going to last? What is going on?" All our energy and concentration was poured into coping day by day. It did begin to seep into our consciousness that this must be a planned movement, well-organized and well-financed. Only in retrospect has history illuminated what was really transpiring.

We were well aware that these Jewish refugees filtering into Germany did not fit the most fundamental criterion for UNRRA support. They had not been in Germany at the end of the war. The term "infiltree" became an official designation to identify those refugees coming into Germany after the end of the war, distinguishing them from "displaced persons" who had been forcibly imported into Germany for slave labor or internment in concentration camps during the war.

There were three groups of these refugees, each with different origins. The first and largest group of Polish Jews were those who fled in the beginning of 1939, in advance of the approaching German army, either to Central Russia or to the provinces of Lwow and Krakow in the so-called Western Ukraine. In late 1939 or early 1940, the Russian authorities collected and transported large numbers of them for forced labor to different districts in Siberia. Upon arrival all adults--men and women--and, in some cases, children of twelve and thirteen had to work as wood cutters in the taiga forests; as laborers at coal and timber-loading stations of trains and ships; or as miners in lead and coal mines.

In 1941, inmates in these labor camps were allowed to leave, so most rushed to the Soviet Republics of Uzbekistan and Tajikistan on rumors of warm climates and abundance of fruits and other food products. A bitter disappointment awaited the new settlers. The native population was hostile, the climate was warm and damp, the land infested with malaria. Jobs were scarce and paid minimum wages. As soon as repatriation was permitted by the Russians, all Polish Jews hastened to join transports for Poland where they met with discouraging anti-Semitism. There they learned of the opportunity to join kibbutz groups being formed in

Lower Silesia.[43] These kibbutzim intended ultimately to begin a new life in Palestine.

The second group came from that part of Poland invaded by Germany, but ceded to Russia as a part of the Nazi-Soviet (Molotov-Ribbentrop) Pact of 1939, and subsequently occupied by the Russian army. At the outbreak of hostilities between the two countries in 1941, they were evacuated into Russia--to the Urals, and Central Asia or Siberia--surviving until they, like the first group, were repatriated to Poland at the end of the war and joined kibbutzim in Stettin or Silesia.

A third group, those who did not manage to escape to Russia, stayed in the German-occupied part of Poland and the West Ukraine. Some of them were sent into ghettos and concentration camps; others managed to hide in the woods among partisans and village peasants. After liberation, the survivors, finding their homes in ruins and property confiscated, also joined the kibbutzim where they received promise of a new life in Palestine. The kibbutzim were organized mainly in Stettin and Lower Silesia--Bielawa, Geszeze, Pusta, Breslau. It was these organized kibbutz groups which were now pouring into Munich, and to the Museum en route to Palestine, although we didn't realize it yet.

Meanwhile, life did go on at Galilei Platz, with some new additions to the team which made it necessary to take over the house next door to No.2. It was a large three-story dwelling in which I could finally have a bedroom to myself. The living room had a big fireplace which in those wintry, snowy days was a great luxury. Again I found myself being asked to assume some domestic responsibilities. With increased housing space and number of occupants, we needed a competent housekeeper.

---

[43] A kibbutz is a collective farm, sometimes including light industry, where all property is collectively owned and communal living is the general rule.

On December 2nd
....found Helena and Mr. Atkins waiting for me to talk to a housekeeper,
Anya. She will be responsible to me and will have complete charge of
both houses. I also noted, *I have talked so much German and French in*
the past weeks that I am getting quite proficient. I don't use an
interpreter now at all.

Anya proved to be an excellent addition to our household,
although it took some sensitive handling to get the existing staff to
accept her, as they had been with the team for some time already.
She was being put in charge of our staff, and it meant that
responsibilities were being redistributed. All were DPs from the
Museum who prized their jobs as they meant prestige, better food
and living conditions--sufficient compensation in their eyes, in
spite of the fact we couldn't pay them. It took some time to
persuade them that Anya's appointment didn't jeopardize any of
that.

Social life with its dates, parties, dancing continued unabated. A
little spice had been added to my life by a new admirer, Bill
Bagnall, one of our Starnberg group. He was a Canadian, a former
"bush" pilot from the wilds of Western Canada, who had served
in the Royal Canadian Air Force during the war before joining
UNRRA. A big, burly guy, a gruff and blustery type who spoke in
colorful language flavored with expletives. Beneath the rough
exterior, he was a real sweetie. He was in charge of UNRRA
transport for the region, what there was of it. Most of his time was
spent acquiring and rebuilding anything on four wheels. Any
word of an accident would be the signal for him and his trusty
young German mechanic to rush out to salvage the vehicles if
possible, or, in the case of a total wreck, to cannibalize parts for
use in later repair of our motley stock. During the war, soldiers
had developed the habit of painting slogans on vehicles of all
kinds, from jeeps to planes. Bill adopted the practice by adorning
anything and everything with my name. Soon he commanded a
fleet of really disreputable Sues; Sweet Sue, Sue Too, UNRRA Sue
and more. I took a lot of kidding. He kept my little car in near-
mint condition; repaired, washed and even polished until the

black paint fairly shone. When Charley invited me to come to Belgium for Christmas with his family, Bill even arranged for me to go in a winterized command car.

On December 7th, Mr. Atkins received word that his wife was ill, so he quickly took off for England, saying he would be back by Christmas, leaving Ed and me holding the bag. By now Ed and I had established a congenial working relationship through the hectic days at the Museum. From Ohio, he had served in the Army before transferring to UNRRA. About my age and of medium build, Ed smoked a pipe which somehow made him look more boyish instead of more sophisticated. While good-natured and well-meaning, Jack Atkins didn't have Charley's special skills or his general competency. And so it was mutually decided that Ed and I would both be Deputy Directors, the better to bolster Jack in his new role of Team Director, which he assumed on his return from home leave.

Changes had also been taking place in the Museum staff as well, as time and life had moved along. Walter had married a Polish girl who was working at the Museum. Other members of the core staff had left and there were many new faces. A special event for me was the christening of my namesake, Susan.

Tuesday, December 18th
In the afternoon I was godmother at the christening of my namesake, Susan, Mrs. Hoven's baby. Interesting service in a chapel in a bombed-out Catholic school. The priest from the Museum officiated.

Palmer Bovie, the *Stars and Stripes* reporter, had met the Hovens at the Museum. Susan Hoven's parents had quite a story to tell, one that her mother had, with some reluctance, shared with Palmer Bovie, saying it was, "just the same old story, don't you know."

Edith Hoven, born and raised in England, persuaded her parents to send her to Vienna in 1936 to study voice. She found the student life to her liking and, feeling she was making progress in her musical development, settled in for an indefinite stay. Then she met her husband, Paul Meyer, who was studying to be a concert pianist. Before long, they were happily living and working together. Although clouds of war were gathering and letters from home urged her to return, she shrugged off the idea that war was really coming. By the winter of 1939, "I saw I was wrong," she conceded.

Paul was half-Jewish, so it wasn't long before the terror against Jews forced them to spend the next few years of their life in a constant effort to keep out of sight and find at least one meal a day. Edith was pregnant, so she stayed in Vienna until the baby was born, while Paul hid wherever he could, helped by friends or secret underground groups. She had only her English passport, Paul had none, so they faced jail or worse if picked up. With the baby, they moved to Germany, from city to city, always on the move, sometimes with the help of kind Germans.

Paul began to lose weight and after they came to Munich, his illness worsened with worry and malnourishment, so he had to go to a hospital, terrified that the authorities would learn who he was and send him to a concentration camp. They were fortunate enough to have found a friend in one of the doctors in the hospital, Dr. Krauer, a psychiatrist who arranged to take on Paul as one of his patients. He saved Paul's life. When his identity was revealed, the doctor persuaded the authorities concerned that Paul was insane and, rather than send him to a concentration camp, to leave him in the hospital as a subject of experimentation. Later, the matter died down and Paul was released from the hospital.

Their life as refugees continued until the Americans arrived in Munich. With sadness, they learned of the death of Dr. Krauer, killed by SS soldiers on April 24th, as he was crossing into the American lines under a white flag of truce. He was going to surrender the hospital of which he was in command. The SS let him get fifty yards from their lines, then they shot him in the back. "He was one German I can call a thoroughly good man. He worked hard all the time to help people, no matter who they were," Edith commented.

She finished her story, saying, "I came to the Museum late in May to help DPs. My husband is quite well now. He is practising again as he is to give a recital here at the Museum next week, and is worried as a kid."

Thursday, December 20th
Learned there was a gale in the English Channel which meant that there was a possibility that Mr. Atkins wouldn't get back for Christmas. That means no chance of my going to Belgium. There was no one else to take over at the house.

Although disappointed at not being with Charley, I think in some ways I was relieved. There had been the nagging question in my mind as to how receptive his wife and children might be to having this strange woman there, one with whom they had nothing in common except Charley. After all, it was their first Christmas together since the end of the war, and his wife was pregnant. So I was not unhappy to plunge into preparations for a Munich Christmas.

Friday, December 21st
Began seriously making plans for Christmas--at the Museum--at home. Planned party at our house for Christmas Eve night; talked with Anya, housekeeper, about the party, Christmas dinner. Discussed Museum Christmas with Walter. Checked Museum food, candy, toys.

On the next day, Saturday, December 22nd, there seemed two events. The Military was in deep mourning as General Patton had died the day before. On the other hand, that same evening, there was a special holiday party at the officers' club, marking the beginning of the Christmas festivities. I was dressed in my new $89.50 Saks Fifth Avenue dress for it, ready to enjoy the evening. It is inconceivable now to conjure up what it meant for me to have a dress from Saks Fifth Avenue, that temple of fashion so worshipped from afar--Alabama--most of my life. Such a dress would have been special had I been in the States, but here in the land of khaki uniforms and drab German dresses it was really goddess-like. And that amount of money spent on luxury for a Depression-oriented female was almost giddily sinful. And in spite of the pall cast cast by Patton's passing, the party went well, even if there was no dancing out of respect for the general.

Sunday, December 23rd
Slept rather late. Got up to learn that a group of one hundred and fifty children had arrived at the Museum the night before. Later got the story from them. They were Hungarian Jewish children, almost all between the ages of 6 and 14. They had been in the Auschwitz Concentration camp, in the Ghetto in Budapest, and in hiding during the war. After the war they were gathered by the International Red Cross into six children's homes--2 in Budapest, and 4 in Seged. Dr. Tibor was the physician. He and his wife and several teachers had brought them to Germany with Palestine as their goal. They had been traveling three weeks from Budapest, to Linz, to Salzburg, to Munich. The trip and movement had been arranged by the "Joint Distribution Committee" (AJDC). The group was well organized, orderly--was of the Democratic Sect. Spent the rest of the morning on the phone--everyone concerned about the children, giving different orders. Ed and I went after dinner to a meeting of the Bavarian Committee for Jewish People. The whole situation was discussed from two until nearly six o'clock. General Truscott had issued orders that the Jewish camp population be reduced to normal in the large camps by December 31st or the Army would move in.[44] It had been difficult to move the Jewish people. Our people would not move until after Christmas. Mr. Atkins came in about two in the morning.

Monday, December 24th
A very busy day. All morning gave out soap, cigarettes to the DPs who lived in town. Planned food menus for the Museum. Children's party at the Museum at 2 o'clock. Received gifts, a lovely handmade handkerchief, flowers. Came home to decorate for the party, to supervise the kitchen--all sorts of goodies planned. Dressed in evening dress. Much small talk tossed from room to room as Kay, Helena, Yvonne, Susanne and I (we all had rooms on the same floor) dressed. Went to the Museum at seven,

---

[44] Lt. General Lucian Truscott.

then to the Personnel dining room for staff party at eight. It was beautifully decorated--Christmas tree--speeches by Walter, Mr. Atkins. (Walter's mother and sister arrived the next morning from Poland. They hadn't seen each other for six years). It was a joy to see the staff, mostly Polish, happy. Everyone sang. A moving experience to hear "Silent Night" sung by everyone simultaneously in four different languages, but all with the same thoughts, same feelings. It seemed to represent something that cut through the barriers of nationality. We had more gifts, much kissing of hands, many wishes for a Merry Christmas.

Came back to the house, found guests waiting. Had much fun getting the boys (Army officers) in the kitchen making eggnog. Real eggnog![45]

A six piece orchestra played, we danced, had lots of food. Lots of Military and UNRRA folk were at the party. At 12 midnight there was champagne and cards. It was very merry.

Tuesday, December 25th. Christmas Day in Munich, Germany.
I was awakened by a knock on my door at eight-thirty in the morning. Helena announced that a phone call had just come in that there were a hundred-fifty Jews just arriving at the Deutsches Museum. Forthwith, I got up, dressed, went down to the Museum. After telephoning the Jewish Committee, locating a couple of trucks, making arrangements, I loaded all of them on the trucks and sent them off in the snow to another camp, SS Caserne.

I got back home about ten-thirty, found almost everybody still asleep. I began to shout, pounding on doors until everyone else was shouting and struggling up. By degrees, all yelling back and forth, we got everyone to breakfast. It took a wet washrag hurled at one of them to do the trick. After breakfast we opened gifts. There were many I had saved from home, unopened. I had many lovely things given me, including a wonderful bottle of real French perfume from Yvonne. It had been a very happy Christmas with no pangs of homesickness.

---

[45]Powdered milk had been mixed the night before and left on the windowsill overnight to thicken for cream. Powdered eggs were whipped. German whiskey was added for the "nog." The officers donned aprons for a ceremonial effect.

The celebrations continued for another day with another Museum personnel party at which I was acclaimed "Miss UNRRA" along with much clicking of heels and kissing of hand. And thus the year drew to a close with the transport of the hundred and fifty Hungarian children off to the Leipheim Camp. The Military pulled an unannounced inspection by General Hickey who found everything in good order. The children from Indersdorf put on a play at the Museum which was quite well done and seemed to mean a lot to the kids. I topped it off, dressed in evening dress, dancing with Bill at the Seehaus and downing champagne with a group of pals.

In a letter to my family dated January 11, 1946, I tried to convey a sense of the unusual times we were going through, which were beginning to attract world attention;

I shall never forget having to go to the Museum on Christmas and New Year's mornings to receive large groups of infiltrees. Since then it has been the same. Almost every day we have had from a hundred to three hundred Jews coming from Poland, Hungary, or Rumania. Now, after two months of it, it has begun to dawn on the Military and UNRRA officials what has been obvious to us for a long time. The Jews of Europe are gathering in the American Occupation Zone for two, maybe three reasons. They want to go to Palestine and think that the Americans will plead their cause with the British. This is based on Truman's recent statement [his pledges of support for the Jewish infiltrees]. *They also know that the Americans here will take care of them, providing for them as no other country will at the present time. There are some anti-Semitic feelings in Russian occupied zones.[46] At first the influx seemed like only large numbers coming to a place for haven. Now it is obvious*

---

[46] "Initially the Americans and British authorities were indifferent to Jewish infiltration, and Jews were freely admitted to the centers. Soon, however, the British took the view that this movement was part of a well-organized and financed Zionist plot to force Britain to relax her restrictions on Jewish immigration to Palestine. The British, on 5 December 1945, prohibited the further movement of Jews into or through their zone via Berlin, and subsequently ruled that those who infiltered through any route would no longer be admitted to the centers." Proudfoot, p.335.

that it is a well organized movement by international Jewish forces. Last week this was all brought out in the open by a very hot article in "Stars and Stripes" quoting our German Operations boss, General Morgan (Chief of Operations for Germany), who stated very frankly that it was an organized movement and that the Jews were well-clothed, well-fed and had sufficient money. That night Leo Bernstein, news correspondent for "P.M." (New York City evening paper), and Ray Daniels from "The New York Times" came to Munich to the Deutsches Museum. Ed and I went down, gave them information, arranged for them to interview some of the people, and had coffee and donuts with them. The next day appeared a reprint of an article from "The New York Times" in the "Stars and Stripes." Also, the next day a Rabbi who had been sent by Eisenhower visited us. We are getting quite famous. I have been interviewing the leaders of these Jewish groups coming through for about a month and have kept copies of their statements. The correspondents go for them in a big way. It is proof of the fact that the whole movement is organized and that the motive is to force the way open into Palestine. I am in hopes that all the facts are made public because I feel that it is something that will have repercussions for years to come. The whole fate of the Jewish race is at a stage of crisis. There is also the question in many of our minds as to whether it is UNRRA's responsibility to play the big part they are playing at this time in the migration of the Jews. It is not a Displaced Persons program. The whole matter will come to a head this week, I think.

Besides that, we have been sending big transports of these people to other camps as they tend to clog our facilities. This means getting to the Museum about six o'clock in the morning, seeing that the people are fed, that they are packed, that food for the journey is prepared in separate cartons for each truck, that hot coffee or cereal is in thermos jugs for each truck, that each person has a blanket, so when the trucks arrive about eight the people are ready to be loaded on them. Last Sunday we sent out four hundred people and the last trucks had not left the courtyard before we received 250 more people. It does get discouraging when there seems no end to it.

It has not been all that grisly. We have a grand gang here at the house. We laugh much and loudly. We have the reputation of being the happiest team in UNRRA.

I am a little weary today--most of us are. I started this Friday night. Yesterday, Saturday, I was going down to Southofen, on the Swiss border, with a gang--leave the car--go up the mountain by sleigh--party-- spend the night, ski today. Just as I was leaving someone came in to say 150 Jews had just arrived. Well, that killed my try. All afternoon we had trucks coming and going, taking them to other camps. This morning 90 more arrived. Someone just called (it is now about 6) to say 200 are coming on the 8 o'clock train. This has been going on for two months and we are all tired. It seems so senseless. They come here by plan, organized, voluntarily--arrive without notice and expect us to do everything for them.

Functioning in this climate of uncertainty, confusion and frustration was transcended by the overwhelming need for action. One sensed that major decision-making must be going on among the "higher-ups," but the details didn't filter down to those of us dealing with the situation on a daily basis. We were aware that there was a sympathetic policy in the US Military reflecting President Truman's stance on the matter of the Jewish infiltree movement. We didn't know, however, the specifics of Truman's policy, although it had been incorporated in a directive from President Truman to the US Military issued on August 22, 1945. The directive ordered the establishment of special camps for stateless and non-repatriable Jews, who were defined as "those Jews who are without nationality or those not Soviet citizens who do not desire to return to their country of origin."[47] Of course this ruling was only applicable to the US Zone. In the French and the British Zones, the Jews were generally segregated in their own camps where they received assistance from the Jewish agencies and UNRRA, but were not provided special privileges to the extent accorded in the US Zone. This distinction often triggered movement of the Jews to the US Zone from the other zones

---

[47] Proudfoot, p.331.

although such migration was illegal, as crossing zone borders violated Military Government Law. Furthermore, Palestine, the recognized goal of the infiltrees, was still under the British Mandate, therefore requiring immigration authorization from the British who were desperately attempting to control a chaotic influx. This posed an awkward and complex position for the British Military in the British Zone, making it a less than friendly reception center for the Jewish groups.

I began to document the individual Jewish groups which arrived at the Museum between December 25th and January 15th in rather primitive reports to Sam Zissman, UNRRA's Regional Director for the XX Corps Area--19 groups in this 21-day period.

January 3rd, 1946
Four large groups of Jews arrived at the Deutsches Museum at the same time on the morning of January 1st. They came by train, a total of 305 people.

One group, composed of 71 people, 4 under 14 years of age, 36 between 14 and 20, the remainder adults. The leader was Mr. Schlinger, the group named "Waltenberg." They gathered together in Krakow in Poland and have been living together for four months. The children are mostly without parents--only five have parents and they are accompanying them. The group left Poland one and a half weeks ago, traveling by train by way of Prague, Asch, Regensberg to Munich. They are in good health and have a nurse accompanying them. Their destination is Palestine and arrangements for their travels were made by the Joint Committee. They comprise a Kibbutz group of the Democratic Organization.

The second group, called the "Reichenbach" group, had for their leader Mr. Wasserzicher. There are 46 in the group; 3 under 14, 26 between 14 and 20, the rest adults. Their story is similar except that they are from the Silesian part of Poland.

The "Ludwigdorf" group, with leader Mr. Gruenwiess, is composed of 34 people, 3 under 14, 31 between 14 and 20. They are also from Silesia.

The other group, the "Krakow" group, has 54 people under the leader,
Mr. Peresada--3 are under 14, 51 between 14 and 30. The majority of
these people have been in concentration camps in Germany and in
Poland. They returned to Poland after liberation.

On January 15th, 1946, I reported a further influx.
A small group of 10 Polish Jews came to the Deutsches Museum on
Saturday night, January 12th. This group had come from Berlin by train.

According to information given by the leader, this group gathered
together in Lodz. Many of them had been with the Partisans during the
war. The leader stated that there were 7000 Polish Jews in Berlin coming
to the American Zone. This group left Lodz five weeks ago, the
movement planned by the "Joint" Committee (the AJDC). They traveled
by train by way of Posnan, Stettin, to Berlin. In Berlin they went to the
city's French Zone. They obtained passes from an office of the
Burgermeister in the railroad station operating for the purpose of giving
passes to refugees. The official stamp on the pass was "Judische
Gemeinde im Berlin." The group stayed four weeks in Berlin in a house
in a special block on Richendamnasstrasse, operated by the Jewish
Committee, in the French Zone.

The people bought their own tickets, came by train by way of Hannover,
Mannheim to Munich. The leader hoped someday to go to America but
first wanted to go to Palestine. The other members of his group wanted to
go to Palestine. They came to Germany because it was better living here,
some had families living here, thought it would be easier to go to
Palestine from here.[48]

Each group had a leader who gave me the bare facts about the
group's composition, route, destination and group affiliation. The
groups ranged in number from ten to two hundred, an average of
82 persons per group. Those groups which were composed of
families traveling together averaged 4 children under fourteen

---

[48] Reports to Mr. Sam Zissman, UNRRA, Regional Director, XX Corps Area, by
Susan Pettiss, Deputy Director, Team 108, Jewish Infiltrees. In Susan Pettiss'
private papers.

years of age. After January 1st, there were four other groups of children unaccompanied by parents, each of which were composed of thirty to fifty children under sixteen years of age. All were Polish nationals collected in Lodz, Katowice, Krakow, Glacice, Stettin, or Reichenbach in Silesia. Generally, the routes were first to Prague, where AJDC operated a reception camp, then via Hof, Asch and Regensberg to Munich. It was stated that the movements were organized and financed by AJDC.

The debate as to whether the growing influx of Jewish survivors of the Holocaust--a word not yet in the literature or jargon at that time--into the American Zone, clearly heading for Palestine, was an organized movement grew in intensity. Evidence was growing. Higher-up officials became involved. National relations became sticky. The military occupiers were left in a quandary. UNRRA teams, being good humanitarian soldiers, instead went about their jobs of rescue and relief, leaving the argument to be addressed at higher levels and focused on caring for those people as they arrived.

Apparently my reports were the first solid information the agency had on the movement. Fitting the pieces of the story together, it was possible to plot the migration from assembly points in Poland and the Deutsches Museum, from where the groups were forwarded to various UNRRA-operated Jewish camps. "And yet, the movement," as noted by Leo Schwarz,

> ...was a well-guarded secret. During almost three years of steady activity there was no leakage of vital information. How was this possible under the eyes of the Army and UNRRA?[49]

"Partly through skill," was his short answer. But he also acknowledged that the participation of people like those at the Deutsches Museum was key to the ultimate success of what must

---

[49] Leo Schwarz, *The Redeemers: a saga fo the years 1945-1952*, New York: Farrar, Straus & Young, 1953, p.234.

be considered a historic accomplishment.

> (T)he movement would have been delayed and
> frustrated without the good will surrounding it... There
> were the officials, American, French, and Italians in
> particular, who closed their eyes to the peculiarities of
> the travel documents and identification papers that they
> scanned. Among the Army and UNRRA officials in
> Germany, those conspirators were legion.[50]

Meanwhile life went on with ordinary events and demands in
addition to the Jewish infiltree phenomenon. These were often
humdrum, always varied; however they added a zest to life
because they required quick and decisive action, meant numerous
interesting personal contacts, and gave a feeling of instant
accomplishment. January 8th was a typical day.

*Arrived at the Museum to be told that 35 Jews had arrived, were to be
followed by 40 others. Also received word that 140 children were coming
in at ten o'clock. Began telephoning. Ed with 3 trucks went to the station
to waylay them and send them to Funk Caserne. A CIC man came to
interview Jews who came in last Sunday. Had to arrange for the cleaning
of the house next door, using six people from the Museum. Also to
arrange for a plumber and a roofer. Mr. Atkins called from the house,
two of our drivers had been arrested. Arranged for two more. The
District Supply Officer called about food, saying a requisition had to be
in that afternoon. Talked with Janusz and the nutritionist. Had a
conference with Walter and Yvonne about plans for the Cafe and a new
medical section. Talked with Irana, my secretary, about going on leave
for a month. She has pre-TB. A boy from Indersdorf, had been beaten by
Poles. Poor child's face was a pulp. Kay and I made arrangements for
him to be cared for. Talked with him. Six students had been arrested the
night before after curfew. Had to call the Police Presidium for their
release. 261 Hungarian children brought in by M.P.s who had picked
them up. Sent them on to the proper agency. A telegram was received
requesting the location of a Jew who had a sister in St.Louis. A*

---

[50] Schwarz, p.235.

Lieutenant was in to investigate the black market. A Sergeant from the Medical Department at the Military Government was in about rat control and monthly reports. Had to decide who was to move into the new house, trying to keep everybody happy. No lights, so to bed early.

Although both of us had left the house in Starnberg at Thanksgiving, my friend Helen Zilka, who had gone to nearby Augsberg, and I managed to see each other frequently during the winter. Before the situation at the Deutsches Museum had become so chaotic, we had applied for and been granted a short leave. We planned to go on a GI R&R (rest and rehabilitation) trip to Switzerland. Urged by Jack, I decided to go, in spite of job pressures.

The train trip through the snowy January countryside was a fantasy ride. On a day's trip to St. Moritz, we rode in a horse-drawn sleigh decorated with bells. Of course we bought watches the first day. I even tried to ski. And the pastries! It was heaven. The contrast between bombed-out Germany and storybook Switzerland overwhelmed me. Everything was so orderly, so clean and freshly painted. There were stores filled with clothes, books, fresh vegetables! I wrote my family that I saw no poor nor slums.

The cities are ultra modern, all very clean. Prosperity everywhere: sleek automobiles, fast smooth streetcars, speeding silent efficient trains. And the people! Happy, healthy, friendly people who seem to have no class distinction — all well-groomed — exceedingly well dressed in clothes that were more American than American. They mostly spoke English and were more than friendly to us Americans. It was such a contrast after seeing for many months only old people, troubled people, people with whom I am only professionally associated; or with whom we have no contact even though we live in their midst--the Germans.

The trip had seemed like a dream, but the effect was short-lived.

In Munich Ed and Mr. Atkins met me. (Tuesday, January 29th)...suggested we sit there (in the station) at the Red Cross Club and

164

have coffee and donuts. I thought they looked a bit serious but was certainly not prepared for all the news they gave me. From eleven o'clock until after one (a.m.) we sat there. Mr. Atkins did most of the talking. The world seemed to have turned upside down while I was gone. The day after I left Mr. Atkins had been asked to leave the team, was replaced in a few days by a new Director, an Englishman, Jim Wilkinson.[51] This was a terrific blow, dealt chiefly because of his failure to control the black market activities in and around the Deutsches Museum. Of course he was just sick about it. He loved Team 108, felt unjustly treated.

Secondly, Cookie, our supply officer, had left town to return home, was sought by the CIC for being involved in black market activities. UNRRA security men had flocked down to the Museum, crawling all over it, turning up all sorts of evil looking things. Everyone seemed to be implicated. The whole DP staff was in a state of very low morale. What had formerly been "scrounging" for needed articles was now put in a different light. There were many new members of the team, now about sixteen in all.

The whole conversation had the effect of a blow with a wet towel. The memories of the Swiss trip disappeared even before I reached the house. As I went in Mr. Atkins put his arms around me and cried. It was tough. Kay was up waiting for me. She and I talked for about an hour, giving me her version of the whole situation. Finally I got to bed about three. The next morning Vera, our maid, had come in to my room to close the windows. She did not know that I had returned in the night. She turned, saw me in the bed, fell on her knees by the bed and wept. The servant staff had put flowers in my room, greeted me like a long lost mother. They were all feeling insecure with the changes, said that had I been there things would not have changed.

I learned that Alfred had been involved in black market activities, and another version of his story apparently emerged during the investigation. Initially he had told us that he had escaped Poland at the age of seventeen, fearful of being recruited for military

---

[51] Jack Atkins was transferred to Erlangen and put in charge of three small DP camps, two Baltic and one Ukrainian, with a total population of 1300.

service by the German occupying army. He had talked his way across the German border in April 1945, hiding out until the American forces arrived. It now appeared that he had been in Germany for a number of years--working, hiding, living by his wits. The real story is still probably a mystery, as his tale of survival modified with changing circumstances.

Immediately after surrender it was smart to appropriate anything by what was called 'organization.' Also, Alfred was fascinated by the American soldiers and would do anything to gain status in their eyes. It all caught up with him--but I can't help but feel he was more or less a victim of circumstances.

The new Director, Jim Wilkinson, was a handsome, somewhat stereotypical Englishman with dark hair, a neatly clipped mustache, dark brown eyes, about thirty-five years old. He was a recently discharged Lieutenant Colonel in the British Army, still with vestiges of military mannerisms, but seemed friendly and welcoming. The next morning we went to the Museum together. I found he had taken over my desk and most of my functions, leaving me pretty much in limbo. I wrote my aunt,

...trying to keep an open mind about it all, I tried working as usual for a few days. It was very difficult as I really had little to do--most of my functions and responsibilities had been taken over by Jim. After a week of it, I went to my Supervisor, told him I wanted to leave Deutsches Museum, be reassigned. I was offered several interesting sounding jobs. I made a lot of inquiries as to the future of UNRRA and found that we are now in the beginning of the closing stages--two or three more months will see the winding up. As soon as the weather is better the Army intends to ship all DPs home.

Three weeks later I wrote,

I had a long talk with myself, reached the decision that what was right was for me to stay put. I was completely satisfied with the decision, had the feeling of 'rightness'. So I did, and it has worked out. The new Director was removed, a bit unjustly, I thought. Ed Broughton is the

new Director and I am Deputy Director. Ed has been Deputy along with me and together we have pulled through the infiltree period. He is a swell guy, very sound, and I like him a lot. We work well together, so that is happily settled for now.

And Munich was coming more alive each day. The Munich Opera House, only a couple of blocks from our billet, reopened. Never mind that there was no heat, that we kept our trench coats on and took blankets for our knees and feet. That first postwar winter had brought record-breaking cold to the continent. Also, the electricity went off early, so the performances started at 5:30. But the ambience of the shabbily-elegant opera house, dimly lit and flooded with beautiful sound, was electrifying.

The same was true of symphony concerts in the bombed-out Munich University Hall. Stepping around debris with sky showing through the ceiling in spots offered a strange thrill. These concerts were always packed with music-starved Germans and non-Germans alike. The two groups eyed each other suspiciously, but when the music started, differences disappeared. Afterwards, the Germans clutched their worn, colorless coats around them, almost silently making their way through the rubble while the uniformed segment of the audience similarly kept together, usually talking enthusiastically about the music. There was no effort at communication between the groups. So life was not all work. And on occasion, I got to see history in the making on a grand scale.

The name "Nurnberg" conjures up three images: the world-renown toys manufactured in that city; a city almost entirely demolished by Allied bombing; and, of course, the criminal trials of the perpetrators of World War II. I was present at these trials on two occasions. The monolithic gray concrete building serving as the Palace of Justice for the occasion was located on the outskirts of the near-obliterated city, ominously guarded by patrolling tanks and MPs. Inside, besides being positively cavernous, the courtroom was much like any other--except that instead of one black-robed judge presiding, there were eight: one British, one

French, one American and one Russian, plus their alternates, although presided over by one Chief Justice. The eight judges were seated behind a long bench on a dais, with the four huge flags of the Allies suspended on the wall as a backdrop. The twenty-two German defendants were seated in two rows in a boxed section against the wall opposite the judges, the second row slightly raised so that all were in full view.

They were so close to us that I could have easily hit them with a spitball, I wrote my aunt. *Goering slouched in his seat with his chin in his hand most of the time. He was wearing a gray suit with a red scarf. Hess surprised me because he was so bald. All wore civilian clothes except the two Generals, Keitel and Jodl. They appeared rather bored, read papers, did some writing, or just sat there. The thing that struck me so forcibly was that they seemed to be just a bunch of tired, insignificant old men.*

Though the tone of my letter was a little flippant, my reaction to the scene was a mixture of revulsion and outrage. I did find it rewarding, however, that for the first time men were being held accountable by law for crimes against humanity.

My second visit to the courtroom was on March 14th. I found Goering on the stand. For me, he was the greatest monster of them all. I wanted to bear witness to his judgement, as a representative of the streams of DPs, infiltrees, and other war victims with whom I had been working every day. While on the stand, Goering was in full uniform, medals and all. This was significant inasmuch as his defense was that, as Commander-in-Chief of the Luftwaffe and an SS General, his actions were merely those of a soldier carrying out the orders of his commander. This big bulldog of a man seemed arrogant, obviously not accustomed to having his authority challenged.[52]

---

[52] The court convicted Goering and sentenced him to death. Two hours before hanging, he committed suicide by swallowing a cyanide capsule. Of the twenty-two defendants, twelve were sentenced to death by hanging, seven were given prison sentences ranging from ten years to life, and two were found not guilty.

And then it was spring. On Saturdays and Sundays, friends often piled in my little car and we took to the autobahns and back roads, snow-capped Alps looming in the distance. One such day was April 26th. It was a Sunday.

It was a beautiful day. We put the top of the car down, Helen and I tied yellow bandana handkerchiefs around our heads and took off down to Prien, a charming village on the Chiemsee. We then drove over some back roads through rolling country with snow capped Alps in the background. I shall never forget it. The fruit trees were in blossom everywhere. All along the roads there were people walking, dressed in their Sunday best--the men and boys in their short leather embroidered pants (Lederhosen)--the women in gay dirndls with white aprons--the little girls with their blond pigtails tied with bow ribbons. The fields were carpeted with masses of yellow buttercups and dandelions. We stopped along the way home, climbed a hill and ate our lunch in the sunshine, in a field of flowers. There was a beautiful view--a peaceful valley with a church, a few houses, people bicycling along the road. We felt so relaxed, almost dizzy from our pastoral surroundings. On arriving home, learned that the first group of DPs had departed today for immigration to the States.

Next came the anniversaries. April 28th, a year since the liberation of Dachau. May 8th, V-E Day. May 11th, Team 108 arrived in Munich. Each date had special memories for every individual, was celebrated by close-knit groups, but there was nothing on a large scale. On Dachau's liberation day,

I went to the Polish Committee Headquarters to see an exhibition of drawings, scenes at the Dachau Concentration Camp, by a Pole, George Zielezinski. I thought them remarkably good.

I also noted on May 8th that,
V-E Day was a strange day in Germany. There were no feelings of the day at all. No celebration--no nothing, but a holiday.

More important, it seemed, was the anniversary of the beginning of my life in Munich.

Arrived in Munich one year ago today (May 11th). In some ways it seems like a long time ago and in others a very short time. We had a conference about a special edition of our Museum "DP Express" which will be printed on June 3rd in commemoration of our anniversary. We talked of all the things that had taken place during the year, the different phases we had gone through--the hard work, the difficulties faced and surmounted somehow.

I was deeply touched by the simple gesture by Yvonne later, when she presented me with a rose in honor of our year together. We were now the only surviving members of the original Team 108.

But there was other evidence and effects of the passage of time, particularly the restoration of the all-but-obliterated city of Munich, as I reported to Aunt Katie in my May 26th letter.

It is hard from here to know what the Germans are thinking, are planning. In the American Zone, the Military Government has consistently stuck to the policy of reestablishing the German economy as soon as possible and has almost entirely turned back to them the governing powers. Many think it was done too hurriedly, too entirely. I don't know. The type of Military Government that we had, or rather that which we established, had officers who have not been very admirable characters in so many incidents that it is almost as well for them to be withdrawn. By July there will remain almost none. The Occupation Forces will consist of constabulary forces which will be here to keep law and order when called upon. There is only a meager Air Force left. If the facts were known (and I don't doubt that the Germans know it very well) we have so few forces here now that it is a very dangerous situation.[53] It is strongly felt that the soldiers were pulled out of Germany and sent home too rapidly. The pressure from families and Congress was too much for the Army.

---

[53] Although Germany was a defeated country, it was still preceived as the enemy who one day could seek revenge against its conquerors, particularly those who were occupying their domain. This was not realistic, but such were the times. There were even rumors about an underground movement among the Germans.

Germany is beginning to rebuild. There is not much in the way of building materials but scaffolding is beginning to appear. As of last month the Germans could legally license automobiles so there are more on the streets driven by Germans, although gasoline is supposed to be issued only for Government use. The people in this part of the country have always been well dressed. There was no sign of suffering in that respect last summer. Housing is about the most critical thing. Here in Munich there is not a cranny that is not occupied. Families live together--refugees have come in from Austria and other countries.

Food again is critical. Here in Bavaria we do not see any starvation. Up until the present there has evidently been enough stored to last. It is also a farming area which is very productive. The rationing is strict and there are many things that are impossible to have. But there seems enough to eat. That is not true in Northern Germany, so they tell us. Also, in the other occupied zones things are different. The Americans are the only ones that feed their armies from home--the Russians, the French and (I think) the British live off the land they are occupying. Every single bit of food we eat comes in cans from the good old USA--that is where your taxes are going. And so help me, if I ever see another canned peach or pineapple when I get home I will scream. Our DPs are fed mostly from Red Cross packages left at the end of the war--those which had been provided for prisoners of war.

As to the future of UNRRA--we naturally are very interested. It seems to be pretty definite that the Agency will fold in December. At the same time it is also realized that the Displaced Persons problem will not be settled by then. There are two alternatives being talked of here. One, the U.N. will take over; secondly, that the Army will assume full responsibility. In either case, it is believed that many UNRRA employees who have the experience will be taken over to continue the programs. So those of us who are not in a hurry to come home will probably have no difficulty in finding our jobs continuing. We know very little about the organization at home. The organization in Germany has improved somewhat but I am still convinced that the real work in UNRRA has been done by the teams in the field.

As summer approached, there was more talk of repatriation. The Military was getting restless, wanting closure to the DP program, to tidy up and get out. The humanitarian aspects of rescue and relief were now becoming undermined by frustration, impatience and the burgeoning costs. In March 1946, UNRRA was caring for 863,000 DPs in the Western Zones of Germany, 337,503 in the US Zone.[54] In my letter of the 26th to Aunt Katie, I had put it this way.

There has been much talk about the huge movements in the spring when the remaining DPs would be repatriated. There have been a few shipments but nothing like those talked of. The bulk of those DPs who are here now will probably not return to their homes. They fall into several categories--many Poles, Baltics (Latvians, Lithuanians, Estonians), some Yugoslavs, many stateless including Ukrainians and White Russians who have not been in Russia since the last war, and the Jews. The Poles don't want to go home while their country is under the domination of the Russians, particularly the intellectual class. The Baltics, for the same reason, claim that they cannot return. The Yugoslavs that are here are the Royalists who would be killed by the Tito group should they return (so they claim). The Jews have now openly acknowledged the fact that we know, that they are trying to force the opening of the barriers to Palestine by congregating in the American occupation zone. We are facing much more of a problem now than in the earlier days, although the situation was more tense then. The continual living in the abnormal camp conditions is beginning to have its effects. Crime is going up--lack of initiative to work, etc. is making the Military and the Germans lose any respect or sympathy with the DPs. The Military Officers in Charge have changed so frequently that it has been extremely difficult for UNRRA. The only answer that I can see is in two directions--one, some political solution to the Russian situation so that people can feel that they can return to their countries without fear; and secondly, opening of the immigration quotas to some other countries. America is the only country now open for immigration--and that is very limited.

The fact that repatriation efforts were not meeting with eager response in the DP population was somewhat of a surprise to

---

[54] Proudfoot, p.289.

many in UNRRA. We had, perhaps naively, assumed that, once the shooting stopped, our job would be to assist the non-German victims to return "home" as soon as possible. Then, on the one hand, there began to emerge the political complexities of the times and, on the other, the recognition of the existence of groups and individuals who had nowhere to go. For instance, there were the Volksdeutsche, the ethnic Germans who had been living outside of Germany, often for generations. The Nazis had been gathering them together, identifying and registering the Volksdeutsche, recording the degree to which they were German in a register called the Volksliste. As explained earlier, they were to be part of the Third Reich's colonisation of eastern Europe. In many cases, they were given German citizenship and, as a result, special privileges not granted their non-German countrymen. Thus, by the war's end, their fate became closely entwined with that of the Nazi regime. Many who were in areas overrun by Allied troops were forced to flee with the retreating German forces. Others were exiled after the German defeat by the governments of their country, who no longer regarded the Volksdeutsche as their citizens. In their eyes, the Volksdeutsche were German--the enemy--and to be expelled into Germany. In the early days after the end of hostilities, some sought refuge in UNRRA camps, as had Helena. However, when regulations for eligibility for UNRRA and Military assistance were formalized, this assistance was disallowed with the understanding that the Germans would assume responsibility for them.[55] If Volksdeutsche were found during the screening of the DP camps, regardless of their nationality, they were transferred by the Military to German-operated refugee camps. (Helena was provided protection as she had become a member of Team 108). It was estimated that twelve million Volksdeutsche were expelled into Germany under the terms of the Potsdam Agreement.[56] As for the stateless, displaced persons who found themselves without a country as a result of the

---

[55] "Table 15: UNRRA and Military Eligibility Criteria for Displaced Persons to Receive or be Denied Assistance in the Western zones of Germany: July 1946 to July 1947", Proudfoot, p.243.
[56] Wyman, p.167.

shifting borders and changing citizenship laws, they were eligible for assistance from UNRRA if they met the Regulations' definition.

> ...persons who had been deprived of their nationality by decision of the government of their country and not acquired a new nationality, and who had been driven, as a result of war from their previous places of settled residence (i.e. Jews).[57]

Although the Deutsches Museum had been only indirectly involved in the repatriation push, colleagues from the camps had filled us in with their trials and tribulations in its regard. We learned about the all-out efforts made to persuade reluctant nationals to return home. It was a clear UNRRA policy that no force would be used in the repatriation of unwilling DPs to their countries of origin. We were aware, however, that in some instances liaison officers used pressure to persuade, but only the Russians were known to be unrelenting.

The most successful measure was the "Carrot Operation" ordered by the then Director General of UNRRA, former N.Y. City Mayor Fiorello La Guardia, which provided returning DPs a sixty-day ration of food and other inducements. I went down to the station one day to observe a train departing with Polish repatriates, seemingly in a jubilant mood as they waved from the open doors of the boxcars which would transport them to their homeland. The cars were decorated with branches from trees and a flag now and then. I had very mixed feelings as I watched the blond-haired, happy, mostly young people, glad to see them ending the bleak era in their lives, but skeptical about the potential hardships which lay ahead, if there was any credence in the worrisome rumors filtering back from Poland.

The Poles who remained behind were very concerned. On May 12th, I went to the Museum to do a little work.

---

[57] Proudfoot, p.244.

George Dyla came in to talk. He is a very honest, sincere person. During the war he worked with the Polish underground, smuggled in American money to bribe German officials for false papers to get Polish officers out of Poland. He was in Dachau for five years. He will go to work for the Polish Committee. We talked of Poland, of the London Poles (those army officers who managed to flee to London before or during the German occupation of Poland), the Warsaw Poles, of the Russians in Poland, the hungry people there. How bread and meat are available at prices which cannot be paid by the common people, how the food shops are only open two days a week, of Poland before the war.

Out of curiosity, I decided to sample the intentions of the University students and staff at the Museum via a poll on May 14, 1946. The results were telling.

They were asked to fill in three questions:
(1) Nationality,
(2) Do you want to be repatriated now, and
(3) If not, why not.

It was an unsigned ballot, so that many people had the satisfaction of putting on paper pent-up feelings. My secretaries, Wolf and Valeria, stayed and counted the ballots with me that night. The results were very interesting. Out of 1,348 people who filled out the ballots, there were 15 who wanted to be repatriated (4 Americans), 75% didn't want to return home because of political reasons (Russian occupation or domination).

With the enormity of problems facing the Museum at the time of my return from the Child Search assignment, I was at first unaware of the budding movement to establish a university on its premises. When I had left Team 108, my replacement was a Polish welfare officer, Halina Gaszinska, who became deeply concerned about the young DPs between the ages of 18 and 25 who had been deprived of higher educational opportunities during the war. Incorporating several DP professors and some eager potential students, a small group had begun to formulate plans for studies, gather equipment and look for resources. On my return to the Museum, my first awareness of the activities was when I was asked for special privileges for the professors and students, such as white bread instead of the usual fare of dark bread, and special and separate eating arrangements at meals. It seemed to me that to agree would have suggested a class system within our general DP population, so I found myself not particularly sympathetic.

Gradually, increasing demands and a "settling-in" process set off warning bells to the Military and UNRRA that the growing institutional arrangement might delay or discourage repatriation. Notwithstanding, over time the now-called UNRRA University became established and functioned, albeit with a limited and precarious status. However, even this did eventually lead to a showdown. The breaking point came when the University demanded that the entire Museum be turned over to the University, eliminating the transient center. This was back in January.

Sunday, January 13th
Mr. Atkins, Ed, our Field Supervisor and I were in conference all afternoon. The Supervisor was telling us that the Museum was to be turned into a University. We did not think it practical or feasible--did not like the manner in which the plan had been worked out without our participation.

The next day,
Conference at Colonel Nelson's house about the University--an unfortunate meeting. The Military should not be involved.

Then, *on Wednesday, January 16th*
Conference all morning with Mr. Burman, Zone Education Head--very satisfactory. And, finally, on Thursday, January 17th the issue was negotiated satisfactorily. Our (Mr. Atkins, Ed and me) lines of thinking are being followed--to limit the living accommodations for students in the Museum, but to hold classes there.

The enrollment of students at the UNRRA University had continued to grow as it did in other DP camp universities. By 1946, some 1400 were enrolled at the UNRRA University.[58]

In May came an unexpected interlude which turned out to be a break in my life and functions in UNRRA. I received a special delivery letter from my brother telling me that my mother had been in an automobile accident resulting in a fractured vertebra in her neck. She was recovering, but we agreed that, if possible, it would be a good idea if I could make it home for a short stint. My bosses agreed that I was due some home leave but the problem was transport. There were no rules on the books at that time regarding transporting non-military personnel back to the states. But I managed, with a tantrum or two and even a few feminine wiles, to get there. Eventually I crossed the Atlantic on a US military transport plane that landed in Washington; then arrived quite unglamourously at Mobile's L & N (Louisville & Nashville) railroad station on the four o'clock afternoon train. Two weeks passed rapidly, and reassured about Mother's health and well being, I was off again for Munich by way of Washington, Newfoundland, the Azores, and Paris. As the C47 from Orly descended towards Munich on that clear summer's day, my whole being was adjusting, shifting gears--from "Mobile Susan" to "Munich Susan." Positively flooded with excitement, "Munich Susan" felt like the real me.

---

[58] Wyman, p.122.

ON TO PALESTINE

The time in Mobile was only two of the six weeks away; the rest was spent getting there and back. Not unpleasant layovers had been necessary in London, Paris--and Washington on return. Needless to say, time had not stood still in Munich. Changes, changes met me on my return on July 27th. The summer was half gone. Team 108 was in flux, old hands departing, new ones moving in.

Kay had gone home--Colette and Yvonne had resigned, were to leave in the middle of August. At the Museum, Walter had returned to Poland that very morning. The Information Section had dropped off, employment picked up. The whole 9th Division Artillery had moved out and the 34th Infantry was in Munich now. Suzanne Weymar and Madame Tschentko were in jail.[59] They had been picked up on suspicion of Communist activities. (Both had been working in the Information Section).

Vera cried with joy when I arrived. She helped me unpack, exclaiming over my new clothes. She was thrilled with the new nylon stockings I brought her.

The next day I was amused at her horror at my appearance in a blouse that had not been pressed since unpacking.

While at dinner she hung around the dining room door with iron in hand, pounced on me the minute I got up from the table. In the meantime she had been in my room and pressed everything in sight.

Vera had become an important person in my life, so loving, so protective. Her devotion to me knew no bounds. As one of the

---

[59] The CIC had advised me and Ed confidentially that Madame Tschenkto was known to be a Russian spy, but they preferred she stay on Team 108 where they could keep an eye on her. "Better the devil you know, than the devil you don't."

DPs in the Museum she had been chosen to work as a housemaid in our billet. A portly, middle-aged woman with mouse-colored hair twisted into a bun on the back of her head from which there were always straying wisps requiring a backhanded motion to clear them from her face. To Vera, even everyday events were high drama in true reputed Russian form, which added zest to life in the billet as there were always crises, emotional highs, and sometimes excitement. She was constantly laughing or smiling, which exposed several gold teeth. Full of energy and good humor, she contributed considerably to order in No. 2 Galilei Platz. And she brought romance. It was a delightful story.

Vera Bogdanova was Russian. She was born and grew up in Latvia, which was part of Russia at that time. Evidently her family was of the landed gentry, as she seemed well educated, and spoke French, German, Polish, Russian and English. The story of how or why she was in Germany during the war is a bit hazy. All we knew was that she had been working for three years as a servant for a farmer's family before liberation and escape to the Deutsches Museum.

At the Deutsches Museum she met Jasha Senkow. Jasha, also Russian, was born in Riga, Latvia, in 1892. As a young boy he accompanied his father, an engineer in the oil industry, to the Caucasus and then to South Russia. He attended the Konstantinowska School of Artillery in Petersburg, graduated as an officer, moving up to become a "high officer" in the White Russian army. He fought against the Bolsheviks in the 1917 Revolution where his army was defeated, forcing him to leave Russia. He sought refuge in Yugoslavia where he worked as a technical draftsman for twenty years until the Germans invaded, uprooting him again, bringing him into Germany for forced labor in the salt mines. At liberation he found his way to the Deutsches Museum where he worked for us as a policeman and guard. There were few signs of the former soldier in the small, white-haired, rather stooped Jasha with his gentle personality, except for his conscientious approach to any job at hand.

And now, the romance. There, at the Museum, he found Vera. They discovered that they had known each other in their youth. When he was a dashing young Russian army officer stationed in the area where Vera's family lived, he, along with other officers, were often invited to visit on Sunday afternoons for tea. Vera played the piano on these pleasant occasions. They had lost track of each other after he was transferred, until fate brought them together again at the Deutsches Museum.[60]

Working in the billet for UNRRA was a haven for Vera and Jasha, who guarded our automobiles and did odd chores around the house. They were terrified by the threat of being returned to Russia as DP camps were being searched by Russian Repatriation Officers and any Russians found were sent off to Russia under the terms of the Potsdam Agreement. Many Russian DPs in Germany went into hiding and/or just disappeared. It was rumored that some even committed suicide.

It was becoming increasingly clear to me since my return from Mobile that the time had come for me to move on, to leave the Museum for another job. It wasn't just that my close teammates were peeling off. Kay had gone, Yvonne was leaving, Ed packing to go. I was ready for a new experience. So I talked with Personnel, eliciting tempting offers of a variety of positions. At their urging, however, I agreed to take a temporary assignment.

The US Zone Child Welfare Officer is on home leave for thirty days so I am in her office for that period, I wrote my Aunt on August 16th. *It is a good spot to get a picture of the whole zone activities. I would not like to be here permanently, as I do not like just policy making and paperwork, but for this crucial period in UNRRA's life it's not bad. In 30 days we should have some idea what the program will be for the next few months, at least. Things have changed somewhat. The Military has tightened--more MP patrols are evident, parades and tanks. They are*

---

[60] Vera and Jasha were married in June 1947. I later sponsored their immigration to the United States.

stricter about uniforms, traffic, etc. Planes seem overhead more. There is a bit of tension, mostly because of Russian feeling.

Then, it was like a TV program in fast forward, skittering through farewells at No.2 Galilei Platz, clearing my desk at the Museum amid tears, festivities and parting wishes. Completing the temporary assignment, I found myself in that romantic city of Heidelberg.

The initial surge of Jewish infiltrees had subsided in the late winter months, but the trend took another guise of unexpected, again unannounced arrivals in late June--groups of children under eighteen years of age, usually between the ages of six and thirteen. A report I prepared for the UNRRA US Zone Headquarters stated explained the situation.

> In June and July 1946, they (unaccompanied Jewish children) started again to "infiltrate" into the Zone with the numbers reaching a peak in the latter part of August and early September. During this period there were authorized Jewish transports entering both from Berlin and through Austria, with the large majority coming through Austria. Estimate of infiltrees from June 15th to Nov. 1st:
>
> | | |
> |---|---|
> | Total | 76,924 |
> | Total children | 13,878 |
> | Total unaccompanied children | 2,458 |
>
> In August, the Child Welfare Section at UNRRA US Zone Headquarters assumed the responsibility for planning and providing care, particularly for the unaccompanied children. (At this point, the position of Child Welfare Officer for Jewish Infiltree Children was established and I was appointed to fill it). It was important to first coordinate efforts of the Jewish Agencies, those particularly interested being the Jewish Agency for Palestine (JAFP), the American Joint

Distribution Committee (AJDC), and the Central Committee for Liberated Jews. It was found that all were eager to cooperate and pool their thinking and resources. Working together, a plan of operation was evolved and with UNRRA approval, was put into effect. The Jewish agencies (by November), especially JAFP and AJDC are providing trained educators. An Educational Board has been established composed of one representative [from each] of AJDC, JAFP, UNRRA, and Central Committee will assume responsibility for coordinating educational facilities, planning a training course for teachers and leaders, approving courses, curricula, and methods of teaching, as well as arranging for printing and distribution of text books.[61]

By September, this new phase of immigration was in full swing. Apparently the various Jewish agencies had spent the summer recruiting the children, organizing them, and planning their movement through Germany towards Palestine. It was clear to UNRRA that immediate measures had to be undertaken to keep things from getting out of hand. Because of my early reports on the infiltree movement and my child welfare experience, I had been promoted to the new UNRRA Zone Headquarters position. This appointment coincided with the move of Headquarters from the Munich area to Heidelberg in order to be closer to the headquarters of the US Military Forces in Germany located there.

I had been offered work in Heidelberg once before, as Relief Services Liaison with the 3rd Army and USFET (US Forces in the European Theater), a job that would have focused on reducing friction between UNRRA and the Military at top levels. I considered the offer, but not for too long. I didn't kid myself. Sure I was able to get things done. Additionally, however, it seemed that I had been selected because I was not too bad-looking, and got along well with men. This seemed an exploitation of my femininity. Certainly I felt no qualms about turning on a bit of

---

[61] Report of Jewish Unaccompanied Children, undated (probably November 1946), in private papers of Susan Pettiss.

feminine charm to get something to further our work, but to be offered a position on that basis was unacceptable to me. I said so. This time around, I was more than happy to say yes. I moved to Heidelberg.

The city was positively idyllic. It had not been bombed, the result of an unwritten agreement, it was said, between the British and the Germans to spare Oxford and Cambridge as well. With narrow, crooked streets winding among the buildings of the University of Heidelberg, the city was straight out of *The Student Prince*. It was nestled at the foot of low mountains along the banks of the Nekar river. On my first evening, I was taken by a friend to see the city from the top of one of the surrounding mountains. At sunset, the scene was breathtakingly beautiful. Flowers were everywhere. Under the rose-colored sky, the Neckar River wound through the valley below punctuated by bridges and church steeples, then snaked across a plain--to infinity, it seemed.

Initially I felt caught up as if in a fog; the shape and size of the problem and my new assignment seemed purposely obscured. Like a B-47, the job took off the day after my arrival, however, and for the next three weeks I spent beating up and down autobahns and back roads, covering Germany from Berlin to Bavaria. With 1,000 children descending upon us daily that September, the need for action to locate appropriate facilities, get authority from the military for taking over the facilities, as well as staffing, equipping and getting centers up and running was tremendous. Thus, the first weeks of my new job were spent tackling that emergency. The UNRRA Social Workers and Team Directors, joined by the Jewish agency representatives, were heroic in seeking out, converting and assuming responsibility for the readiness of installations to receive the children. There was no time to be lost. Things had to happen or I had to make them happen. In one instance, I was notified on a Wednesday that we could take over a caserne with a capacity for 3,000 children. The army unit which had been occupying it moved out on Thursday. I was there on Friday with the area UNRRA Team Director, and rounded up staff to supplement the personnel the quickly appointed Center

Director had brought with her. This provided a nucleus to arrange for food, beds, supplies and run the place. On Monday, the first 1,000 children arrived from Berlin.

I wrote about the introduction to my new job in a letter to Aunt Katie on September 30th.

I'm dead tired. I have turned into a traveling saleslady or just a traveling lady. For three weeks I have been in Heidelberg and I have only slept here four nights in that time, and no two consecutively. From one end of Germany to the other--Berlin to Rosenheim! Maybe I had better tell you about it diary-like.

On Monday morning, I had a meeting in Munich with the Jewish agencies, lunched, packed the car, started off (for Heidelberg). The next day, Tuesday, I went to our office which is in the big caserne used by the army as the US Military Headquarters for Germany. After no more than a look, I took off for Wiesbaden as I had called a meeting there for two o'clock. We met all afternoon so that I could explain the plans that had been worked out for the care of infiltree children coming into the zone. The Child Welfare Officer there is a Canadian, Margaret Newton. She was a Major in the Canadian Army and has an excellent social welfare background.

Wednesday morning I got up early and drove back to Heidelberg. Friday morning Jack Whiting [UNRRA US Zone Director] and I left in his car for Frankfort at 8:3o in the morning. We went to Eschon Airport and took off about 12 o'clock. At two we landed at the famous Templehof Airport which is right in the middle of Berlin. Mr. Doughty, Field Supervisor, and Mr. Nordby, District Director met us there. They had a meeting with the Military so I was taken to the camps in the neighborhood. I was eager to get as much information as possible about the number of infiltrees coming in, and anticipated. There are about nine thousand now in camps in Berlin and nine thousand living in the city. They are expecting about ten thousand more to come. The camps are new, are barracks and overcrowded. I talked to the welfare officers and took a look around.

The next day, Saturday, I went back to the camps, inspected a Children's Center, condemned it, worked out arrangements for registering the children and having them sent into the American Zone immediately so we could provide more adequate care for them. I had a conference with the Jewish Agency for Palestine and met Jack and Mr. Nordby for lunch at the home of the representative of AJDC.

In the afternoon Jack and I slipped away and finally got to see a little of Berlin. The most interesting thing we saw was the official black market. It is in a wooden building and is rather crude but fascinating. Jack and I nearly went crazy in it. Americans can take articles of food, cigarettes [from the States], clothing and any essential articles and get points for them. In turn, Germans take luxury articles, glass, china, silver, linen, cameras, radios, etc. for which they get points. All are displayed on counters and there you trade your points. There was lovely china and so many interesting things. Unfortunately we had nothing to trade so we couldn't get anything. There were lots of officers and their wives who were having a picnic.

The huge city must have been beautiful at one time, I thought, its wide streets lined with trees which obscured the rather uninteresting architecture. Vast parts of the residential sections were in shambles. The city center was completely bombed out, block after block in ruins except for a tiny shop or cafe here or there. Although Berlin was divided into zones of occupation by the four Allied armies, there were no clear lines of demarcation or signs of difference, except perhaps that the Russian zone didn't seem to have large hotels, officers' clubs or VIP residences. I saw the battered Reichstag building, home of the Bundestag or Parliament, where some of the final, fierce battle for Berlin took place. And the famous Tiergarten, at this time only a cluster of "victory gardens" along wandering paths. It was divided by a wide street formerly lined by trees which had been cut for fuel, at one end of which was a marble statue rising out of a potato patch -- an eerie sight. I saw, too, the air-raid cellar where Hitler was supposed to have died. Everyone to whom I talked seemed convinced it was true.

We returned to Heidelberg the next day.

Tuesday, I left immediately after breakfast and drove to Kassel. Got to Kassel in time for lunch with the UNRRA Field Supervisor and left for Hofgeismar. There we inspected a camp that we wanted to use for a Children's Center, talked to the UNRRA Team Director, acquainting him with the total planning for the children, arranged for staff, movements and conversion of the camp. I then came back to Kassel and went on to Hess Lichtenau. At Hess Lichtenau we inspected another installation for a Children's Center. It was formerly a German Children's Orphanage, was used during the war as a hotel for German officers, later by American officers and now has some adult Jewish infiltrees in it. Again, we had to talk to the team, arrange for the conversion into a Children's Center. Fortunately they were very enthusiastic about having children.

Wednesday I got up early and drove over to Frankfurt for a ten o'clock meeting with some Jewish Agency people, leaving about twelve for Heidelberg. I got up at 4:30 a.m. on Friday and started for Munich and Rosenheim. I had breakfast in Stuttgart, stopped for an hour at a new Children's Center we had just opened at Dormstadt and whizzed through Munich and down to Rosenheim. There they were having a two day meeting of District Child Welfare Workers where I was to discuss with them at three o'clock the Jewish infiltree children plans and problems. After meeting for awhile, we went down to see the Rosenheim Children's Center which is the reception center for the whole Zone. It is a fascinating place because of the stories of the children there. Back to Prien for dinner and afterwards we sat around a big table and swapped children. It sounded like a life and death bargaining. Some worker would have fifty children in her District belonging to one (socio/political) group which had an institution in another District.

Saturday I went back to Rosenheim as I wanted to talk to the Director in more detail.

After next week I think my plans for the Jewish children will become crystallized enough so that I can transfer into something else, or at least take on other duties. I think I would like to spend the winter in

Heidelberg.

From the outset of the flow of children into the zone, each group unannounced and unexpected, it was clear that this was a planned movement which could not be proceeding so smoothly without a system of grapevine communications. It occurred to me that it would be efficient to set up a children's reception center near one of the popular entry points to the US Zone, then send out word over the grapevine that it was available and ready to receive the children. That is exactly what was done. The Rosenheim Center in Bavaria, near the Austrian border, between Salzburg and Munich, was established. It was a former German military facility previously occupied by a US Army Engineers Unit. Much like hundreds of similar complexes of solidly-constructed concrete buildings it was austere but livable. The Armed Forces had equipped it with good recreational space which was later upgraded by UNRRA, and again, like the Deutsches Museum, the coldness of the installation was diminished by the warm atmosphere created by the staff who were determined to welcome and comfort the arriving children. The plan was that incoming children would rest, undergo complete registration and documentation, receive medical examinations and immunizations, TB x-rays if indicated, and disinfection. They were provided with clothing, and for the first time in years (and in many cases, ever), these tired and fearful youngsters found sheets, pillows and hot water awaiting them. After three weeks, they were to be fanned out to appropriate children's centers throughout the Zone according to their kibbutz affiliations.

It took me some time to understand this kibbutzim system. Each kibbutz was affiliated with one of six or seven youth movement organizations. It was usually a well organized group averaging about seventy, under the care of a youth leader, or madrich.

Leo Schwarz explained the system as follows.

> The children had been organized into political cadres at
> their point of origin and indoctrinated into every variety

of Zionist philosophy: some belonged to the Aguda and Mizrachi of orthodox persuasion. A number of Hungarians in particular adhered to the Dror or Revisionist youth organization and others to socialist parties like the Hashomar Hatzair. While it seemed objectionable from a professional angle, the UNRRA leaders realized that these allegiances had created an emotional security for the children, thus accepted and encouraged their continuance.[62]

From a Western social worker's point of view, perhaps it would have been more logical for the children to be planned for by age groups, or by language and regional backgrounds. But I soon saw the value of the system. The group pattern had been adopted before the children came into Germany and would undoubtedly continue in Palestine. By breaking it up during the interim stay in Germany, there was danger of destroying the fragile sense of security initially developed. It also facilitated the usage of facilities and personnel, i.e. Kosher kitchens, selected vocational training for adolescent groups, educational curriculum, et cetera. And it anticipated emigration when the children would proceed in their assimilated groups for resettlement. I have to admit that I was often amused at myself trying to convince a General why we needed a new installation for the Hashomar Hazairs (or another kibbutz) when he pointed out, "but there are vacancies in already existing centers." "But one doesn't mix the Hashomar Hazairs with the Drors," I explained.

The story of Wolf, a Polish boy, was typical of the way Jewish children found themselves in a kibbutz, with Palestine as their goal.

Wolf was born May 5, 1932 in Dubienko, Gublin, Poland. His whole family left their home in September 1939 (before the advancing German armies) to go to the Eastern Ukraine. The father had worked as a fruit merchant, owned a small house. In June 1940, the family moved from the Ukraine to Siberia and in the winter of 1941 to Turkestan in

---

[62] Schwarz, p.165.

Karakstamt, where they remained until 1946 when they returned to Stettin. Wolf joined the Hashomar Hazair Kibbutz and left with a group in June for Berlin, later coming into the US Zone of Germany, to the Rosenheim Center.[63]

Before the end of November, we had 12 Children's Centers in operation in four of the five Districts of the US Zone, caring for just over 3,000 children.

In selection of Center sites, consideration was given to the grouping under area UNRRA teams with specialized child welfare personnel, accessibility to medical facilities, besides good physical accommodation The following installations had been opened and in operation:

<u>District 1.</u>   *<u>Bleidorn</u>*
near Ulm--(x-6682) Team 1007
Capacity 350--For Aguda Kibbutz

<u>Darnstadt</u>
near Ulm--(x-6488) Team 1008
Capacity 500--for coordination, or children not belonging to any political or religious group

<u>District 2.</u>   *<u>Lindenfels</u>*
near Lampartheim (M-7621) Team 1021
Capacity 450--For Hashomar Hazair Kibbutz
An installation composed of separate hotels and houses located in one village

<u>Schwebda Castle</u>
near Eschwege (H-3890) Team 1025
Capacity 200--For Hashomar Hazair Kibbutz

<u>Goldcup</u> (planned but not yet in operation)
Near Hess-Lichtenau (H-3890) Team 1025

---

[63] Report of Jewish Infiltree Children.

Capacity 450--For Mizrochi children

District 3.   *Struth*
Near Ansbach (T-1095) Team 1041
Capacity 400--For Dror (Hungarian) and
Hashomar Hazair

District 5.   *Indersdorf*
Near Dachau (x-6980) Team 1067
Capacity 300--Dror Kibbutz

Bayrish Gmein
near Traunstein (Z-6632) Team 1070
Capacity 250--For Gordonya Kibbutz

Aschau Youth Center
near Muhldorf (Z-4366) Team 1068
Capacity 350

Purtan I.
near Muhldorf (z-4867) Team 1068
Capacity 500--For I chud (Moar Zioni
children)

Some Jewish unaccompanied children are in International Children's Centers at Prien and Aglasterhausen.

Of course staffing these centers was a heavy responsibility. Fortunately the UNRRA personnel was supplemented by Jewish agency personnel and the *madrichim*, the youth leaders accompanying the kibbutz groups, who facilitated many functions. As a matter of fact, the *madrichim* played a key role. They were young men and women in their early twenties who bore with great stoicism the heavy responsibility for the children under their wings--most of whom were undernourished, many of them sick. The *madrichim* had been appointed by their own organizations and so were not always amenable to supervision by

Jewish youth on parade

the military or UNRRA. Some were imbued with idealistic fervor to the point that they were overzealous in protecting their charges. Yet their potential seemed practically boundless, thus, one of the first things I planned with the UNRRA district welfare officers and children's center social workers was a series of training courses for the *madrichim* to discuss child welfare principles which were pertinent to the circumstances. This also provided the opportunity for the *madrichim* to meet each other, to share experiences and sometimes solutions to problems.

After the initial push, I was able to visit the centers in a somewhat more leisurely manner than at first, and to become acquainted with the children and the *madrichim* at each. This was not always easy, as I didn't understand Yiddish or most of the other languages spoken by them. I had been eager for some personal connection but it didn't happen. I realized that I was an unknown adult, always with the supervisory personnel, undoubtedly invoking the suspicion of strangers developed over the years of terror. Usually their faces were expressionless, their voices silent. I couldn't help but make comparisons with children in the institutions in Mobile where I had functioned as caseworker. I missed seeing what I thought of as normal children's behavior--shouting and laughter, spontaneous games and songs--and fretted constantly about their lack of exuberance. Frankly, I would rather have seen them making a little mischief now and then. These kids were serious, focused, even militant; marching in formation to meals and special activities, eating in silence. Most kibbutzim were uniformly dressed--the girls in white shirts and navy blue skirts, the boys in white shirts and either navy blue or khaki shorts. Education was a "must," and rigorous study time taken extremely seriously as most of the children had not been able to go to school during the war years. Skits, in which the actors wore adult clothes and the scenes were invariably set in Palestine, seemed to be a favorite activity. Although the script was in Hebrew and I couldn't understand the content of the performances of those I saw, it was clear that they were not comedies.

My supervisory responsibility for the Children's Centers introduced me to many new challenges. There were always crises. Some of them, for instance, children disconsolate over the loss of parents and family, were beyond the power of UNRRA to remedy. Others were easy to repair. One cold winter day, I received a call in Heidelberg from a center just outside of Stuttgart, which was faced with a serious and urgent problem. Could I come immediately? Although Stuttgart was several hours' drive from Heidelberg along snow-covered roads, I bundled up and jumped in my jeep. (I had been assigned a jeep on my move to Headquarters in Heidelberg and used it on trips like this, through snow and bad weather, rather than my Wanderer). When I reached my destination, I was warmly welcomed and explained the dilemma faced by the center. Each day a supply of food rations was delivered so that the required number of calories for each person was provided. On that day the center had received an article of food utterly unknown to them. The cooks had no idea how to prepare it, but they had to use it or else the calorie count could not be met. I was taken to the kitchen by a staff member, who opened a big sack. Bewildered, I took one look and laughed. It was hominy grits! I assured the staff that they had called the right person, as any Alabamian would certainly know about grits. I suggested they include it with the stew or flavor it with the gravy and all would be fine.

During this period of limbo, while they waited until they could move on to Palestine, our purpose was to provide the best care possible under the circumstances. For instance, services to meet their needs included,

Registration, *consisting of complete documentation under supervision of Child Search Teams with copies sent to the UNRRA Tracing Bureau.*

Medical Services, *included initial physical examinations, special attention given to children needing individual medical treatment. Each Center had its own medical dispensary and infirmary, and approved hospital facilities easily accessible.*

Dental Care, *administered in the individual Center by traveling clinics.*

A Mental Hygiene Program *whereby two approaches to the problems were to be followed:*

1. A recognized psychiatrist will visit the centers to work with staff personnel in recognition, interpretation, and understanding of general emotional problems of the children.

2. A trained psychiatric social worker will be attached to one of the centers to which children with outstanding behavior problems will be referred for observation and treatment.

Educational Needs. *One of the most difficult phases of care because of the lack of trained teachers and text books. The task was complicated because of the language differences, the lapse of the children's education during the war years, and the impermanence of the situation. The Jewish*

Agencies, especially JAFP and AJDC, provided trained educators to help alleviate the situation.[64]

The exodus of the infiltree Jews from Poland and other central European countries had been dubbed the "Bricha," the Hebrew word for "flight." It was an apt and descriptive term for the masses of individuals fleeing war, persecution, and then the disillusionment faced on return to their pre-war countries and homes where they encountered continuing anti-Semitism, loss of property and even threats on their lives. The Bricha took many forms. We never knew the rationale for the organization of groups of unaccompanied children as one of these forms. We initially assumed the children were either orphans or given up by their parents in the fervor to establish a new Jewish homeland in Palestine.

We soon found, however, that a significant number of those coming into the US Zone were not orphans or abandoned, but had one or both parents either in Poland or traveling in different transports. As a matter of fact, it was estimated that fifty or sixty percent of the children had parents. Apparently the families had placed the children in the kibbutzim to enable them to get out of Poland more quickly, feeling that better care would be administered to such groups and hoping that unaccompanied children would be given priority for entrance to Palestine. When families found that children were not moving immediately through Germany, they began appearing at Centers to reclaim the children, causing unnecessary confusion of movement, as well as setting up an emotional conflict within the child who had become strongly attached to the group. Additionally, many relatives arrived or wrote to request to take children, causing burdensome decisions as to whether the child should be released. In such instances, consideration was given to the matter by UNRRA and the Jewish agencies, with the final decision made by the UNRRA welfare officer.

---

[64] Report on Jewish Infiltree Children.

As time went on, the Children's Centers began to function smoothly, and the flow of children into them dwindled. Then commenced the outflow, the illegal underground movement towards British-controlled Palestine in the footsteps of the adult infiltrees who had made the journey during the preceding year. Again, this was something that one felt in the air, but couldn't distinguish the precise form or substance. It was just as well. Because of the diplomatic implications, being a party to it was highly imprudent. I walked a thin line as it was, coordinating the activities of the Jewish agencies in the US Zone while representing UNRRA. As I wrote in a letter to my mother, "If someday Parliament calls me on the carpet, just don't know me." But I had begun to feel that remaining in Germany was detrimental to the well-being of the children and there seemed no other answer than Palestine.

Now, I know that, for the children, two hubs for collection and departure from Germany had been set up--one in Leipheim near Munich, and the other in Bad Reichenhall near the Austrian border, the gateway to the Alps. As Leo Schwarz explains, the path of the infiltrees generally wound through the mountains towards French and Italian ports, whence ships sailed to the Middle East. Children stole away during the night in small groups. I asked only that they leave me a note stating how many had gone so I could bring some order to my chaotic record-keeping. There were no good-byes.

WINDING DOWN

It seemed that during my sojourn in Germany I was living two lives, in two worlds, both of which had deep meaning for my personal development and setting a compass for my future. One, the engrossing life of work, if it could be called that. It was not the usual concept of "work." There was not the traditional framework--hours, offices, bosses, accountability in the usual sense. It was intensive, ground-breaking, challenging, inspiring, exhausting. There were no guidelines, no tools; few limits, restraints or deadlines. I found myself forever learning, experimenting, testing new sets of values and priorities. Each day brought new challenges. I reveled in the freedom to create, to draw on my imagination in lieu of following an imposed credo. There were also disappointments, and some disillusions which helped to shrink my naiveté.

My other life was one of parties, dancing, sightseeing, swinging from deep subjects of conversation--real conversation--to gaiety and laughter. This life was a mixture of my Southern background with its emphasis on social niceties and surroundings which set the stage for them, and the Europeans' extravagant celebration of almost any occasion or for any excuse. And then there was the constant availability of male companions which undoubtedly helped in the healing process of a failed marriage, a restoration of my self-confidence and a reassurance of my feminine attractiveness. The surreal backdrop for the nightlife included lavish officers' clubs and messes, often in former German mansions or cabarets, with live music, cheap bars, and sometimes spectacular German floor shows. Money was never an issue. The military was eager to make life pleasant for its troops, as was UNRRA, with its international flavor.

The thread which ran through both lives was the people with whom I worked, shared experiences and dated. Enough can't be said about my gratitude, or the admiration for and humility learned from those deep, close relationships which have strengthened me throughout the rest of my life.

Although times and circumstances constantly shifted, I made some lifetime friendships. There was Helen Zilka, of course. She and I had shared so much; crossing the Atlantic on the *Koda Gede*, London, Jouluville, early Munich days. We had collaborated in our social welfare work, shared trips to Switzerland and Czechoslovakia, and often double dated. I was the more serious, she the more worldly. Our friendship had special meaning for me at a time in my life when I was making a critical transition. So it was a blow when on September 3rd, Helen came by to tell me she was going to get married to a Polish ex-POW, Stan Jaworski. The simple wedding took place in Munich. My little blue taffeta hat that I had acquired on my trip to Mobile was the ultimate bridal touch, perched saucily on Helen's beautiful brown hair above a happy face. Stan lightened the occasion with his teasing and infectious laughter. They made a handsome couple, and departed soon afterwards for home, Chicago.

The fact that Helen's wedding and her departure coincided with my move to Heidelberg softened the loss somewhat. So did a trip to Brussels where I saw Charley again. In Heidelberg, one of my new friends was Virginia Coker, who was on the UNRRA Headquarters staff. Organizing Helen's wedding seemed to have established my reputation for putting on weddings, so, when Virginia announced her intentions to marry, I was corralled and even persuaded to serve as the bridesmaid. So I must have a proper dress. We agreed to go to Brussels for it.

"You look so civilized!" I exclaimed when we met. Charley was dressed in a dark blue beautifully-tailored suit with a homberg hat, a far cry from the unpressed uniform pants and khaki shirt I had been accustomed to seeing him wear. Despite a relentless cold drizzle, we had a wonderful day in Brussels, wandering the narrow, winding streets and commenting on the similarity of the city's central square and town hall to those in Munich. At lunch I was introduced to snails, which at first intimidated me, however when I got up nerve to take a bite I found them delicious. Next came the shopping spree, first for lace for the bride, then for the dress for me. While we worked together in Germany I had not been aware that Charley was of noble lineage, so imagine my surprise when he was regularly greeted as " Baron del Marmol" upon entering shops.

We soon established a routine. Charley--Baron del Marmol-- would introduce Virginia and me (still wearing our uniforms) and describe the dress in which I was interested. The saleslady would look at me rather skeptically, clearly struggling to imagine me in such an elegant garment. Nevertheless she would bring out a series of gorgeous dresses made from fabulous materials. Usually we sat on dainty, satin-covered settees to view these offerings, bug-eyed. Charley would scrutinize each one, giving a little toss of his head to indicate it wasn't quite right. Then we would thank the saleslady and proceed to the next shop, where the routine was repeated. Charley was enjoying every minute, particularly my unrepressed excitement at the vision of finery so different from what I had been accustomed to during the past two years. Each shop seemed more elegant than the last. I never asked a price. Finally we settled on some heavenly blue silk material which we took back to Heidelberg to be made into my bridesmaid dress.

Naturally, Charley wanted news of the Museum, friends and colleagues, of my present status--and plans for the future. He was getting back to being a Professor of Law at the University of Liege, overjoyed to have been reunited with his family, including a new baby. It was the last time I ever saw him, a person whom I will always hold in the highest regard and with deep affection.

Meanwhile, changes were taking place in Heidelberg. Military "dependents," wives and, in some cases, children, were beginning to arrive; those of the highest ranking officers first. They often brought the latest model American automobiles with them, and the P.X. offerings suddenly took on up-scale standards. I had looked forward to meeting some women from the States, maybe putting my feet under a table spread with an American home-cooked meal. It never happened. The dependents formed an enclave that excluded the rest of us women, and I will never know whether they suspected us of previous "fraternizing" with their husbands or merely thought of us as second-class citizens. My greatest annoyance resulted from the fact that only these just-arrived wives were eligible for articles in the P.X. like irons and toasters--the very things we had been deprived of since arriving years before.

In Heidelberg, since I was working in the US Military Headquarters, my associations were mostly with officers and, at some point, I realized that I was no longer in awe of high rank. Those stars and birds now meant little to me. After all, the shoulders sporting them belonged to human beings who really liked to be treated as such. They liked to be flirted with, even subjected to irreverent jesting.

For instance, on my earlier trip to Heidelberg with Jack Whiting, Jack took me to General Truscott's house, a gorgeous estate on the side of the mountain. General Truscott was the Commanding General of the 3rd Army, the US Army of Occupation. He was in bed, ill with a heart ailment. He was awfully nice--had a drink with us--joked a lot. It did my heart good to see a commanding general of a tough military machine so gentle, so human.

One night in an Officers' Mess, a general called my date, a major, inviting us to join him at his table. My conversation with the general was the usual giddy sort. Afterwards my date commented, "Susan, I never heard anyone talk to the general like that." "But he loved it," I replied. Sure enough, the general urged us to come over to his billet after dinner for drinks. We even stayed to watch a film out on his terrace.

Christmas came and went pleasantly in Heidelberg's picture-postcard setting. For a different New Year's holiday, Margaret and I decided to venture into the British Zone of Occupation, to a British Officers' "Rest Hotel." This installation had been used by Nazi officers for what they called "strength through joy." In other words, it was a spot where selected Aryan girls were made available for sex and entertainment, and incidentally to produce beautiful babies to augment the Master Race. The hotel was a three-story building decorated externally by exposed beams, its grounds bare of any trees or evident shrubbery beneath the Christmas snow. From the outside, the appearance was rather somber, however big fires glowing in the reception and lounge areas brightened the interior, further warmed by the hearty joviality of the British and Scottish officers in attendance. And as there was still a shortage of women around, our welcome was an enthusiastic one.

The snow was enchanting. I was still fascinated by it. This was very clean, very white snow that crunched with each step. The bright sunlight created a heavenly playground which I found irresistible, and Margaret eagerly taught me how to fall with my arms outstretched to make angels in the white softness. Having lived most of her life amid deep Canadian snow, however, she soon grew disgusted at my endless delight.

I was deeply grateful for Margaret's friendship. Helen's absence had left an empty spot in my life. A Canadian, with a social work background, Margaret had joined UNRRA after serving as a major in the Canadian Woman's Army Corps (CWAC), and after ending a love affair. She was an attractive brunette with the traditional Canadian openness and marvelous sense of humor. Coupled with sensitivity to peoples' feelings and competent social work and management skills, this made her an exceptional person. We had immediately established congenial bonds, marveling at the similarity of interests, tastes and values between two people with such dissimilar backgrounds--one from a small town in Quebec and the other from a city in the Deep South. It was a propitious way to start 1947, a year which was to bring another shift in my life.

One morning in March 1947, at Heidelberg Headquarters I was summoned to the Director's Office where I was introduced to two gentlemen, who, it seemed, had come to ask permission to visit some Children's Centers. Did I have any plans to visit some Centers, and if so, could they accompany me? Oh, sure, I always had reason to make supervisory visits.

The two gentlemen were Fred Zinnemann of Metro-Goldwyn-Mayer and Richard Schweizer of the Swiss Praesens Film Company. Two Swiss photographers, Berna and Furrer, were to accompany us. They planned to shoot a feature film in that part of Germany and were looking for sites, individuals to be in the film, and stories to help flesh out the script. Fred was to direct the film, Richard was the script writer.

The big deal for me was that we were assigned a Chevy pick-up truck for the trip. You had really arrived when you got a Chevy truck! You knew it would get you there and your status promptly escalated. Every day at five, the generals, colonels and other officers would emerge from the buildings, their big cars driven up by G.I. chauffeurs to sweep them up and off they would go. The UNRRA personnel would be picked up by our old beat-up little jeeps or battered German civilian cars.

So we took off the next morning for a two-week trip through villages and bombed-out towns, visiting a number of Centers. Fred, Richard and I usually sat in the front seat with Fred driving, although we all took turns sitting in the open back part of the truck. Fred had an Austrian background so he spoke German and was fluent in French. Richard, being Swiss, was bilingual and spoke both French and German, as well as impeccable English. It wasn't so easy for Berna and Furrer, who only spoke French, but we all managed to communicate somehow. We often drove through badly or completely bombed towns, a sight all too familiar to me. So, I was amused to hear someone yell out, "Hold it, wonderful ruins!", stop the car and start shooting film.

Fred and Richard were wonderful companions, always thoughtful and sensitive. Fred was particularly kind and understanding with the children. Being Austrian and Jewish he had a great deal of empathy for them, and the ability to communicate easily. He would play with them a bit to get acquainted, and then ask if they would like their pictures taken, lining up everyone so no one was left out. Realizing that identifying numbers might recall concentration camp experiences, he devised some way for his camera to record identification without their knowledge. Although all of the kids weren't potential subjects he went through the picture-taking process only pressing the trigger selectively to keep everyone happy. Fred began to call me "Queenie, the Queen of Alabama" or der König (which actually translates as "the King,' but, oh well, his German wasn't very good), and this was picked up by Richard and the Swiss guys. As time went on it became obvious that they were not only looking for kids to play parts in the movie but also interviewing UNRRA personnel. One day, Fred said to me, "Der König, I'm embarrassed not interviewing you. I can't have you in the movie. You are too glamorous."

The movie that eventually was made was *The Search*, starring Montgomery Clift, the Metropolitan Opera Czech singer Jarmila Novotna, and the British star, Aline McMahon. It tells the story of a little Czech boy separated from his parents in a concentration camp, discovered among the ruins by a G.I. (Montgomery Clift), and made a mascot by the Army unit which eventually received orders to return to the United States. The little boy was taken to a Children's Center (Rosenheim) where the social worker (Aline McMahon) finally is able to reunite him with this mother.[65]

---

[65] About a year later, in January 1948, I had the unforgettable experience of seeing *The Search* for the first time, in New York. Fred had arranged for me to go to a preview screening in a small room in a Broadway building. I had real trepidation about going, fearing that the movie would distort the reality of Germany. I had been too close to it all. As I sat there in that little dark room seeing it unfold, I was relieved, moved; and on leaving the building had to walk fast in the cold darkness of the street to get hold of my emotions. Subsequently, I had several letters from Fred, "Hi, Queenie"; and from Richard in New York, "Dearest Queenie, You are here, YOU ARE HERE, That's G R A N D!" I recently saw the movie again and it brought total recall, as well as appreciation for the talents of the two responsible for it, Fred and Richard.

Early in the new year, 1947, the flow of the infiltree Jewish children had subsided, and I was asked to take on a position as Deputy Field Operations Officer at UNRRA Headquarters. A Memorandum from R.W. Collins, Deputy Zone Director, Department of Field Operations, to the Personnel Section described the transition in assignments, citing my child welfare function vis-a-vis the Jewish unaccompanied children.

It was ...*a particularly important function, insomuch as there were 10,000 Jewish unaccompanied children who came into the Zone as "infiltrees" during the three months of the fall of 1946. Children's Centers and proper classification and intake policies of the various centers had to be established. Mrs. Pettiss performed an excellent job in these functions, and was very popular with the Jewish agencies as well as with the UNRRA field personnel. More than this, she was able to work under great pressure and was able to orient the field operational aspects of the program to the cultural needs and problems of the Jewish infiltree children.*

In February, due to an extreme personnel emergency, caused by the resignation of my own deputy, Mrs. Pettiss was brought into my office. She acted as my assistant in all matters of field operational and social services character. She was excellent in an administrative way in assisting with the handling of the volume of paper and the preparation of procedure on dealing with the various eight staff divisions under my general administration.

Spring brought not only blossoms, but a flurry of activity to bring hope and solutions to those tens of thousands of DPs still languishing in camps. A final campaign went into effect to repatriate those opting to return to their home countries, mostly Poles and Yugoslavs. This required careful registration and assurance that it was the individual's desire, as UNRRA had the firm policy that no one would be returned against his or her will. The returnees were brought to collection points from which they were loaded on trains for their destinations. These trains, in fact, carried the passengers in boxcars equipped with food, water,

Polish Refugees leaving for Poland

blankets and toilet facilities; and accompanied by UNRRA escorts for the day or two day trips. Somehow the travelers always seemed to manage to get greenery, branches of trees and shrubs, to decorate the cars and the groups usually left singing.

Kathryn Hulme, Deputy Director of the UNRRA DP camp, Wildflecken, traveled as an escort on one of these repatriation trains. She described her experience in *The Wild Place*.

> I rode out of Wildflecken in a boxcar bound for Poland, with two hundred and twenty repatriates, one lieutenant and eleven G.I. guards and two large American flags tacked on both sides of the military escort car, ... with a French nurse from another camp. I rode in what was called the 'hospital' car because a huge red cross outlined in white was still visible in its scarred and scaly interior.... The cities of Germany and Czechoslovakia were just freight yards to us.... We slid into their sooty gray sidings and set up housekeeping on their narrow

cinder paths between tracks, doing all the things that could not be accomplished while we were shaking along in the seventeen boxcars with no communication between. ... Claudette, the French nurse climbed down with a medical kit of aspirin and soda bicarbonate tablets, bandages, iodine, and laxatives.... She made her 'home visits' down the string of boxcars.... Perhaps it was the singing that turned Claudette, the Irish lieutenant and me into DPs going home to Poland.... The last night ... before entry into Poland, ... as the men began to sing ... the male voices lifted strongly above the iron clatter and presently you did not hear the train at all..., only the folk songs of Poland...

How could you have heard above that virile uplift of joyous home-going voices the creaky rustle of an iron curtain swaying insidiously westward? How could you have guessed that what you really were taking in was the haunting material for heartbreak? Your only thought was, how beautiful are people going home.[66]

During that spring, tensions escalated in the camps, as the DPs felt the pressures of choice closing in on them. It was now firm. UNRRA would close on June 30th and the new U.N. body, the International Refugee Organization (IRO), would be taking over. The shape of things to come was therefore very hazy. Each DP became a Hamlet, "To be, or not to be"--to go or not to go. The choice was particularly painful for the Poles with their passionate love of their country and the close bonds of their Catholic religion. Sixty-eight percent of the more than one million DPs in the western zones of Germany in September 1945 had been Poles.[67] Their dash for home at the end of hostilities had been tempered by the political upheaval taking place in their country--confusion backed by rumors of Soviet oppression and ambitions for dominance.[68] As time went on, the choice became even more harsh

---

[66] Hulme, pp.135, 136, 137, 141, 142.

[67] Proudfoot, p.281.

[68] During the war, a pro-Allied Polish Government-In-Exile had been established in London who came to be known as the "London Poles." Upon their occupation

with the news of jockeying for power among the different political factions in the country. Non-Polish DPs were more or less facing the same options with trepidation. On the one hand, the specter of remaining in the camps with an unknown future, especially in light of UNRRA's closing, was daunting. On the other hand, news seeping back into the camps from repatriated compatriots was discouraging. Although the word "resettlement" was creeping into the vocabulary, there was little evidence of opening doors.

It was obvious now that those still in Germany would not, or could not return to their country of origin, thus shifting UNRRA's emphasis from repatriation to efforts to locate countries willing to welcome this "hard core" as new immigrants. These were mostly Poles, Baltics, Yugoslavs, Jews, the stateless and a few Russians who had managed to escape earlier forced return by the Russian military. My job as Field Operations Officer was to work towards consolidation of camps, and to carry out projects such as issuing new identification cards, writing administrative orders, dealing with correspondence and team communications.

With resettlement planning came contact with representatives from those few receiving countries who came to Heidelberg to set up selection procedures--initially Belgians, Canadians and Norwegians. In addition to the work involved, it often offered pleasant diversions. For instance, two UNRRA Officers I had met in Berlin arrived in Heidelberg accompanied by a delegation of eight over-six-feet-tall lusty, handsome Norwegian men. They had come with a plan for a program to resettle 300 Jews in Norway. In

---

of Poland, in July 1944, the Soviets had established in Lublin a communist-dominated government known as the Provisional Government, or the Lublin Government. Subsequently, at the conference held in Yalta in February 1945, agreement was reached on the formation of a new Polish Government of National Unity, which became known as the "Warsaw Poles," as the site of the Provisional Government had been moved from Lublin to Warsaw. A unicameral parliament was established in 1946, after a referendum, with an election on January 19, 1947 (reputed to be notoriously rigged), awarding an overwhelming majority to Boleslaw Bieurt, a Pole who was a Communist and a Soviet citizen.

order to entertain them one evening, I gathered some of my female colleagues for dinner enlivened with much singing and *Skolds!* (a Norwegian toast), followed by an evening of the most athletic dancing I had experienced. I was picked up and whirled around--polkas, waltzes, jitter-bugs, winding up in a state of exhaustion.

But resettlement was a dream for most of the anxious, remaining DPs, feeling forgotten and unwanted. The upcoming deadline of June 30th just exacerbated their fears.

My job in Field Operations began to become a drag. So an opportunity to return to the Child Welfare scene was welcome. I wrote my mother on April 26th,

As to my job, I go back next week to Child Welfare--to the Jewish children's problems. I feel very flattered that the Jewish agencies made such an appeal to have me back, plus the fact that for the present and for the next two months it will be a very interesting job. I don't know how much is in the papers at home, but most of the Jews here are illegally going to Palestine. By the time that UN gets around to making a decision, it will be all settled. As you know, last year a large percentage of Jews in Central Europe came into the US Zone of Germany for haven and to raise pressure to have Palestine doors opened. Now, after they have been in DP camps for about a year and nothing has happened, they are going illegally in large numbers to Palestine. They have several routes. Some go through Austria to Italy and across by boat. Some go to France and by boat. The groups of children for whom I planned, and we cared for in Centers, are also on the move. We have no part in the movements, do not know when they take place. Rumor has it that within the next two months most of the children will be gone. My job will be to supervise the eleven Children's Centers, consolidate when necessary, work through any legal repatriation or resettlement plans. It is very ticklish job on account of diplomatic implications. After all, England is a member of the United Nations (our organization in charge) and Palestine is under their governing mandate. I will be in the middle, coordinating the Jewish agencies sponsoring the illegal movements to Palestine, representing UNRRA and working with the people themselves. I personally feel that being in Germany is a deteriorating experience for the children. There seems no other answer, so if they want to slip across the border to Palestine, I will do my darndest to see that they have good care here, that we can give as good training for the future as possible. It is impossible to see any other solution. So I start back on the road next Tuesday, first to Regensberg to see about opening a new institution there, then on to Munich for several days.

My other job was getting to be just a desk job. I can't see sitting around with not much to do at this stage of UNRRA, so if you don't hear often within the next few weeks.

The Collins Memorandum described the move from Field Operations.

> Late in April it became necessary again to re-establish the position of Child Welfare Officer for Jewish Children. At some loss to my own office we transferred Mrs. Pettiss back to this position, this time to consult on matters of education and training, to reestablish the Advisory Committee on Child Care for Jewish Children, and to work out programs on transport and movement for the children to various European countries where the children were going on legal visas for convalescent care and treatment.

I was pleased to be back in my Child Welfare job. The kids were now beginning to move out of the zone and rumor had it that most would be gone within two months. So, as soon as I was back in my old job, eager to get out in the field to see what was going on in the Children's Centers, I took off with a fellow UNRRA staff member, Ruth Feder (from the Public Relations Staff), and our Latvian driver.

Tuesday, April 29th
We left after lunch, driving through Nuremberg to Regensberg arriving about eleven at night, going straight to the UNRRA billets for the night.

*Wednesday, April 30*th
I spent the morning talking about opening a new Children's Center so we could consolidate, closing two others. We worked out staff problems, equipment, transfer of children, etc. After lunch I left, accompanied by several others, to see the potential center--about an hour's drive from Regensberg. It was an ideal location except for the fact that it was adjoining a former ammunitions depot where there were still a few undetonated mines lying around. It had everything--infirmary, lovely kitchen and dining room, shops for vocational training, separate unit dwelling places, swimming pool and excellent recreational facilities. We worked it all out so that within a week it could take up to 250 children.

Ruth and I took off from there and drove on down to Munich. The car wasn't driving too well so we had to stop in Landshut for a little work but we limped on into Munich about ten that night, going on to Pasing, our old UNRRA Headquarters. Although it was long after dinner, Eugene, the chef who had been with us in Starnberg fixed a luscious cold plate for me. I stayed in Jack Whiting's old house which almost made me homesick.

*Thursday, May 1*st
Had a two hour session on the subject of closing the Children's Center at Kloster Indersdorf with the Zone Field Representative. We did not agree on the matter. Then a meeting the rest of the morning with the Jewish Agency for Palestine representatives. I am so deep into this whole Jewish problem that it scares me sometimes. A historical move and drama is being played out here, the equal of which has not taken place for generations. The Jewish race here in Europe has suffered not only in the war years but for decades--suffering that we Americans cannot conceive. Jewish forces which are powerful and stronger than imagined have organized to take advantage of opportunities presented by the postwar adjustment period to establish what they sincerely feel as the only solution to the Jewish race, a homeland of their own in Palestine, and incidentally move most of the remnants of Jews from Central Europe. I am sympathetic to the move, as it seems the only alternative for their salvation. England's position on the whole matter has been shameful. Some of the methods used by the Jews I do not agree with, but think I understand.

As for the Jewish children here in the US Zone, there are definite plans for their getting to Palestine this summer. There are several different methods which I won't go into. I am amazed at the confidence that the Jewish agencies have in me and I would be much happier if I didn't know so much. UNRRA policy, and I think US policy, unwritten, is to know nothing, participate not at all, but not to restrict any movement out of the Zone. We are all hoping that the UN will be able to reach a rather quick solution as ... two years in DP camps is most unwholesome for individuals.

So now I am in the process of closing and consolidating Children's Centers that I opened about eight months ago.

Friday, May 2ⁿᵈ
Drove out to Indersdorf with Blake Cox, the Team Director with operational responsibility for the Center. He wants to close the Center too, and move some Balts in. It is about an hour's drive from Munich, near Dachau. We inspected the place, talked to the staff. I still maintain it should not be closed.

Got back to Munich about one and took off immediately for Rosenheim, getting there in time (about three-thirty) to talk about closing it, working out the details. Then on down to Seigsdorf for dinner and a talk with the Team Welfare Officer, and afterwards drove to Berchtesgaden to see the Team Director. I reached there about nine and was immediately cornered by a Jewish girl who had been working in a Children's Center and who was at that time very emotionally disturbed. The Director and I talked until midnight.

Saturday, May 3ʳᵈ
Having called a meeting in Munich for ten o'clock I got up at six, leaving Ruth, started out at six-thirty from Berchtesgaden. Everything went fine for about two hours then all of a sudden the car sounded like it was losing the engine. Fortunately I was near an Army garage (they have them along the autobahn at intervals) so pulled in. This was about eight-thirty. They were awfully nice to me, started looking for the trouble. To make a long story short, it went on all day, thinking it would be fixed any minute. And what a day I spent. Sitting in an Army garage,

telephoning, answering the telephone for the G.I.s, reading a book I had along, etc. I reached several conclusions before the day was over. The American Army is a "bust" as far as an army of occupation. G.I.s under age 25 should not be allowed over here. I was green with envy of all the "dependents" (military families) driving up in smooth running, slick looking American automobiles with husky males to look after them. Well, by three-thirty they said my car was ready so my Latvian driver and I climbed in, started--got about fifty feet and part of the whole engine block fell out. That did it. We left the car, got a ride into Munich with a very nice G.I, in a jeep. When I got to Pasing, Annie the maid took one look at me, began bringing me coffee and food--sent me to bed. I had to laugh at myself later. I don't know when I felt so feminine and in need of protection. I recovered quickly, however, and after an hour's rest went out for dinner.

The comment about the social behavior of the US occupying forces pointed up changes in the troops from the time when the shooting stopped until the present--two years later. It had been gradual, as the fighting guys were shipped home only at the rate shipping space became available. The replacements arrived on the returning ships and planes. The fighting guys were older, more mature, more responsible. Many were draftees, therefore better educated than their much younger successors, and seemed more worldly. The new fellows brought a freshness, some excitement about being in a foreign country, a sense of adventure. They found that the glamor of uniforms in the eyes of the lonely German frauleins, as well as the ubiquitous P.X. goodies, meant female company was easy to come by. The cheap liquor and military clubs were conducive to overindulging. They never had it so good. The term "gentlemen" seemed to have disappeared from their mantra. Whereas there were some few marriages, the most obvious evidence of the occupation on the local population was the burgeoning number of illegitimate births of half-American babies.

This artificial lifestyle of the soldiers did bother some. One night at a club, a couple of guys approached me, just wanting to talk. They were concerned about themselves, concerned that they and some of their buddies were just becoming "no good drunkards." They had set a target of two weeks to see if they could "straighten up." They were dead serious and I was glad to give them a pat on the back and a "right on." One of the challenges to an army of occupation is how to deal with the morale, morals and the abnormal lifestyle of young soldiers functioning in an unfamiliar culture with lax social constraints. It will always be thus, I suppose.

But to continue. *Sunday, May 6th*
So, without a car, I bummed a ride back to Heidelberg with Carl and Blake Cox who had to go to a Team Director's meeting. We had a most pleasant trip--good company, good conversation, no hurry or strain as Carl had a Buick with an excellent driver. Leaving at ten thirty in the morning we arrived about five in the afternoon. I changed, we had dinner and went around to a party for the visiting directors which was very dull. We finally got away and Carl, Blake and I went to my house where we fixed coffee and snacks, sat up until two talking.

Having been together on the drive all day, one wonders what topics of conversation were still left untouched, that we could talk until two in the morning! This indulgence in good conversation with my international colleagues was one of the most meaningful aspects of my experience in Germany. It changed my life. I realized that in Mobile where I usually felt remote from the ongoing banter and small talk, I had thought there was something odd about me. Here I began to realize it hadn't been me, it was because I had been bored.

Wednesday, May 7th
Ruth and I drove up to Lindenfels. Lindenfels is one of my Jewish Children's Centers, a lovely little German village where we have four pension-type hotels in which the children live. It was the celebration of a Jewish holiday, Lag m'ber, celebrated in boy scout manner. Kids from all over the zone had gathered, all dressed in white shirts, the girls with kerchiefs. At dusk they lined up, marched to a spot on the side of a hill cleared for the purpose. There were over a thousand of them. I wish I could describe my emotions a I stood there in the quiet little town and

watched them go by. They were serious, had such old, almost sad faces. There was so little of the natural spontaneity of children about them. Most appeared husky, but very small. As one youngster was walking by the man standing next to me asked me how old I thought she was. I guessed eight and he poo-pooed me, saying she couldn't be more than six. I stepped over and asked. She was nine.

We went up the hillside and watched while they lit a bonfire, sang songs. It might have been Camp Nakanawa (a girls' camp in Tennessee where I spent several summers), *with the peaceful mountains around, the valley stretching out in the twilight. The difference was startling, though. The songs weren't happy. They were intense, almost martial. The little drama enacted was fiercely emotional. It was all too orderly, too mature for juveniles. I don't know when I have been so moved. Going home in the car Ruth and I were both quiet. Ruth is Jewish and a very sensitive person....*

Thursday, May 8th, V. E. Day
So here, two years from the day I left the coast of France to come to Germany, I seem another person. A lot has happened in those two years. I have been more than fortunate. I am certainly a different Susan Pettiss.

Tuesday, May 13th
Up at six, off by seven to Munich. They had provided me with a Chevrolet pick-up which delighted me because I was pretty sure it wouldn't break down. I had a good driver, a Frenchman who had come to Germany at the same time I had two years ago, so he took good care of me. We got to Munich in time for lunch and I spent the afternoon in conferences. We drove on down to Bad Weisee where the UNRRA Training School is located, to spend the night. A special course was being held to train a group of displaced persons who are working in camps and children's centers as welfare workers. I was to help out during the week. Bad Weisee is a beautiful spot. A colorful little Bavarian village located on Lake Tergensee with the Alps in the background.

Wednesday, May 14th
I lectured on "Institutional Care" and had a discussion lasting all morning. The group of thirty was a keen, alert group so it was a lively discussion. I used an interpreter, of course.

After lunch I went into Munich again (about an hour's drive) and was all afternoon with the Jewish agency trying to work out staff problems, setting up a system whereby Idersdorf could be administered by a DP. Dinner at Pasing and back to Bad Weisee to give another lecture at eight on Jewish children's problems.

Saturday, May 17th
Finished my business in Munich and drove back to Bad Weisee, Dinner that night was the graduating exercise for the welfare group. There was one girl that I found especially interesting. A Jewish girl, age sixteen. She was Polish. She had been forced to hold her mother in her arms while the German soldiers shot her. She had seen her father hung. She was thrown in a ditch with a lot of half dead Jewish people and later taken to a concentration camp. She escaped and got into Russia. There she joined the Partisans, lived in the woods with them and fought with them. She was decorated twice for bravery. Her only relative was a brother whom she had lost track of. When she was called to Minsk to receive the Red Star decoration, the names of the people receiving them were called out alphabetically. The name after hers was her brother. He is in Germany with her now and they are planning to go to Palestine. There were eleven G.I.s taking the course for D.P. camp administration along with the DPs, a very interesting experiment.

Sunday, May 18th
So I came back to Heidelberg. I felt as if I had been gone for months. Summer has come. People are leaving in droves as the staff is cut down to fit the prospective I.R.O. budget. Now it looks like I will stay on until the middle or latter part of the summer.

The significant date had been set--June 30th, the date of UNRRA's official termination. I had decided it would also be the date for the end of my job with UNRRA. Margaret had settled on the same schedule. We set about planning a trip to see unvisited parts of

Europe before returning to our respective countries, casually leaving details to be worked out as we traveled. A target for final departure from the continent was established after perusing shipping schedules--the sailing date of the Queen Elizabeth from England on August 12th. I passed this on to my brother, Stewart, who worked for a shipping company in Mobile, asking him to "work it out."

Meantime, there was the push to tie up loose ends at the office, with the Children's Centers, and the Jewish agencies with whom I had worked so closely. The latter was a wrenching experience as we had shared so much together, had really bonded. The meeting where I announced my decision to leave took place in the small, rather sparsely furnished office of the Jewish Agency for Palestine, attended by a number of representatives of other agencies. After the meeting, Dr. Chaim Hoffman, the JAP Director, asked me to stay for a few minutes. He was a rather serious, but gentle man, dedicated, with a zeal for getting things done. He and I had not always agreed but both respected each other. Now, with a certain amount of formality, he told me that his agency would like to invite me to visit "their" country, Palestine, as their guest as an expression of their gratitude for all I had done for them and the Jewish children. I was quite moved and had to fight to keep the tears back. We realized it wouldn't be easy to get there but as soon as I arrived I would be taken over by the Jewish community to see the land that had played such a part in my recent life, and the one which will be the home for "my children."

During the next few weeks, as we made future plans for the Children's Centers we intermittently discussed details for the Palestine trip, most of which had to remain hazy as the British/Palestine situation was heating up. I was unwilling to go illegally, so it meant that I would have to go to Geneva to request a visa from the British Embassy to enter the country.[69]

---

[69] In February 1947, the British had conceded that their mandate was unworkable and turned the issue over to the United Nations which in April established a U.N. Special Committee on Palestine (UNSCOP). As I was in Geneva requesting

In Heidelberg, it was a time of farewell for a number of us who were departing, so there was a spate of parties in homes and clubhouses, and the atmosphere in our UNRRA mess in the Hotel Shreider was a mixture of excitement and sadness. The hotel, in the center of the town, had provided our meals, breakfast, lunch, and dinner, as well as serving as the social focus for all UNRRA staff, taking on an international flavor. The round tables with their white tablecloths were spread with the best that could be produced from army rations (and always potatoes), held bottles of local wines which undoubtedly stimulated the babble of voices in different languages discussing day's events accompanied with much laughter. I knew I would miss this camaraderie which had meant so much to me.

The time passed quickly, often filled with competing emotions. The last day and the signing of final documents seemed to symbolize the closing of my life and experiences in Germany. My personnel records showed that I had started at Grade 7 with a salary of $3050 per year and wound up at Grade 11, salary of $5750. I was most gratified to see my rating stated as "Superior." Departing UNRRA personnel were given the option of returning to their home country for final termination or to go to the UNRRA Office in Paris for that procedure, where a voucher would be given for home-country transportation to be utilized within a two-month period. Needless to say, Margaret and I opted to go to Paris. On June 26th, after a farewell luncheon at the Shreider, and a drive to Frankfort, we boarded the six-thirty train for Paris.

---

a visa at the British Embassy, this Committee was assessing the situation which led to their unanimous recommendation that the British give up its mandate for Palestine and that the country be divided into two states, one Arab and one Jewish. This recommendation, although rejected by the Arabs, was approved by the General Assembly on November 29, 1947. The British began to withdraw, completely ending its responsibility for the country. On May 14, 1948, the State of Israel came into being.

FINALE

> On October 30, 1948, the US Army Transport, *General Black*, nosed into New York harbor, decorated with flags of many nations and carrying Displaced Persons immigrating to the United States. It was a thrilling occasion. Whistles blew, fire boats sprayed water into the air, as the Statue of Liberty held aloft her torch of greeting. This was the first ship bringing DPs to America under Public Law 774, passed by the 80th Congress.

So I wrote in an article, "Immigrant, 1948," published in the Fall 1948 issue of the New York School of Social Work alumni newsletter.

> US Immigration, Public Health and Customs authorities boarded the ship at the point of quarantine and processed the passengers while the General Black slowly made its way to the pier. As it tied up at the dock, press representatives and photographers poured aboard. Public officials and dignitaries made speeches of welcome which conveyed a meaning to the newcomers whether the language could be understood or not. The rails of the ship were lined with passengers, their eyes searching for friends or relatives--many shedding tears, all drinking in their first glimpse of America. They were quiet, waving now and then, seemingly dazed by it all. First down the gangplank came the orphan children accompanied by a representative of the US Committee for European Children. Then followed families, all wearing identification tags of a voluntary agency.

> Mrs. Rowinski steps off the gangplank and a representative of the United States for New Americans comes forward to greet her, exchanges handshakes and smiles, and steers her toward her baggage. Every individual or family is met by an agency representative who assists them through customs, plans with them for their travels to their destinations in the US Customs

officials proceed about their business of inspection in a patient, friendly manner. The pier hums with orderly activity. The Red Cross rolls a table bearing coffee, milk and doughnuts to the groups as they wait for this or that. The Travelers' Aid is busy making travel arrangements with a railroad agent who is on the pier. The Church World Service worker is interviewing the Zalinkas to find out if they prefer to go on to Tennessee that night. The National Catholic Welfare Conference staff is grouping all the families going to Detroit, having arranged a special car on the train for them. The Hebrew Sheltering Immigrant and Aid Service is assisting one of their families to meet a relative who has come to the dock to meet them, with the help of an International Institute staff member. The federal D.P. Commission representative busily goes from group to group to see if all is O.K.

After several hours, the pier cleared, the ship pulled away, and the DPs were on their way to their destinations scattered throughout the United States.

The arrival of the *General Black* signaled the Intermission for me was over. The Second Act had begun. It actually began on a brisk autumn day, October 1st, when I turned up at the Dupont Circle Building in Washington D.C. to report for my new job as US Resettlement Officer in the Washington office of the IRO. The drama, started with UNRRA, was playing itself out, but with a new cast of characters in a different setting. I was shown to my office, formerly that of my friend, Helen Wilson, and found on my desk a big rubber thumb. From some fun shop, I presume. Under it was a sign, "Welcome Susan. My best advice, just go by rule of thumb." So much for any briefing or orientation for the job! The advice came in handy, however, since again I was functioning in a situation with no precedent, no past model. I quickly realized, though, that I had landed in another set-up not unlike UNRRA Team 108--a small, closely-knit staff with General Walter A. Wood, Jr. in the role of Charley del Marmol.

General Wood, a slightly built man with a taut, erect carriage one would expect of a military officer, had started his military career in World War I after graduating from West Point, continued with distinction in World War II at the end of which he retired for health reasons (emphysema). I soon appreciated his exacting military precision, usually softened by a lurking warm humor and twinkling eyes. Not only was he a great boss, he was superb in dealing with the highest level of US government and army officials on shipping, policy and congressional matters, as well as being notorious for producing results beyond expectations. He had created a highly supportive and hard-working staff. It wasn't long before I fell into step, increasingly impressed and inspired by his leadership. It was from him that I picked up the quote which became my mantra: "The difficult will be done at once. The impossible may take a little longer time."

During the Intermission, I had polished my professional social work credentials by spending the year in study at the New York School of Social Work, Columbia University. The time had passed pleasantly, providing an antidote for any pain of transition from Germany to my home country in the form of the excitement of living in New York. I ended the year with a Masters degree in Social Work. I didn't have to look long for a new job--there it was.

One night, returning from a date, I found Helen ensconced on a cot she had requested brought to my tiny room at the Beekman Tower, as she planned to spend the night in New York. She had something on her mind. After greetings and an exchange of personal news, she came to the point of her trip.

"Since you'll be finishing school in a few weeks, Susan," she said to me, "how about coming to Washington to replace me at IRO?"

She had transferred from her European position with UNRRA to the newly opened Washington Office of IRO, but she was getting bored with her new job. She wanted to get back to the more exciting European operation. To effect this transfer, she figured it would be easier to persuade General Wood if she had an immediate replacement. I was the obvious choice. I had the UNRRA experience with DPs and was even writing my master's thesis on recent US refugee legislation.[70] Plus the fact that I needed a job. So we worked it all out. She returned to Washington the next day, discussed the proposition with the personnel officer, and contacted IRO Headquarters in Geneva regarding a transfer. Finally, she presented General Wood with a *fait accompli*. Much amused, he said, "I would at the very least like to meet this Susan Pettiss." So I went to the capital, gussied up in a stylish (I thought) black linen dress, a new hat, dressed to meet my potential boss. It worked.

The International Refugee Organisation had just been established as the United Nations specialized agency to succeed UNRRA. Eighteen member governments formed a Governing Council with a mandate "to solve that part of the world refugee problem represented by the 'displaced persons' who were uprooted by the Second World War and by political disturbances which followed in its wake."[71] The organization became operational on July 1, 1947, picking up seamlessly from UNRRA--even inheriting its Headquarters in Geneva and a significant portion of its staff. It immediately became the base of operations for DP resettlement which included masterminding the movements of thirty-six ships under charter, ten of them former US Navy troop transports, and a fleet of chartered planes taking refugees to receiving countries. The Washington Office was responsible for the US end of the resettlement operations, as well as serving in an important liaison role with US Government. Not only was the US one of the IRO Council members, it was also the largest donor to the IRO, and the country offering resettlement to the largest number of refugees, although many other nations also took in DPs, including Canada, Australia, Britain, for example.

---

[70] The thesis was about the DP Act of 1948, a legislative measure passed by the US Congress on June 25, 1948, providing for the admission of 205,000 refugees and displaced persons in a two-year period.

[71] "Introductory Forward", *Migration from Europe… a Report of Experience,* IRO General Council Document, GC/199/Rev.1, p.v.

The mass movement of newcomers to US shores, which had commenced on that October 30th, set a record in that it was an unprecedented operation carried out in such a short space of time. There was no prescription for accomplishing the task, no receiving camps. We invented as we went along. The basic principles incorporated in the DP Act of 1948 permitting the issuance of special visas were that families should be kept together, and each individual and family had to be sponsored by a family in the United States with assurances for shelter, employment and a guarantee that they would not become a public charge. In the next three years, a half million refugees were welcomed under these circumstances and absorbed into the landscape without a ripple.

This could not have happened without the voluntary agencies which brought to the program not only commitment but private funds, operational staff, resources and the support of their constituencies. There were religious agencies--Catholic, Protestant and Jewish. There were ethnic organisations, such as the Russian, Polish, Ukrainian, Armenian. Additionally, there were secular groups, the International Institutes, Councils of Social Services and Travelers Aid Societies. These organizations were a lifeline for a number of the waiting DPs in Europe, headed for a "home" in the United States. The final settlement for each took place in cities, towns, villages, communities of all sizes and across America, so that American citizens throughout the country were involved.

My major assignment was to serve in a liaison capacity with these voluntary agencies. That meant meetings, meetings, meetings in order to be available for advice, information and assistance in matters which would facilitate the program or remove any glitches which arose. Both IRO and the federal government, through its DP Commission, provided subsidy and support to the agencies, as well as help with publicity to whip up interest in offering resettlement opportunities. To accomplish this latter, I found myself criss-crossing the country, sometimes with one of the three DP Commissioners, making speeches about the plight of the DPs still needing "assurances," the magic ticket for immigration visas to our shores. Although timid at first about standing on a podium facing a large audience, I gradually developed enough self-confidence to be comfortable. And, of course, it required new hats, strong arms for carrying baggage, and an intensive search for a feminine-looking briefcase. It seemed that the only briefcases on the market were the ugly, hunky ones designed for men. I made a fetish of going into luggage stores, asking for "a woman's briefcase," on the premise that, if there was enough demand, something might be done about it. It was only several years later that I found a lovely green leather briefcase in Paris.

As time moved on, however, my life seemed more and more involved with ships. All the IRO-chartered Army troop carriers were named for generals. I still have the image of the huge chart on the wall in General Wood's office listing the "Generals" with statistical information about dates of departure, arrivals, ports of entry, number of passengers, et cetera. I have to confess that this chart took on special significance for some of us on the staff (led by General Wood), as it enlivened our daily tasks by providing an ongoing lottery with bets placed and collected at regular intervals. We could never be accused of not being completely informed as to the exact status of any ship at any given time!

From the day of the arrival of that first ship, I often found myself standing on a dock waiting for the thrilling sight of the first DPs to come down the gangplank onto American soil. Standing there with the breeze ruffling my hair was a thrill, listening to the lap of water against the pilings as the big hulk gently nudged alongside the dock, alive with individuals waiting in suspense for the lines to be thrown ashore to tether the creature. Always the rails were lined with crowds of people of all sizes and stages of animation. The pattern for welcome was set. Newcomers were cleared through Customs, Immigration and Public Health, then greeted by the sponsoring voluntary agency representatives. Their baggage identified, they were whisked off to trains and airports for cities and towns across the country. My only regret was that I was never able to see the DP actually arrive in his or her new home, or sense their feelings at the end of the line.

Subsequent to the arrival of the *General Black* in New York, the scene was repeated in the ports of Boston and New Orleans. By December, four ships a month were docking, then seven, then nine. In August 1949, sixteen ships arrived, as well as forty-nine plane flights transporting pregnant women, small children, the handicapped and the elderly. In September, nineteen ships landed during the month. From one of those ships, just a year after the arrival of the *General Black*, the 100,000th DP came ashore.

I had visited Boston and New Orleans before the first ships arrived in their ports, to discuss the arrangements involved and to help work out any kinks in the system. I sure learned a lot. For instance, the curriculum of my masters degree hadn't included knowledge of how to develop a SOP (a military acronym for Standard Operating Procedure) for off-loading baggage and passengers in sync, so that the flow from ship to dock to inland transport moved smoothly. (Just for information, baggage should be loaded in reverse alphabetical order so that, on docking, it is unloaded with the "A" luggage on top--the same order that the passengers flow down the gangplank. Passengers can then identify their luggage and move out while the unloading proceeds without a backlog.)

The pattern of ship arrivals was broken by a dramatic event in 1949, shifting the scene from the east coast to the west coast. The *General Meigs* landed in San Francisco, bringing 228 refugees, mostly European Jews, rescued from Shanghai by the IRO, as China had dissolved into civil war. I was given the responsibility of escorting the refugees on a so-called "sealed train movement" across the country. There had been no time, nor the facilities, to produce US visas to cross the country, so the IRO had negotiated a plan for their movement from coast to coast by train, restricting the passengers from disembarking at any point, enforced by the presence of armed guards on the cars.

At about noon on March 13, 1949, a typical, bright, California-blue-sky kind of day, the train carrying those 228 passengers pulled out from a track siding in Oakland, across the bay from San

Francisco, for an unforgettable journey across the vast landscape of the United States. To the rhythm of the wheels chattering over the rails at dizzying speed behind the monster of an engine, I watched through the windows which framed my country like a film on a screen. I was seeing it with two sets of eyes--mine and those of my fellow travelers who had no country, only memories of past homelands, maybe Germany, maybe Austria, and more recently, China. I felt wonder at the differences. I felt their excitement at seeing America.

Who were these refugees? Why Shanghai? That city had not only one of the world's greatest seaports, but was the largest city in China. Because of its strategic place in international trade, it had attracted foreign interests. In the mid-1800s, the British, the United States and France had dominated a section of the city which was eventually designated as an "International Settlement." It required no entry visas and became a haven for exiles fleeing political upheaval around the globe. Russian monarchists, for instance, had sought refuge there in revolutionary days during and just after World War I. Later, as Ernest Heppner vividly documented,

> The city became a beacon of hope to European Jews fleeing the Nazis. The first Jewish European refugees arrived from Austria in March 1938, after the Anschluss, when Austria accepted annexation by Germany. Despite the fact that the Japanese were Axis partners of the Third Reich and occupied sections of Shanghai, European Jews used every means of transportation available to reach this haven from persecution. The refugees came by boat, some via Kobe, Japan and large ocean liners shuttled between Europe and Shanghai bringing thousands. Others came by train via Poland, the Soviet Union, Siberia and Manchuria. In 1939, the trickle increased to a flood until there were more than 18,000 European Jews in Shanghai.[72]

---

[72] Ernest Heppner, *Synopsis: Shanghai - The Temporary Haven.* (unpublished manuscript).

Heppner himself, at age seventeen, barely escaped from Breslau, Germany, with his mother, successfully obtaining passage by ship to Shanghai. Other members of his family remained, with the result that his father and sister were never heard from again, and a brother was sent to the Buchenwald Concentration Camp. The father of a friend, Lieselott Marcus, managed to obtain a place for her (at age seventeen) on the last Siberian Express train from Germany across Russia to Harbin. From there, she went by ship to Shanghai to a waiting fiancee. Her family were all taken to a concentration camp. Only a sister survived. Similar stories were told to me over and over, as our train sped across the country those five days.

I had dropped Fred Zinnemann a note, telling him about the anticipated drama of the Shanghai refugees, inviting him to join us for part of the trip. Arriving from Los Angeles, he gave me a big hug and a European-style kiss on each cheek. I was too busy to spend much time with him, but it was great to see him and get caught up on his latest movies. (He had just finished producing *The Men*.) Fred was deeply interested in the refugees and wandered the pier in his quiet, unobtrusive way, talking to a few of them. His ride with us from San Francisco to Los Angeles was only a short leg of the journey, but his presence gave me a boost at the start.

We sped along the California coast, past seemingly-unending rows of grapevines, cabbages, and orange trees, with boats like toys on the sea in the distance. Texas seemed just empty space. Cows seemed the only occupants of the land. We roared through a few small towns, stopped briefly at Dallas, then continued on to New Orleans.

As the train sped across the country, the passengers relaxed, wandering up and down the aisles and between cars, joking, singing at times, or just sitting quietly, observing the landscape. The guards in the cars put their guns out of sight and often joined in the conviviality and singing. Clearly, the greatest treat was the dining car. To be seated at tables and served second helpings on china plates by genial waiters was unmitigated joy. And at every city where the train stopped, there were groups organized by Jewish agencies to greet the passengers. Gifts and mail were brought on board, and food. If I ever saw another banana, I thought it would be too soon--whole bunches were presented. I suppose the stereotype was of the starving refugee.

After New Orleans, it was on to Mobile for another stop at the very station from which I had exited my former life almost five years before. I had no advance knowledge of our itinerary, so only managed to get a quick telegram to Mother about the Mobile stop, but, bless her heart, there she was, albeit somewhat befuddled as to what was going on. Preoccupied with my responsibilities, I could only offer her a hasty kiss and a few words of appreciation for having shown up. A stop in Atlanta, then up the Atlantic coast through the Carolinas. On through Virginia to Washington, where the excitement became palpable. The last stretch of the journey was through an unbroken stream of civilization: shops, factories, and finally Manhattan's distinctive skyline on the horizon.

The report I filed with the IRO stated,

> It was a tedious trip for the refugees, terminated by an emotional day on Ellis Island when relatives and friends were allowed to visit.

An understatement, to say the least. After five days in transit, we pulled onto a siding in New Jersey, near Ellis Island, where passengers were scheduled to detrain, spend the afternoon and night, before sailing the next morning, March 18th, on the *General Ballou* for the IRO resettlement processing center in Naples. Ellis Island, for most Americans, is somewhat of a hallowed place, as the entry point for the hordes of immigrants making up the population spine of our country. By then, it had ceased to function, but the facilities were still intact.

Two until four o'clock in the afternoon were visiting hours, and the Great Hall, a bare, high-ceilinged room, was thronged with relatives and friends of the Shanghai refugees. There were hugs, tears, hands holding hands. Reunions with siblings, children with parents, many who had thought they would never see each other again. I have never observed such emotion. It tore right into my gut, almost unbearable. The worst part of it was watching the good-byes at the four o'clock deadline.

Walking up and down the train's aisles on the train every day, all day, had left me with the feeling that I had walked the distance from San Francisco. I was physically exhausted. The emotional rollercoaster of that afternoon had left me drained. I was more than happy to pass the official documents over to the Army officers in command of the *General Ballou*, thus relieving me of my responsibilities, and head back to Washington. However, it wasn't long afterwards that I found myself on a plane, headed for Europe. It was still a matter of ships. I was on a special assignment to assist in sorting out a problem regarding escort staff on the IRO ships.

Personnel on the ships bringing refugees to America had called my attention to shortcomings of the IRO escorts assigned to assure a smooth passage. It was a traumatic time for the passengers, filled with the gamut of emotions--anxiety, fear, anticipation, excitement, insecurity. The language difference between ship staff and passengers often resulted in misunderstandings, tensions and frustrations. Innumberable personal problems among the DPs surfaced on the voyage, calling for sensitive counselling. On the other hand, it was a period which offered an opportunity for briefing and orientation, which could ease the transition to the new homeland.

This information was relayed to Geneva Headquarters by General Wood in frank, but diplomatic terms. In a letter assessing the problem, he ended with,

> I feel that the matter of provision and training of suitable escort officers is of such overall importance to the transport problem that, should you desire it, I would be

> willing to arrange for Mrs. Pettiss, of this office, to make
> a trip to Europe for the purpose of assisting in the
> establishing of a pool of escort personnel, as well as
> instituting a brief orientation course, to be given to such
> individuals.

The response was amusing. Bureaucracies haven't changed in centuries when it comes to matters of turf and, according to the Shipping Director, the Personnel Division didn't take kindly to the idea of calling someone from the field to advise Headquarters. He went on to say, however, that it was not Personnel's responsibility, but that of Shipping, therefore,

> ...hope you will be willing to send her (Mrs. Pettiss) as
> we require her services for whatever time you can make
> her available.

So, with that request and the potential for a prickly reception, I took off, looking forward to seeing old friends from UNRRA days, to enjoying the ambience of Geneva in the spring, and to meeting the challenge of assuring smoother passage for the DPs. I visited the embarkation port in beautiful, sunny Naples, stopping by the Rome Office, then proceeded to the major embarkation center in Bremerhaven. While there, I visited some of the nearby DP camps. I walked between the barrack-like buildings, stopping now and then to talk to some of the DPs sitting around or at their work. Superficially, not much had changed. There were the same dreary, brick exteriors to the buildings, peopled with waiting individuals. It was now four years since liberation. There were some changes, however. A few flowers had been planted here and there. The residents seemed less crowded, more relaxed. Many were working either on their own enterprises or in administrative jobs running the camps; in jobs with the armed forces, or getting experience in skills and democracy in preparation for anticipated resettlement. The striking change was in the faces. Smiles came more easily. There was more openness. There was trust and hope, especially for those in Bremerhaven, who had been lucky enough to have been already accepted for a country of resettlement.

The 1950 termination date for the US DP Act of 1948 was approaching and still 250,000 DPs were anxiously waiting in IRO camps, with about the same number outside of camps who were eligible for legal and political protection and for assistance in resettlement or repatriation.[73] So early in 1949, steps were set in motion for an extension of the Act. An amendment was finally passed by Congress on June 18th, 1950, giving two more years of life to the DP program. In the meantime, the IRO Governing Council had extended the life of that organization for two years. The end of 1951 was set as the deadline for DP activity, a goal demanding all-out action to reach it successfully.

We were caught up in this last effort to empty the camps. Ships kept coming, planes flew like magic carpets. One of those efforts was an attempt to rescue the last remnant of refugees still in Shanghai, now stranded, stateless and homeless, as the Chinese Communists were moving in. A group of Americans, refugees, and non-Chinese nationals were permitted by the Communists to go by rail to Takubar, Tientsin, for a dramatic escape via sampans and junks to a waiting IRO rescue ship, the *General Gordon*. So, about a year after my first "sealed train" experience, I found myself on a second such trip. With much more savvy this time, I insisted that the train cross the country directly, in four days, and with improved accommodations.

The *General Gordon* slid under the Golden Gate Bridge and sidled up to the pier about noon on May 23, 1950. I couldn't help being struck by the differences between these Shanghai refugees and those I had known in Germany. They were older and better dressed, with significantly more baggage. Some were even carrying gold bars. They had been living independently and, in most cases, earning their living for many years. The war that had mangled their lives was more remote. Most were now just seeking peace and a relatively comfortable way to spend the rest of their lives.

---

[73] Statement by J. Donald Kingsley, Director General, IRO, before the Second National Resettlement Conference, Chicago, June 23, 1950.

Susan Pettiss interviewing a refugee couple from Shanghai

Stories of individual passengers emerged. The 61-year-old George Lissner and his wife, Katie, 55, told of the day in 1939 when the Nazis closed Katie's Berlin dress shop, leaving them with no money and no visas. They managed to get to Shanghai, where they had lived through the Japanese occupation, always moving from place to place for security. "Now to Berlin," they said, "but only to get visas to return to America. How long from now? Nobody knows. But we will come back." And then there was Heinz Paul, who had owned a nightclub in Berlin. Sent to Dachau, and later to Buchenwald, he was let out in 1939 and managed to get to Shanghai, where he opened a nightclub, the Silk Hat, by saving up enough from selling macaroni. When the Communists came, he had to shut down the club. So the stories went.

> This move involved 261 refugees and was more
> complicated because of inadequate documentation,
> diverse travel arrangements and political pressure in the
> US.

So read my official report to IRO. During the trip, considerable agitation had developed in the United States regarding the on-forwarding of the Jewish passengers back to the source of their oppression--Germany. Many had assurances for US resettlement, but were being required to proceed to Bremerhaven for visa issuance anyway. As a result, an outcry had been raised by Jewish voluntary agencies, citizen groups, and some congressmen, as well as the media, arguing that they should be allowed to remain in the United States, especially if they had the necessary assurances. Isolated on the train at the very center of the controversy, however, we were not aware of the debate. And so, according to schedule, the train pulled onto a Statten Island pier alongside the *General Ballou* about noon on May 25th. The passengers quickly boarded the ship, found their assigned cabins, then had lunch. After a period with visitors, things began to settle down. Suddenly a voice came over the loudspeaker, calling all passengers to the mess hall. When they had assembled, a message read in German and English announced that they had been granted a stay of ten days by order of US Attorney General McGrath. After a dazed moment of silence, there was a combination of shouts of joy and tears of emotion. Finally, in somewhat quavering voices, they broke into "God Bless America."

It was just over three years since the *General Black* had brought those first DPs to New York. Over a million refugees had been resettled by IRO since the agency's beginnings on July 1, 1947. Mr. Kingsley, in his Chicago speech, commended the United States for its generosity and efficiency in the provision of new homes and new lives to approximately 500,000 left in limbo when the shooting stopped at the end of World War II.[74] He put this task in

---

[74] Speech by J. Donald Kingsley, Second National Resettlement Conference,

perspective, when he said,

> The Organization has cared for nearly a million and one-half people in camps, providing food, clothing, shelter, education, medical services, medical rehabilitation, vocational training, and all other necessities of civilized life. It has operated the largest civilian shipping fleet ever assembled in time of peace, one of the largest housing programs every run by a single authority, and tremendously complex health and educational programs.... Already it has carried out a movement of people greater than any previous mass migration in history, except in war. By the time it is liquidated next year, the figure will be well over a million men, women and children, transported by IRO to approximately eighty different countries, colonies, and dependencies from one end of the world to theother.[75]

He concluded with the prophetic comment,

> When IRO came into being, the Displaced Person problem and the refugee problem were almost synonymous. This is no longer the case. In the world today, there are many more refugees than there were then, and more people are becoming refugees every day....
>
> [I]t is possible, I think, to make a number of coordinated approaches to the problem, which, with sufficient imagination might go far to help the situation. New international methods can and will be worked out to ease migration from one area to another, to apply the 'surplus' talent of the refugees to the development of under-developed areas, to rationalize immigration laws and procedures, and to bridge the social no-man's land into which ultra-nationalism has now thrown the stateless.

Chicago, June 23, 1950.
[75] Speech by J. Donald Kingsley, Second National Resettlement Conference, Chicago, June 23, 1950.

The problem is complex, and there can be no simple or single solution. But it is one which cannot be dismissed by refusal to recognize it. In the final analysis, it will be met, as the Displaced Person problem is now being met, through the combined creative efforts of Governments, international bodies and voluntary agencies. In that effort, I am sure you will play a major role and will take the lead in this as you have in meeting and solving the great human problem of the displaced.[76]

---

[76] Speech by J. Donald Kingsley, Second National Resettlement Conference, Chicago, June 23, 1950.

ISBN 141203882-0